A Debt of Gratitude

MODERN WAR STUDIES

William Thomas Allison
General Editor

Raymond Callahan
Heather Marie Stur
Allan R. Millett
Carol Reardon
David R. Stone
Samuel J. Watson
Jacqueline E. Whitt
James H. Willbanks
Series Editors

Theodore A. Wilson
General Editor Emeritus

A Debt of Gratitude

HOW JIMMY CARTER PUT VIETNAM VETERANS' ISSUES ON THE NATIONAL AGENDA

Glenn Robins

University Press of Kansas

© 2024 by the University Press of Kansas
All rights reserved

Published by the University Press of Kansas (Lawrence, Kansas 66045), which was organized by the Kansas Board of Regents and is operated and funded by Emporia State University, Fort Hays State University, Kansas State University, Pittsburg State University, the University of Kansas, and Wichita State University.

This book will be made open access within three years of publication thanks to Path to Open, a program developed in partnership between JSTOR, the American Council of Learned Societies (ACLS), University of Michigan Press, and the University of North Carolina Press to bring about equitable access and impact for the entire scholarly community, including authors, researchers, libraries, and university presses around the world. Learn more at https://about.jstor.org/path-to-open/.

Library of Congress Cataloging-in-Publication Data

Names: Robins, Glenn, author.
Title: A debt of gratitude : How Jimmy Carter put Vietnam veterans' issues on the national agenda / Glenn Robins.
Description: Lawrence, Kansas : University Press of Kansas, 2024. | Series: Modern war studies | Includes bibliographical references.
Identifiers: LCCN 2024007586 (print) | LCCN 2024007587 (ebook)
  ISBN 9780700637836 (cloth)
  ISBN 9780700637843 (ebook)
Subjects: LCSH: Carter, Jimmy, 1924– | Vietnam War, 1961–1975—Veterans—United States. | Veterans—Services for—United States—History—20th century. | Georgia—Politics and government—1951– | United States—Politics and government—1977–1981. | BISAC: HISTORY / Wars & Conflicts / Vietnam War | HISTORY / United States / 20th Century
Classification: LCC E873.2 .R63 2024 (print) | LCC E873.2 (ebook) | DDC 959.704/3—dc23/eng/20240708
LC record available at https://lccn.loc.gov/2024007586.
LC ebook record available at https://lccn.loc.gov/2024007587.

British Library Cataloguing-in-Publication Data is available.

*Dedicated to all of those men and women
who served honorably in Vietnam.
You are not forgotten.*

CONTENTS

List of Abbreviations, ix

Acknowledgments, xi

Introduction, *1*

1 Illuminating Vietnam Veterans, *9*

2 The Vietnam Campaign, *20*

3 The Vietnam Agenda, *44*

4 Battling Expectations, *76*

5 Losing Control of the Agenda, *98*

6 The Revolt of the Veterans, *121*

Conclusion, *143*

Notes, 149

Bibliography, 177

Index, 185

LIST OF ABBREVIATIONS

GA   Georgia Archives
JCL   Jimmy Carter Presidential Library
MCP   Max Cleland Papers
PPPUS   *Public Papers of the Presidents of the United States*
RG   Record Group

ACKNOWLEDGMENTS

I never intended to write this book—or any book, for that matter, on Jimmy Carter. While researching a Vietnam War–related project, I ran across a reference to Carter and the court martial of Lieutenant William Laws Calley Jr. In the course of investigating the Calley reference, I discovered a completely different and untold story. *A Debt of Gratitude* is that story. Venturing into policy history has been a new experience for me. Consequently, I had to rely on the advice and guidance of the archivists at the Jimmy Carter Presidential Library and the Georgia Archives. Brittany Parris, Sara Mitchell, and Joseph Hollis at the JCL were particularly helpful, as was Hendry Miller at Georgia Archives.

Joyce Harrison at University Press of Kansas was an early and eager supporter of this project even when I wasn't completely sure where I was headed. It has been a pleasure to work with UPK and Erica Nicholson, Derek Helms, Karl Janssen, and Michelle Asakawa. Bill Allison, the Modern War Studies series editor, has been a good friend and always seems to be the right guy, at the right place, at the right time. Gregory Daddis reviewed the manuscript and offered not just scholarly input but also practical advice. Greg's firm but supportive interpretive suggestions saved me from making a self-inflicted mistake. I'm glad he cared enough about me and the project to offer the advice.

At Georgia Southwestern State University, Jimmy Carter's first alma mater, I've found a comfortable academic home. The university has provided generous faculty development grants to facilitate my research. Over the past few years, I've benefited from the comradery of a small writing accountability group at Georgia Southwestern that included Alaina Kaus, Susan Bragg, and Mohammad Dehzooei. D. Jason Berggren has become my Carter whisperer. He has fielded every question that I have thrown his way and generously shared his own research on our fellow Georgian.

I'm thankful to my parents Marvin and Phyllis Robins for supporting unconditionally my pursuit of a writing life and to Buddy and Virginia Douglas for continuing to look after me.

[xi]

My final debt of gratitude is to Dr. Irina Toteva for showing me how to live life differently and for encouraging me to be curious.

Introduction

On December 15, 1972, as rumors swirled of a pending peace agreement between the United States and North Vietnam, Governor Jimmy Carter issued an executive order creating the Georgia Advisory Committee on Vietnam Veterans (GACVV). His reasoning was simple: "The citizens of the State of Georgia and of the United States of America owe a debt of gratitude to these veterans who have served the Nation in an unpopular war."[1] In response to this call, government officials, physicians, psychiatrists, and Vietnam veterans convened in Atlanta to testify on an array of problems including unemployment, drug addiction, and mental health needs.[2] The GACVV was not Carter's only foray into the realm of veteran politics during his time in the governor's mansion. He also designated a "Jobs for Veterans Year"[3] and sponsored a "Salute to Vietnam Veterans Week." These endeavors represented his desire to ensure that the service of the war's veterans "not go unrecognized or unappreciated." To those ends, he deliberately conveyed the message that "their sacrifice" was emblematic of prior generations of "Americans who have fought, died, or been wounded in the cause of this nation's struggle for freedom and dignity."[4] Carter's efforts followed trends occurring across the country as a host of states contemplated their responsibilities to Vietnam veterans by considering such benefits as cash bonuses, educational stipends, and free hunting licenses. Through his words and actions, Carter joined this broader debate regarding society's obligation to Vietnam veterans.

A Debt of Gratitude examines Carter's role in the creation of Vietnam veterans' issues as a national agenda item. This study covers virtually the entire decade of the 1970s, from the Georgian's one term as governor to his single term as president of the United States. Throughout this period, Carter distinguished himself as one of the country's most important decision-makers concerning Vietnam veterans' policy. To be sure, Carter assumed office, on both occasions, with a large agenda, and he had higher priorities than Vietnam veterans. Nevertheless, in addressing Vietnam veterans' issues and by communicating his positions and views, Carter made a substantial political investment in moving these items from the level of public debate to the level of policy prescriptions. He contributed to this historic development in several ways. Carter campaigned on and governed according to a recognizable and definable Vietnam veterans' agenda. In sponsoring or endorsing consequential legislation, he raised public awareness, generated concern, and promised government attention. In addition, Carter engaged in commemorative activities and public events to honor and thank Vietnam veterans. On these occasions, he employed a rhetoric of gratitude that proffered a revisionist history of the American experience in Vietnam.[5]

Carter's rhetoric of gratitude conveyed multiple themes. To begin, he placed patriotism at the center of his war narrative, and he privileged the heroism and selflessness of Vietnam veterans. He separated the war from the warrior, thereby avoiding controversies concerning US military intervention in Southeast Asia and the widespread destruction wrought by the war. In addition, Carter reaffirmed "American's perceptions of their national character as hardworking, beneficent . . . and just."[6] These rhetorical choices produced "a new identity and a new direction" for Vietnam veterans,[7] by presenting them as idealized citizen soldiers in contradistinction to the narratives promulgated by the antiwar movement. Carter adopted redemption strategies that infused "the war with a nobility that it lacked during the actual conflict." Moreover, he integrated Vietnam veterans into the larger community of American veterans who had fought for noble causes, and his rhetoric of gratitude framed their service as "a positive event."[8]

Carter's rhetoric of gratitude often competed with a countervailing characterization of the Vietnam veteran as victim. According to the expositors of the narrative of victimhood, those who served in Vietnam were first victimized by an unfair system of military conscription that afforded white middle-class and affluent young men the privilege of deferments. As a result, the sons of the nation's poor and minorities and those of the working class were sent to Vietnam to face an extraordinarily difficult set of circumstances.

While serving in that country, these unfortunate sons confronted a peculiarly savage form of combat; some battled drug addiction, and some were subjected to a racist military culture and command structure, the argument goes, that so degraded them that many were physically and emotionally damaged forever by their ordeal. The victimization continued upon their return stateside when those who served perceived the absence of a homecoming welcome as a signifier of a societal disregard for their ongoing struggles. A historically bad national economy and high unemployment rates compounded their post-service victimization. They were even, according to some narrators, emasculated by their participation in the war because their multi-year absence from civilian life had afforded women an avenue to bypass them in the race for jobs and social standing. Eric T. Dean Jr. has questioned the merits of these characterizations, but he has shown how the media in particular cast the Vietnam veteran "as *unique* amongst veterans of all American wars."[9]

Unfortunately, scholars have not devoted meaningful attention to Carter's rhetorical choices on the Vietnam War and that war's veterans.[10] He was generally regarded as a poor communicator and formal public speaker.[11] A common complaint, as noted by scholar Mary Stuckey, was that Carter's rhetoric was often flush with "strategic ambiguity," in part from his proclivity to stress his values and judgment over "specific policy proposals."[12] This line of criticism does not describe accurately his rhetoric on Vietnam or the veterans of that war. Indeed, he employed targeted and focused language on the subjects throughout the entirety of his elected career. In this vein, Carter navigated with intentionality the cultural and political debates about the readjustment struggles of those Americans who fought and served in Vietnam.

A Debt of Gratitude does not suggest that Vietnam veterans' issues as a national agenda item originated with Carter or that he was solely responsible for defining and implementing Vietnam veterans' policies. In fact, an entire network of Vietnam veteran advocates that coalesced in the late 1970s contributed to the process. In Congress, members of the bipartisan Vietnam Veterans in Congress caucus constituted a unique and authoritative participant. Activist groups such as the Council of Vietnam Veterans, later reconstituted as Vietnam Veterans of America, as well as Agent Orange Victims International pushed various agendas. Finally, some of the nation's most prominent journalists—such as *Washington Post* editors Philip Geyelin and Colman McCarthy, as well as Ward Sinclair, Bernard Weinraub, and Charles

Mohr of the *New York Times*—helped to frame the agenda-setting processes. At times, Carter lost control of the Vietnam veterans' agenda to this newly formed activist network. On other occasions, his presidential administration disagreed on the best way to define and implement policy. And like many politicians, Carter sought to manage expectations regarding the promises that he made. His motivations for advancing Vietnam veterans' issues as a national agenda item were not always clear or singular. Generally speaking, some combination of personal, practical, or political reasoning guided his policy decisions. Regardless of his motivations, the evidence clearly shows that throughout Carter's time in elective office he wanted to be viewed as supportive of Vietnam veterans and wanted credit for his initiatives; his administrations waged a multi-front public relations battle to rebut those who criticized his efforts.

Taken in its totality, *A Debt of Gratitude* differs considerably from works by Gerald Nicosia (*Home to War: A History of the Vietnam Veterans Movement*), Myra MacPherson (*Long Time Passing: Vietnam and the Haunted Generation*), and Wilbur J. Scott (*Vietnam Veterans since the War: The Politics of PTSD, Agent Orange, and the National Memorial*). These works have defined the conversation on Vietnam veterans for a generation. Each author takes a bottom-up approach highlighting the emotional and physical toll of the war, and they sometimes concentrate on volatile personalities or groups. Scott writes from the perspective of a trained sociologist and that of a former Vietnam combat officer. His account highlights stories of protest from "the major social movements among Vietnam veterans from 1967 to 1990." MacPherson, a journalist, covered Vietnam veterans for the *Washington Post* in the 1970s and 1980s. She was drawn closer to their plight after viewing the film *Friendly Fire*, a cinematic account of two distraught and embittered Iowa parents who fought a government cover-up to learn the truth about the death of their soldier-son who was killed in Vietnam. MacPherson, by her own admission, adopts a motherly perspective to explore "the effect of the war *as it was* on the generation asked to fight it." Each of these works relied quite extensively on oral history interviews and tended to amplify the depiction of the frustrated and victimized Vietnam veteran. While useful in a variety of ways, there is certainly room for both an alternative approach and different lines of inquiry into the Vietnam veteran story.[13]

Toward that end, *A Debt of Gratitude* offers a methodological and perspectival contrast to most works on Vietnam veterans. It makes an archival contribution by bringing to light overlooked and neglected materials. The vast reservoir of archival collections at the Jimmy Carter Presidential Library, primarily the Records of the Domestic Policy Staff, the Media Liaison Files, the Veterans Affairs Files, the White House Central Files, the White House Press Files, and the Max Cleland Papers, provide sources for fresh insights into the debates over the nation's obligation to Vietnam veterans. The Domestic Policy Staff, in particular, produced an avalanche of documents that Carter meticulously poured over, sometimes adding handwritten comments or instructions for follow-up actions. These records, more than any other source, reveal the president's thought processes as his administration pursued various policies related to Vietnam veterans. The reliance on archival materials avoids one of the common pitfalls of presidential studies: an over-use of oral history interviews, something that imposes a worrisome risk of revisionist or retrospective accounts of past events and decisions.

Similarly, the wider interpretive arch and decade-long time frame fills a noticeable void in the scholarly literature on policymaking and the Vietnam veteran. For too long, Ronald Reagan and his affirmation of Vietnam has cast a long shadow over the study of the war's veterans. In a noteworthy address to the Veterans of Foreign Wars convention in 1980, Reagan declared that American involvement in Vietnam "was, in truth, a noble cause. A small country newly free from colonial rule sought our help in establishing self-rule and the means of self-defense against a totalitarian neighbor bent on conquest."[14] Scholars see Reagan's noble cause speech as a transformational moment in the contested memory of the Vietnam War.[15] For example, in his history of veterans in America, Joseph Darda writes that a transfiguration of the Vietnam veteran from a victim or "minoritized outsider" to a new form of war hero occurred in the 1980s.[16] Others, such as Jerry Lembcke, point to a new "mythologizing of the Vietnam War" that gained "prominence during the first years of the Reagan presidency." This orientation to the Reagan era has relegated the mid- to late 1970s to a zone of "grey space."[17] In actuality, Carter colored in this space and both facilitated the transfiguration of the Vietnam veteran and contributed to a revisionist view of the war. As *A Debt of Gratitude* argues, Carter's policy prescriptions and his rhetoric of gratitude form an earlier junction point in the ascendency of the celebratory discourse of Vietnam War veterans. In addition, Carter's political career overlaps a crucial period in the Vietnam veterans' readjustment story, one that has been mischaracterized as "a decade of virtual silence about Vietnam veterans."[18]

Without question, many veterans, for a variety of reasons, did not talk about their war experiences. There were those who encountered difficulties with their homecoming readjustments and can legitimately claim their needs were not fully met or their service appropriately honored. However, there is little validity that a prolonged period of silence prevailed when there was no meaningful dialogue about the war or the nation's obligations to those who served in Vietnam. Thus, *A Debt of Gratitude* functions as a corrective to the myth of silence and improves our understanding of a formative period in America's collective memory of the Vietnam veteran.

The book is divided into three chronological periods: the Georgia years, the presidential election of 1976, and the Carter presidency. Chapter 1 examines Carter's time as governor and how Georgia functioned as his training ground with respect to Vietnam veterans' policy. The chapter chronicles his appointment of the Georgia Advisory Committee on Vietnam Veterans and the ensuing two-year legislative debate over a free college tuition proposal for Georgia's Vietnam veterans. This foundational chapter concerning the state's responsibility to Vietnam veterans provides a crucial understanding of Carter's approach to Vietnam veterans' issues. In chapter 2, a discussion of the 1976 presidential election shows the continuing political reverberations of the Vietnam War. Although Carter supported the war in Vietnam while governor, he began his quest for the Democratic nomination by making a politically calculated decision to present himself as an antiwar candidate. Consequently, he fielded questions about his prior stances. His attempt to parse the meanings of pardon and amnesty for Vietnam draft evaders drew critical scrutiny, as did revelations that he had formally declared American Fighting Men's Day as a response to the My Lai massacre court-martial verdict. After securing his party's nomination, Carter accused incumbent president Gerald Ford and the Republican Party of abandoning Vietnam veterans and promised that if he were elected president he would push forward a comprehensive agenda to meet their many needs. His condemnation of his opponents and corresponding pledge of commitment raised expectations among Vietnam veteran activists and became the standard upon which they judged Carter throughout his presidency.

Most of *A Debt of Gratitude* examines the Carter presidency. Chapter 3 looks at his first year in office and the launching of his Vietnam veterans' agenda. On the day after his inauguration, Carter pardoned the Vietnam War draft evaders, and a few months later he waded into an even bigger controversy when he proposed upgrading the discharge status of 100,000 Vietnam-era military deserters. These discordant moves were offset by a substantial job creation initiative for Vietnam veterans, which he announced as part of a national economic stimulus package. Carter made another consequential decision when he appointed the first Vietnam veteran, Max Cleland, to head the Veterans Administration. Despite these early efforts, Carter faced a barrage of criticisms when the jobs program failed to produce immediate results. Critics also faulted him for not providing leadership on his own discharge upgrade program when bipartisan opposition killed the plan. At the end of his first year in office, Carter faced serious doubts about his commitment to Vietnam veterans.

Chapter 4 covers the critical second year of the Carter presidency. In 1978 he approved a Presidential Review Memorandum on the Status of Vietnam Veterans (PRM), the first such study originating from the executive branch since the war began and one modeled on the Georgia Advisory Committee on Vietnam Veterans. The PRM concluded that for the most part, Vietnam veterans had made a successful readjustment to civilian life. This celebratory narrative of the Vietnam veteran proved to be a pivotal moment for the administration. From this point, Carter linked his policies to the successful readjustment of Vietnam veterans. Furthermore, he claimed to have fulfilled his major campaign promises to Vietnam veterans. Subsequently, the administration concentrated more narrowly on dealing with high unemployment rates among disabled and minority veterans, to enhancing GI Bill services and benefits, and to promoting public recognition of Vietnam veterans. The PRM set the tone and direction of Carter's Vietnam veterans' policies for the remainder of his presidency.

During the third year of the Carter presidency, the administration made a deeper commitment to showing appreciation and gratitude to Vietnam veterans through public ceremonies, proclamations, and special occasions such as Vietnam Veterans Week. Chapter 5 explores the various reactions to these commemorative endeavors. Most notably, Robert Muller of Vietnam Veterans of America and Representative David E. Bonior (D-MI) of the Vietnam Veterans in Congress caucus challenged the authenticity and credibility of the administration. These groups subsequently proposed the Vietnam Veterans Act, a comprehensive benefits package that dwarfed, both in scale and scope, the recommendations of the Presidential Review Memorandum.

Chapter 6 chronicles the final year of the Carter presidency. As he faced reelection in 1980, Carter had a substantial record to run on, and he firmly believed that he had strengthened the nation's commitment to all veterans and had fulfilled his promises to Vietnam veterans. Therefore, it came as a near complete surprise that Republican challenger Ronald Reagan and the former national commanders of several influential veterans' groups hit the campaign trail and accused Carter of being a hypocrite on Vietnam veterans' issues. This politically contrived veterans revolt marks a pivotal moment where two presidential candidates and two political parties staked a claim to being the guardian and defender of Vietnam veterans. It is highly unlikely that this climatic episode would have occurred had Carter not first played a leading role in establishing Vietnam veterans' issues as a national agenda item.

A Debt of Gratitude demonstrates that the quantity and scope of Carter's legislative and commemorative efforts positioned him at the forefront of fixing Vietnam veterans' issues on the national agenda. Indeed, even his numerous critics recognized him as the leader of this important debate, and the battles with Congress, the media, and the various activist groups over the direction of the Vietnam veterans' agenda testified to the growing vitality of these issues. Moreover, Carter's rhetoric of gratitude created an image of the Vietnam veteran that stood in stark contrast to the narrative of victimhood. In short, Carter's career as an elected official provides a lens for reevaluating the Vietnam veterans' readjustment story and provides a basis for analyzing the political rhetoric that animated the national discussion over the meaning of the Vietnam War and the responsibility of the federal government to Vietnam veterans.

1

Illuminating Vietnam Veterans

The signing of the Paris Peace Accords on January 27, 1973, prescribed an exact timeline for the withdrawal of the US military from the Vietnam War. The war itself, however, was not over. The North Vietnamese still held every intention of unifying the two countries under Communist rule. An abundance of editorials contemplated what military responsibility the United States still owed South Vietnam. However, the biggest story to accompany the signing of the Paris Peace Accords, at least in terms of media coverage, was the release of the American prisoners of war (POWs). On February 12 the first group of prisoners left Hanoi, and the last major release occurred on March 29. Many Americans wasted very little time in appropriating the almost six hundred former captives as the heroes of a lost war. Corporations and private citizens lined up to shower them with gifts and favors. Major League Baseball presented the POWs with lifetime passes to every major league ballpark. The POWs received offers for courtesy cars from automobile dealerships, free admission to movie theaters, country club memberships, and paid vacations to Disney World.[1] Hoping to capitalize on these outpourings of generosity and tribute, President Richard Nixon, who was starting to feel the pressure of the Watergate investigation, invited the POWs to the White House for a patriotic extravaganza.[2]

The concern heaped upon the prisoners of war following the signing of the Paris Peace Accords invigorated the debate over society's obligation to Vietnam veterans, with some journalists assailing the effusive gift-giving and the "red carpet" celebrations that had been afforded the POWs. For example, Tom Wicker of the

New York Times admitted some of the outpouring "may be well-deserved," but he was angry by the disproportionate response, calling it an example of "a warped sense of priorities." He wanted the focus placed on the troubled survivors, the ones in a new battle against unemployment and drug addiction, and he wanted to see increased federal spending to help the hundreds of thousands of deserving and vulnerable Vietnam veterans. Wicker concluded his column with an admonition, "So let us honor the P.O.W.'s and be glad their ordeal is ended; but let us remember also those who shall have borne the battle, those who need a new Ford less than a decent job, those for whom the only bracelet is a band of needle marks."[3] This final jab was a jarring statement. The bracelet reference was meant to epitomize the hypocrisy of the moment. Wicker contrasted one of the most enduring cultural symbols of the war, the VIVA (Voices in Vital America) bracelets that contained the name, rank, and date of loss of a POW or MIA serviceman, to the needle marks on the wrist of a drug-addicted veteran. His intentions were clear. Wicker fashioned a narrative of the Vietnam War that centered on the victimized veterans, the unemployed, the physically and emotionally mangled, the dope heads.

Mainstream newsweeklies painted a somewhat different picture of the plight of Vietnam veterans.[4] From this journalistic genre, *U.S. News & World Report* produced the most comprehensive coverage. Such articles as "For Veterans Seeking Work, the Picture Is Brighter" and "How Aid to Veterans Is Rising" portrayed employers as "taking special pains to hire Vietnam-era servicemen" and a federal government that was steadily increasing its efforts.[5] Its series of articles, however, did not ignore the "deep physical or emotional scars of war" that left some men struggling to readjust. Citing psychiatrists, and psychologists, *U.S. News & World Report* suggested that Vietnam veterans had "unique problems." Nevertheless, the publication recommended "civilian employment" as one of "the best and fastest ways of easing the transition."[6] The perception of veterans was fundamental to how politicians, the media, and activists framed policy considerations as part of the overarching conversation about the nation's responsibility to those who had served.[7] Moving forward, both left-leaning journalists and the more mainstream newsweeklies validated the assertion that the Paris Peace Accords marked another juncture in the debate over societal obligations to Vietnam veterans. Amid this cacophony of competing voices, important questioned remained. How would the American people and their elected political representatives respond to this opportunity to address Vietnam veterans' issues, and what exactly did Vietnam veterans think they were entitled to and why?

Georgia's Debt of Gratitude

Against this cultural and political backdrop, Governor Jimmy Carter created the Georgia Advisory Committee on Vietnam Veterans (GACVV) in order, as he stated, to repay "a debt of gratitude."[8] When he made the announcement, there were approximately 110,000 Vietnam veterans in Georgia, with more returning to the state each month.[9] Accordingly, Carter tasked the GACVV with three goals. First, "identify" problems faced by returning Vietnam veterans as well as families of POWs, KIAs, and MIAs. Second, "communicate" these problems to the general public. Third, "propose solutions to the Governor."[10] In the second year of his only term in office, Carter declared a societal debt of gratitude to Vietnam veterans with several things in mind. Without question, he adhered to a value system that held that military service was part of one's patriotic duty, an obligation of citizenship, and an essential experience of manhood. Carter's family had taught him these tenets through words and deeds. Both his father and an uncle, Thomas Gordy, were veterans. Inspired by Gordy, Carter decided, at age six, to pursue a career as a naval officer, eventually receiving an appointment to the US Naval Academy. Upon graduation, he served as an officer in the Navy from 1946 to 1953, completing deployments in both the Atlantic and Pacific fleets. He resigned from active duty in October 1953 to take over the family peanut business upon the death of his father. Carter's oldest son, John William (Jack) Carter, followed family tradition. In 1969 Jack voluntarily joined the Navy and completed a tour in Vietnam, a fact his father often alluded to in political speeches and when wooing certain voters.[11]

Proud of his family's martial heritage, Carter, the politician, nevertheless recognized the importance of veterans as a constituency. In 1970, the year Carter successfully campaigned for governor, roughly one million Americans had exited military service.[12] As governor, Carter could not ignore such a large influx of Vietnam veterans populating the state. He was cognizant of trends occurring across the country as a host of individual states debated their responsibilities to Vietnam veterans. Illinois and California had tuition assistance programs, and at least nine states already offered cash bonuses to

Vietnam veterans, ranging from $100 in Illinois to $750 in Pennsylvania.[13] During Carter's term as governor, cash bonuses were a hot topic in several states, with a total of fifteen states and the Territory of Guam offering such payments. Ohio approved $300 million in bonds to pay bonuses of $500 to each Vietnam veteran, and West Virginians authorized $40 million in bonds to cover a $400 bonus to each of the war's veterans. Other states, such as Massachusetts and South Dakota, which had created bonus programs in the late 1960s, ensured solvency of their programs through additional bond measures or appropriations in the amount of $15 million and $4 million respectively.[14] The Western Conference of the Council of State Governments convened in San Francisco to identify problems faced by returning veterans, to propose specific legislative and programmatic solutions, and to determine how best to coordinate efforts between the private sector and federal, state, and local representatives.[15] Thus, it was for personal and practical reasons that Carter created a state-level executive committee to examine the readjustment problems faced by the newest generation of war veterans and make them part of his administration's agenda.

The governor tapped Max Cleland, a Vietnam veteran and triple amputee, to chair the committee. Cleland sustained his catastrophic injuries in the aftermath of Operation Pegasus, an overland relief mission to break the siege at Khe Sanh during the 1968 Tet Offensive. After completing a prolonged and difficult rehabilitation journey, he decided to run for a seat in the Georgia Senate. He scored an upset victory in 1970, becoming the only Democratic candidate to defeat an incumbent Republican; his own district voted Republican, eschewing Carter, in that year's gubernatorial race. At the age of twenty-eight, he entered the Georgia Senate as the youngest man and only Vietnam veteran. He won a second term in November 1972. Carter's selection of Cleland to guide the GACVV was a logical choice. His résumé included serving on the advisory council of the US Senate Veterans' Affairs Committee, and he had testified before the US Congress on several occasions.[16] For Cleland, "the very purpose" of the GACVV was to impress upon all Georgians the "grave responsibility" that they had to Vietnam veterans. He wanted everyone to relate to the war's veterans "in a more positive way" and to assist them in making "the most of their benefits and lives."[17]

The GACVV convened formal hearings on February 9 and 10, 1973, in Atlanta. To better manage such a wide-ranging investigation in the middle of a legislative session, the GACVV created subcommittees to gather information and to render findings on drug abuse, disability issues, and employment concerns.[18] However, the dominant discussion to emerge from these efforts concerned education benefits.[19]

For some time, questions surrounded the parity of the Vietnam GI Bill. Signed in 1967 by President Lyndon Johnson, the Vietnam GI Bill followed the basic template of benefits offered to World War II and Korean War veterans. As such, Vietnam veterans were entitled to educational, vocational, and housing assistance as well as home loan guarantees, aid for farm purchases, preferential treatment for federal jobs, employment counseling services, and various types of medical treatment and care. One major concern with the Vietnam GI Bill was its perceived lack of parity with its forerunners in the area of educational benefits. In short, Vietnam veterans received a higher educational stipend in dollar terms than previous generations of veterans. However, the explosive rise in tuition costs coupled with the lack of low-cost affordable housing, which most colleges and universities made available to World War II veterans, meant that the value of the educational allowance was considerably less for Vietnam veterans. Although a great deal was accomplished on behalf of Vietnam veterans, historian Mark Boulton concludes, "the reality remained that the benefits being offered did, in fact, fall well short of the previous iterations of the GI Bill." He further maintains that all through the debates, "there was little consideration given in Washington to the specific needs of returning Vietnam combat veterans," and argues that the Johnson-era bills "were providing some education for most, but not a good education for all, as the previous [GI] bills had done."[20] When Carter led Georgia into the discussion over the nation's obligation to Vietnam veterans following the Paris Peace Accords, he did so with a series of parity questions foregrounded into the debate.

In real terms, the Vietnam GI Bill "covered only 58.2 percent of the average single veteran's annual [educational] expenses," which entailed tuition, living expenses, and other costs. Nationally, 60 percent of returnees had not taken full advantage of existing educational offerings, which was slightly lower that the participation rates after either World War II or the Korean War.[21] In Georgia, the nonparticipation number was an astounding 80 percent.[22] A survey of two thousand Vietnam veterans in Georgia, both enrolled students and nonstudents, revealed that for over 90 percent affordability was the main reason they could not pursue additional education. For those veterans currently enrolled in college-level programs, 83 percent replied that the GI Bill provided no more than half of the income they needed to stay in school, which forced them to seek employment "or borrow heavily into debt." Roughly two-thirds of the surveyed student-veterans worked "full or part-time to stay in school," which hampered their academic success.[23]

At the time there were 13,000 Vietnam veterans enrolled in Georgia's colleges and universities. The University System was strongly in favor of increasing those numbers because of recent declines in enrollment.[24] Support for education reform was also strong among activists Vietnam veterans.[25] The most extensive effort was led by Bert Westbrook, a former West Point graduate and officer who resigned from the Army in the summer of 1971 because of his opposition to the war in Vietnam. Concerned about how education and employment issues impacted Georgia's Vietnam veterans, Westbrook secured funding from the Rockefeller Foundation and the Hazen and Whitney Foundations for a comprehensive statewide study. The completed research was publicized under the auspices of the Georgia Veterans Project and included a recommendation of free college tuition for Georgia's Vietnam veterans. The recommendation was drafted into a formal legislative proposal known as Senate Bill No. 172 (SB-172).[26]

Free College Tuition Debate

As Carter's designated head of Vietnam veterans' issues, Cleland assumed the legislative point position for SB-172. He introduced the measure early in the 1973 legislative session. It called for the state to grant tuition scholarships, "not to exceed $150 per quarter, for any person who served in the Armed Forces of the United States since August, 1964, who was a resident of Georgia at the time of entry into the service, and to dependents of POW/MIAs." To qualify, a veteran had to "begin a program of study within four years after leaving the service, or within four years after enactment of the bill (whichever is later)." Based on current student-veteran enrollment, projected tuition costs, and an anticipated enrollment increase of 25 percent, SB-172 carried an annual price tag of $5.8 million. As conceived, the program had tight eligibility parameters, a relatively short life, and a modest price tag.[27] By comparison, small states such as West Virginia and South Dakota and even the Territory of Guam were investing millions of dollars more in Vietnam veterans' programs.

Not everyone agreed with the broad inclusiveness of the bill. "I don't know if I favor giving a veteran who spent two years at Ft. McPherson in Atlanta the same consideration as a man who spent nine months in Vietnam," retorted Senator James Lester. The Democrat from Augusta recommended limiting the tuition grants to those who actually served in Southeast Asia. Other legislators suggested a more restrictive Georgia residency requirement. Cleland disagreed with such amendments but did not formally oppose them in order to move a meaningful bill forward.[28] To his relief, a compromise was not necessary. On March 6, 1973, the Senate passed SB-172. Cleland praised the body for its commitment to Vietnam veterans, saying, after everything they "have gone through, it is only right that the State help them. . . . I think the State can absorb this cost for a few years for these men."[29]

When SB-172 arrived in the House, members of the University System Committee voted "overwhelmingly" to table the measure for further study. This decision meant the measure had no chance to reach the floor for a vote during the 1973 General Assembly session. Cleland erupted, viewing the setback as a personal insult as well as a slap in the face to all Vietnam veterans.[30] Frustrated on many levels, he chided his colleagues for blocking the tuition scholarships while allowing proposed legislation "regulating astrologers" to reach the floor for debate.[31] Despite the derailment, Cleland vowed to continue fighting, and his optimism seemed justified.[32]

There was considerable support for SB-172 among various Georgia constituencies. Administrators at Georgia colleges and universities needed higher enrollments at their institutions. Sensing an opportunity to boost its numbers, the University System indicated that its existing "administrative structure" could accommodate a new scholarship program with "no difficulty."[33] Likewise, those concerned with economic development recognized that creating an educated workforce had tangible benefits for the state. The media lent its support. Atlanta's WAGA television station and Elmo Ellis of WSB Radio issued on-air appeals, and journalists around the state wrote editorials backing the plan.[34] SB-172 captured enough public interest that the Georgia Federation of Women's Clubs formally endorsed the measure as one of its "legislative priorities" at its 1973 annual state convention.[35] Everyone seemed to agree that the proposal was a worthwhile endeavor.

Illuminating Vietnam Veterans

For the final six months of 1973, Cleland traveled throughout Georgia, talking about the tuition measure with college students and speaking to various veteran organizations.[36] Although he received enthusiastic receptions, Cleland foresaw that compromise was an inevitable conclusion. He admitted to one student-veteran that presenting the original proposal to the 1974 General Assembly "would be like throwing the bill back to the lions." Cleland based this concession on several political realities, of which the most important was the governor's "hard line against new programs."[37] The intervening year had also shifted the legislature's focus to other matters, and "the big issues" included a tax cut discussion and funding for the World Congress Center, an Atlanta convention and meeting venue.[38] Given these substantial headwinds, Cleland backed a Carter-endorsed proposal that gave Vietnam veterans "a preference for loans and grants as opposed to free tuition." The alternative plan drew from an existing state program that received matching federal funds.[39]

On February 19, 1974, roughly one year after SB-172 was first introduced, the Georgia General Assembly passed a bill that amended the Georgia Higher Education Assistance Authority and gave Vietnam veterans "preference" in two existing state scholarship programs. The maximum award allowed to each student-veteran was $450 per academic year, and recipients were not required to repay the awards. Anyone with a greater financial need was encouraged to apply for state loans. The combined annual funding for the two scholarship programs was $800,000, well short of the figures associated with the original goals of the SB-172 measure. Very few details were released to gauge the potential impact of the compromise measure. Everyone spoke of the need to support Vietnam veterans, but no concrete alternatives to the compromise emerged. Rather than admit defeat, Cleland proclaimed victory. "I feel that it is a solid step forward in giving our boys who served their country, the dignity, honor, and recognition that they deserve." In this sense, he cast the tuition measure as a tangible sign that the governor had made Vietnam veterans part of his legislative agenda.[40]

In appointing the Georgia Advisory Committee on Vietnam Veterans, Carter signaled his concern for the readjustment struggles of the war's veterans. Although he authorized Cleland, the committee members, and other advocates in his office to pursue policy options on his behalf, he provided an underlying set of instructions. Early in the process, Bert Westbrook, the

Vietnam veteran whose work led to the free tuition proposal, accepted a position as a paid consultant to the governor. In that capacity, Westbrook wrote to Cleland prior to the hearings asking him to concentrate on "identifying the problems by illumination rather than undertaking a quantitative analysis." He added, "given the confining parameters of time and money we will not be able to offer an in-depth analysis of program alternatives." Westbrook also shared his view that "the main reason" for the committee's "existence—is to propose viable solutions to the Governor." Viable solutions were not defined specifically in the communique, but the inference was clear. There needed to be a balance between idealism and pragmatism.[41]

For example, the GACVV's Subcommittee on Employment came away from the hearings with few concerns. It found that Vietnam veterans had positive attitudes, for the most part, and wanted "nothing more than parity with other veterans," and it concluded that Vietnam veterans' employment issues were not "as serious" as some individuals and groups alleged. Consequently, the subcommittee made minor recommendations. It suggested making the private sector more aware of the work experience and abilities "obtained" by veterans while they served in the military, and it encouraged the Georgia state government to hire more Vietnam veterans "whenever possible."[42] In truth, the situation in Georgia was unique and was not indicative of the unemployment struggles of Vietnam veterans nationally. The main reasons, according to several reports, were "patriotic" feelings among employers who believed they owed veterans "something" and the Atlanta-based industrial community that created a favorable job market especially compared to Midwestern and Northern states.[43] These conditions allowed the governor to accept policy solutions that did not require long-term budgetary outlays. Instead, he relied on public relations and job counseling services to connect veterans with employers. Carter's "Jobs for Veterans Year" epitomized this approach. Although consistent with his commitment to fiscal conservatism and his preference for private-sector solutions, the "Jobs for Veterans Year" was also a response to a federal initiative that asked governors, mayors, and local communities to conduct job fairs and appoint task forces so that recently discharged veterans were properly informed about the current state of the job market, on-the-job training programs, and employers committed to veterans' preference in hiring.[44]

The governor's "Salute to Vietnam Veterans Week" represented another example of the illumination strategy. In early September 1973, once again following an initiative started by President Nixon, Carter signed an executive proclamation designating the third week of September as an opportunity for the state to recognize and show appreciation to Vietnam veterans.[45] Cleland served as the co-chair of the Salute, and the organizing committee's main task was preparing public service announcements and media kits for the commemorative celebration.[46] One radio/TV spot exemplified the endeavor.

Ok, you're a veteran. You've spent three years in the jungles of Southeast Asia, and now you're back home wondering what to do about your future. There are some people waiting to help you find answers—about education, benefits, jobs. Call 800/282-9278 and tell them you're a veteran looking for answers. They'll give you a line to your future.[47]

Through these special observances, the "Salute to Vietnam Veterans Week" and "Jobs for Veterans Year," Carter determined that his primary responsibility was to honor those who had served in the nation's most unpopular war by showing "gratitude" and "appreciation."[48]

In hindsight, Carter formulated an approach to handling Vietnam veterans' issues as governor of Georgia that foretold the approach that he adopted as president of the United States. The promise to "study" their problems was a way to express concern, and his appointment of the executive-level Georgia Advisory Committee on Vietnam Veterans made the governor appear action oriented.[49] The proclamations, commemorative events, and job programs conveyed his preferences to rely on the rhetoric of gratitude, avoid expensive new polices, and eliminate unnecessary bureaucracy. He used this formula for making Vietnam veterans' issues part of his governing agenda.

The Road to the White House

The Watergate scandal and the Vietnam War cast dark clouds over the 1976 presidential election.[50] Timing was a key variable in Carter's decision to make a run for the White House. "He was the right man at the right time at the right place," remarked pollster Pat Caddell. "I don't think he would have been successful in 1972. He'd have gotten eaten up in the Vietnam War issue. He was a product of Watergate in a way."[51] Vietnam, in particular, had not only "increased cynicism about government and the presidency," but the war, as historian Laura Kalman has written, divided America "along the lines of race, religion, and, above all, class" in ways not seen since the Civil War. She rightly suggests that some in the country wanted to forget Vietnam, thinking that "amnesia might unify" the nation. Yet, Kalman recognizes that Watergate and Vietnam would not be so easily effaced. There were segments of the population who did not wish to forget. In her estimation, the most important was the political right, which "delighted" in blaming liberals for leading the nation into war, for losing "their nerve" when things got tough, for reversing course by embracing the war's resisters, and for retreating from the challenges of Communism.[52] Kalman might too have added that the political left was equally determined to keep the debate over the war alive. It no longer focused on ending American involvement in Vietnam. Instead, the left wanted to provoke a national reckoning over America's tragic misadventure in Southeast Asia and to plot a new course in US foreign policy. For many who had been part of the antiwar community, addressing the troubled readjustment of Vietnam veterans was part of that political and moral imperative.[53]

During his four years as governor, Carter navigated the controversial Vietnam War by taking "the easy route," according to his biographer E. Stanly Godbold. For the most part, the Georgian played the role of a hawk. He defended the American presence in Vietnam, he supported the troops, and he muted any criticisms of the war that he had.[54] However, when he left office in 1975 and began his campaign for presidency, Carter briefly presented himself as an antiwar Democrat, temporarily jettisoning his hawkish political and cultural positions. Certain members of the media recognized his personal revisionism and challenged him to explain the sudden shift. He was not always persuasive in answering his critics, but he spoke more clearly and convincingly when he cast himself as a strong supporter of Vietnam veterans.

2

The Vietnam Campaign

On December 12, 1974, Jimmy Carter appeared before the National Press Club in Washington, DC, to officially launch his bid for the Democratic Party presidential nomination. He described himself as a "farmer, an engineer, a businessman, a planner, a scientist, a governor and a Christian." He spoke of shared national values such as "courage, compassion, integrity, and dedication to basic human rights and freedoms." The major theme of his remarks was how government had failed and betrayed the American people. Carter staked his campaign to his own personal integrity and pledged to make government honest and more efficient. In terms of policies and programs, Carter promised to protect the environment, to reduce energy consumption, to support military preparedness, to tackle individual and corporate tax reform as well as welfare reform, to promote a comprehensive national health-care program, to curtail nuclear proliferation, and to negotiate arms reductions. He covered virtually the entire political spectrum. Carter even made an implicit reference to the Vietnam War when he stated, "The time for American intervention in all the problems of the world is over," but he made no comment on the veterans who had served in that conflict.[1]

The Georgian sprinted out of the starting blocks with an eye toward taking advantage of changes in the nominating process. Following the 1972 presidential election, the Democratic National Committee amended its rules and the new guidelines put in play a record number of pledged delegates in a record number of state primaries.[2] To capitalize on these changes, Carter committed to entering every state primary contest. He was the only Democratic candidate to do so. As he campaigned, Carter presented himself as a political outsider. He tended to eschew the "policy orthodoxies to which most Democrats subscribed."[3] This practice translated into a political strategy that focused on "unobjectionable values instead of specific issues and exploiting the nation's anti-Washington mood."[4]

For two and one-half years, Carter tried to be all things to all voters. On one level, he succeeded. Opinion surveys by the *New York Times* and *CBS News* revealed that conservative voters viewed Carter as conservative, moderates deemed him moderate, and liberals considered him liberal.[5] The results were not completely unexplainable. Carter's "politics defy categorization—perhaps intentionally," observed Elizabeth Drew, who covered the 1976 presidential primaries and general election for the *New Yorker*. She considered the dark horse candidate's success more a function of his ability to appeal to voters on a personal level than a result of an ideological connection. Drew also noted that Carter was intentional with his words, careful of unnecessarily offending any constituency.[5] After he won four of the first five primaries, journalists and political commentators pushed the candidate to clarify his positions.[7] Carter had invited the scrutiny by repeatedly telling voters, "I will never tell you a lie" or even make "misleading statements."[8] In early 1976 Carter sat down with representatives of the *Washington Post* for a discussion on a wide-range of topics including a set of Vietnam-related questions. The first of the war-related questions covered how he would handle the legal cases of Vietnam draft evaders, something that had deeply scared the Democratic Party in 1972.[9] To understand the importance of this political issue and how the broader topic of the Vietnam War resonated during the campaign, it is necessary to first examine the amnesty debate during the 1972 presidential election.

The Taint of Amnesty

Somewhere between 40,000 and 50,000 men had illegally evaded the Vietnam draft. Their resistance took many forms. Some played an active role in the antiwar movement and were arrested, prosecuted, and convicted for their actions. Others took a less conspicuous approach, forfeiting their identities to live underground. Some even left the country for places like Canada,

England, and Sweden, where they became high-profile political exiles. Although these draft evaders had violated the law, many in the antiwar community judged their defiance as a heroic and legitimate form of political protest. Indeed, as journalist Barry Werth has written, "The political exiles were to the antiwar movement what the POW/MIA were to the VFW" [Veterans of Foreign Wars].[10] This admiration and approval of war resisters played out in the halls of Congress.

In the early 1970s, proposing amendments to grant amnesty to draft evaders functioned as a type of congressional antiwar activism comparable to proposing amendments to cut off defense funding in order to end the war in Southeast Asia.[11] While these efforts attracted bipartisan supporters, the amnesty issue became most closely identified with the antiwar Democratic senator from South Dakota, George McGovern. Starting in the fall of 1971, McGovern used the promise of amnesty for draft evaders as a rallying cry in his quest for the Democratic nomination for president. His speeches on this issue drew "wild applause" on college campuses and enticed student activists to join his campaign.[12] These advantages may have helped McGovern secure his party's nomination, but many Americans viewed the South Dakotan as the defender of radical feminists, homosexuals, Black militants, welfare recipients, and countercultural hippies.[13] In fact, detractors in both parties labeled him a dangerous liberal and the standard-bearer of "acid, amnesty, and abortion," a charge that was grossly misleading. McGovern rejected abortion on demand, believing individual states should decide the matter, not the federal government. He did not support the legalization of marijuana, although he favored decriminalization of the drug for casual users. Only with respect to amnesty did the Democratic nominee take an unequivocal position, one that was at odds with the majority of the American people.[14] A June 1972 Gallup Poll, focusing only on those draft evaders who left the country, revealed that 60 percent of Americans felt they should not be let back into the country "without some form of punishment." This attitude was bipartisan in nature, with 71 percent of Republicans and 59 percent of Democrats calling for the imposition of a penalty. An August presidential candidate poll found that 62 percent of respondents were less likely to support a nominee who would allow draft evaders to return to the country without punishment.[15]

Acid, amnesty, and abortion were "the terms on which many voters viewed" McGovern, historian Robert Mason contends, and as a result Richard Nixon "worked hard to ensure that this image of McGovern dominated" the campaign. In the end, McGovern never polled above 35 percent of the vote, and the 1972 presidential contest turned into a rout. Nixon received the greatest plurality of the electorate in American history; even 42 percent of self-identified Democratic voters cast their ballots for the Republican incumbent. Moreover, polls indicated that McGovern's antiwar positions, which were the basis of his entire campaign, hurt him with most voters, with only one in four Americans thinking he would handle the war better than Nixon.[16] Neither Nixon's reelection nor the signing of the Paris Peace Accords in January 1973 did anything to make the general public more sympathetic to draft evaders. Interestingly, the number of Americans favoring some type of punishment climbed to 67 percent, with the percentage among Democrats rising slightly.[17] A national survey released in March 1973 indicated that amnesty ranked "second after school busing as the most delicate political issue in the nation."[18] Not until spring 1974 did attitudes begin to soften, but still the number of Americans favoring some type of punishment stood at 58 percent.[19]

Amnesty by Pardon

From the outset of his bid for the Democratic presidential nomination, Jimmy Carter sought a middle ground on the festering draft evader question that avoided the political controversies of the past. As he explained, he opposed "blanket amnesty because this would equate illegal defection from service in Vietnam with sacrificial service there by many who objected to the war but went regardless. I believe that those who have lived in exile for many years have been adequately punished, I favor a pardon for them."[20] Carter drew a distinction between the meaning of the words "amnesty" and "pardon," telling journalists and voters, "amnesty says what you did was right. Pardon says, whether what you did was right or wrong, you are forgiven for it." With these explanations, Carter tried to persuade Americans that his proposal reflected their values and differed from the one offered by McGovern. Carter did not defend the decisions made by the draft evaders. In fact, he criticized them, referring to their actions as an "illegal defection." As for the necessity of punishment, Carter held that the draft evaders had served an appropriate sentence for their transgressions through living "in exile for many years." Moreover, he affirmed the "sacrificial service" of the many who went to Vietnam, despite their misgivings, and offered their patriotic example as a shared ideal worthy of the nation's gratitude.[21]

The US Supreme Court had previously ruled that no legal distinction existed between presidential amnesties and pardons. Carter's parsing of "pardon" and "amnesty" was an attempt to navigate the politics of the draft evader question.[22] Some believed the Georgian's choice of terminology might work. William A. Strauss, the deputy director of the Vietnam Offender Study at the University of Notre Dame, identified the salient considerations in a letter to Peter Bourne, a long-time Carter advisor. "Amnesty is an issue which can be more harmful than helpful to a candidate," Strauss wrote in mid-February 1976. "I think Governor Carter's early comments on the issue were very good. He widely deflected the issue from 'amnesty' to the same thing under another label ('blanket pardon'). This is the only way a lot of middle-of-the-road people can be persuaded to do anything."[23] Strauss's "same thing under another label" designation seemed to confirm what journalist David E. Rosenbaum suspected about Carter when he wrote in the *New York Times* that the candidate utilized "subtle semantic distinctions" to convince people on "both sides of a question to believe that he is on their side."[24] Jody Powell, a campaign advisor and spokesperson, admitted in an interview with journalist Martin Schram of *Newsday* that the "answer on amnesty is a classic example of how to say something and not piss off people." Schram did not feel Powell's "shorthand explanation" did Carter justice, describing the move as "an art form—carefully constructed so as to diffuse the emotions of the subject and come up with something for everyone."[25]

Some in the media thought Carter's rhetorical sleight of hand might convince middle America that he offered a common-sense solution to a vexing problem. There were others, such as conservative columnists Rowland Evans and Robert Novak, who believed Carter was trying to compensate for the lack of an identifiable ideological core. They saw his pardon policy as an attempt to appeal to former McGovern supporters while avoiding the other "pure left positions" that had been "fatal" to the South Dakotan's 1972 presidential run. Helen Dewar of the *Washington Post* reached a similar conclusion. She judged Carter's pardon policy as an effort to pacify the left wing of the Democratic Party, which was "suspicious of his ideological moorings."[26] Without question, Carter had a problem with McGovern supporters.

During the 1972 Democratic Party presidential primary campaign, he attempted to block McGovern's nomination. Carter maintained that the South

Dakotan was too liberal to win the general election against Nixon. To make this case, he offered various disqualifying positions, including some related to the war in Vietnam. These attacks were inflammatory. Carter derided his fellow Democrat for once delivering a public speech while standing beneath a Viet Cong flag. When McGovern advocated a precipitous withdrawal of all US forces from South Vietnam without requiring the concomitant release of American prisoners of war, the Georgian accused the candidate of abandoning the POWs.[27] Unwilling to let the issue rest, Carter successfully lobbied the Democratic Platform Committee to adopt a plank requiring the return of the POWs as a condition of any resolution to the war.[28] Given the absence of a clear-cut ideological stamp and Carter's subterfuge in 1972, former McGovern supporters had every right to be deeply suspicious of the southern Democrat.

To be sure, Carter took more moderate positions on such issues as full employment, national health insurance, busing, women's rights, and abortion in comparison to the party's liberal wing. Yet, for those who cared strongly about amnesty for draft evaders, his pardon promise at least set him apart from the major Democratic challengers, all of whom were dancing around the amnesty issue or were rejecting it outright. For example, Morris Udall of Arizona, who availed himself to liberal voters, favored some type of clemency program that absolved draft evaders if they first signed sworn statements "that they violated the law or military orders because they were conscientiously opposed to the war." Hubert Humphrey, the 1968 nominee and a man considered by some to be an unannounced candidate in 1976, advocated "some form of alternative civil, social or humanitarian service . . . as a condition for repatriation." He thought unconditional amnesty "would be a disservice to the memory of those who fought and died in Vietnam." Likewise both Robert C. Byrd of West Virginia and Henry "Scoop" Jackson of Washington opposed general amnesty because, as Byrd put it, the move might suggest vindication of those "who fled the country." Sargent Shriver came closest to the McGovern position, saying, "We must put the scars and divisions of the Vietnam War behind us" by granting unconditional amnesty to those "who in good conscience" refused to serve.[29] Shriver had been McGovern's running mate in 1972, but his candidacy was dead in the water in early 1976, leaving Carter as the only viable candidate in the amnesty camp.

Against this backdrop, Carter sat down with a team from the *Washington Post* for a thorough discussion of campaign topics. For one thing, the journalists sought clarification on Carter's pardon policy, particularly his insistence that there was a difference between granting a pardon and granting amnesty to the draft evaders. When the interviewers suggested that a pardon was typically "given after a finding of guilt," the candidate bristled and quipped, "I don't remember Richard Nixon having been found guilty." Not satisfied with the candidate's response, the journalists pressed with a follow-up. Carter acknowledged that he wanted "to draw a subtle distinction" between the two terms, but without elaborating shifted the conversation to when he would issue the pardon, stating he would do so during his first week in office. Perhaps convinced that this particular line of questioning was going nowhere, the *Washington Post* panel then asked how and why he arrived at the position. Here Carter was more forthcoming.

In the area of the country where I live, defecting from military service is almost unheard of. . . . So for a long time it was hard for me to address the question in objective fashion, but I think it's time to get the Vietnamese war over with. I don't have any desire to punish anyone. I'd just like to tell the young folks who did defect to come back home, with no requirement that you be punished or that you serve in some humanitarian capacity or anything. Just come back home, the whole thing's over.[30]

The explanation, more than anything else, revealed the political conundrum that the candidate faced.

Carter had long believed the Vietnam War had been an albatross around the Democratic Party's neck. In December 1975 he told political writer Steven Brill that McGovern's "biggest mistake" in 1972 was that he "made the Vietnam War an issue." The taint of amnesty hanging over the McGovern candidacy was not the only problem that Carter faced. He harbored no admiration for the draft evaders, consistently referring to their actions as a form of defection or dereliction of a societal duty. Most importantly, Carter did not want to revisit or debate their actions. As he said, he did not want to "criticize" them or "punish" them; he just wanted to "issue a blanket pardon without comment."[31] The influential pro-amnesty forces in the Democratic Party did not share this perspective. They saw the war resisters as affirmation that Vietnam had been a tragic and immoral mistake. From the *Washington Post* interview, it was apparent that the Georgian was not interested in leading a national reckoning over Vietnam. The questions, however, persisted, and two months later during a campaign swing through Nevada, Carter's past and present views on the war were cast under a much brighter spotlight.

The Ghosts of Vietnam

When the Democratic front-runner entered the Silver State in May 1976, he faced accusations that he had dedicated a day of "honor" to Lieutenant William Calley, the man convicted of murder for his role in the My Lai massacre, a grisly killing spree that had resulted in the deaths of more than five hundred Vietnamese civilians. Hank Greenspun took Carter to task in a page-one editorial in the *Las Vegas Sun*. His motive for reviving the five-year old national controversy was to discredit Carter's campaign. Calley's court-martial trial had taken place at Fort Benning, Georgia. At the time, the vast majority of Georgians opposed the life sentence given to the Army lieutenant and demanded that the verdict be set aside. Amid the public outcry, a grassroots movement quickly formed. Alabama governor George Wallace and Georgia's lieutenant governor Lester Maddox, two of Carter's fiercest political rivals, sought to capitalize on the unfolding drama. Their opportunity came as the featured speakers at a Rally for Calley event near Fort Benning, which drew a crowd of 2,500 participants. The resulting momentum led to the scheduling of an additional seventy-five Rally for Calley demonstrations throughout the state. To counter these efforts and to accommodate hordes of angry Georgians, Carter organized American Fighting Men's Day. Through an official proclamation, he instructed Georgians to drive with their headlights on as a sign of support for the members of the US military. Additionally, they were to display American flags as an expression of renewed patriotism. This executive call to action was the basis of Greenspun's case that Carter had staged a day of honor for Lt. Calley. In a transparent display of contempt for Carter, Greenspun urged Nevadans to confront the Democratic front-runner at an upcoming Las Vegas campaign event and ask whether it had been appropriate for him to pay tribute to the perpetrator of "one of the most barbarous acts ever committed" by an American.

No one stepped forward to do Greenspun's bidding. Nevertheless, the editorial stung Carter, and he reacted quickly to defend himself. At a news conference, he called the allegations in the *Las Vegas Sun* patently false, arguing that proclaiming a William Calley Day in Georgia was something he "never considered." He added that when he was governor, he "never felt any attitude towards Calley except abhorrence. And I thought he should be punished and still do. I never expressed any contrary opinion."[32] Charles Mohr, who was covering the primary campaign for the New York Times, witnessed the dust-up between Carter and Greenspun and initiated his own review of the case. Mohr's investigation found that Carter had called Calley a "scapegoat" of the My Lai tragedy and had predicted that the guilty verdict would be used by those "both within this country and without . . . to cheapen and shame the reputation of American servicemen and to shake the faith of Americans in their country." These pronouncements and the significance of American Fighting Men's Day convinced Mohr that "Mr. Carter never explicitly or implicitly condemned Lieutenant Calley or his actions." Why did this matter now? Mohr was convinced that Carter, who he characterized as "one of the most prolonged and persistent" supporters of the war among those Democrats vying for the presidency, was running from or attempting to hide from his record on Vietnam. The journalist offered further proof of the candidate's Vietnam revisionism drawn from campaign stops in Indiana, Kentucky, and Illinois.[33]

At the Second Christian Church in Indianapolis, which included a large African American audience, Carter referred to Vietnam as a "racist" war and believed that America lacked any remorse for firebombing villages and killing women and children because the victims were Asian. Americans may not have thought the war was racist at the time, "but it was," Carter said. These remarks were well-received by the congregants. The church's pastor, the Reverend T. Garret Benjamin, praised the candidate for stepping "outside traditional politics" and for speaking "from a spiritual base." Jimmy Carter, the cleric beamed, "has got soul." The racist war message was repeated in Louisville and Chicago. When called to account for his remarks, Carter allowed for the development of "different perspectives" over time as well as an internal "dichotomy" about the war that was "hard" to explain. Nevertheless, he vehemently denied allegations that there were contradictions or inconsistencies between his past record and his current opinions on the war.[34] In his reporting, Mohr painted Carter as an avowed hawk while he was governor of Georgia, someone who had clearly chosen not to align himself with the antiwar wing of the Democratic Party. Now in the party's presidential primary the candidate tailored his statements on the Vietnam War for the purpose of winning the nomination, with the draft evaders issue being the most obvious of several examples. Indeed, as *New York Times* senior political correspondent James Reston wrote, "Pardon doesn't start with *a*, as in acid, abortion, and amnesty, the three *a*'s that defeated George McGovern."[35]

Mohr also brought up Carter's recent remarks on the "inequalities of sacrifice borne" by those Americans who served in Vietnam. "I think," the candidate confided, "the most heroic young people we've ever seen were those, in a way, who went to Vietnam thinking or knowing the war was wrong but because of their ignorance because of their lack of education because of their lack of prestige because they didn't know where Sweden was or didn't want to go to Canada or didn't have enough money to hide in college—they went." He continued, "I've always felt . . . a very deep sense of appreciation in my mind of the young people who were in Vietnam, who were castigated at home, who were despised because they were obeying the law, who went because they didn't want to hide."[36]

Vietnam was becoming a bit of a political quagmire for Carter, with segments of the press rehashing his one-time support for the war in light of his newly minted antiwar rhetoric and his offer to pardon draft evaders. Yet, the statements that most worried Carter's campaign managers were the characterizations of those who served in Vietnam as being too ignorant or too poor to avoid military service. An internal campaign memorandum specifically identified Mohr's piece in the *New York Times* and warned that Carter's words risked alienating a large bloc of voters, including Vietnam veterans and their families.[37] During the final months of the primary, Carter modified his statements and used his own son's decision to volunteer for service in Vietnam as a way to personally identify with and convey sympathy and respect to Vietnam veterans.

The Pardon Platform

Although Carter completed the primary season by winning the most states and accumulating the highest delegate total, he stood just short of securing the nomination outright. On the verge of victory, the Carter team quickly convinced his rivals to release their delegates and endorse the former Georgia governor. The nomination became a mere formality to be made official at the Democratic National Convention. In the meantime, designates and officials assembled to discuss the party's platform. They deliberated over a draft platform that they received from the Carter camp. As historian Daniel K. Williams has written, the Carter document "avoided nearly all the polarizing social issues that had damaged George McGovern's campaign four years earlier, and instead it focused more narrowly on economic uplift and government management." Party leaders were determined to present a united front and avoid the combative conventions of 1968 and 1972, which entailed acrimonious platform fights. After only a few days of deliberation, the platform committee gave the presumptive nominee most of what he wanted.[38] The "language" concerning such explosive issues as busing and abortion was "deliberately low-key," the *Washington Post* editorialized, and "the Vietnam issue, formerly divisive, appeared only as a fading shadow." Although the press hailed the party's achievement as a "unity platform," there had been one moment of contention, a debate over the party's position on draft evaders and military deserters.[39]

The trouble began when Sam Brown of Colorado, a one-time antiwar activist and leading proponent of unconditional amnesty, urged the adoption of a plank that gave a "full and complete pardon" to both draft evaders and military deserters.[40] Commonly misunderstood as someone who fled the battlefield in order to escape combat, a charge of military desertion was applied to any individual who was absent without leave (AWOL) for more than twenty-nine days. The number of individuals discharged from military service for desertion and at-large fugitives accused of desertion was over 100,000.[41] In 1974 President Gerald Ford instituted a clemency program to reduce the legal penalties faced by both draft evaders and military deserters. The stringent process required applicants to turn themselves in to the appropriate civilian or military authorities, take an oath of allegiance to the nation, and accept a two-year term of alternative service subject to reduction by the appropriate authority if warranted by mitigating circumstances.[42] Controversy marred the short life of the Ford clemency program, and in the end less than 20 percent of those draft evaders and military deserters eligible for clemency even completed the necessary application.[43]

Throughout the primary campaign, Carter had been unwavering on the question of draft evaders and military deserters. Regarding the former, he pledged a presidential pardon. Regarding the later, he consistently held that he favored a case-by-case or individual review, believing that military deserters were not "entitled to all the rights and benefits earned by men and women who served their full tour of duty."[44] Interestingly, the document that the Carter team presented to the Democratic Platform Committee failed to mention either draft evaders or military deserters. Not surprisingly, Carter representatives objected to Brown's plank calling for a blanket pardon for all military deserters. However, Brown made such an impassioned appeal that the committee presented the Coloradan's amendment to a voice vote. The platform chairman was unable to render a verdict due to the closeness of the voice vote, and he referred the matter to the first roll-call vote of the entire proceedings. Brown's proposal carried by a 55 to 44 vote. Carter representatives responded with a compromise granting the would-be president the option to consider deserters on a case-by-case basis. Brown, though "not enthusiastic" about the modification, consented in the interest of unity.[45] The official plank, tucked into a section on Civil and Political Rights, read: "We pledge . . . a full and complete pardon for those who are in legal or financial jeopardy because of their peaceful opposition to the Vietnam War, with deserters to be considered on a case-by-case basis."[46] The ability to resolve this issue persuaded Democrats that the party convention would be harmonious and celebratory. Certainly no one anticipated that an exiled draft evader would officially be nominated for vice president.

A Draft Dodger for Vice President

Unity and optimism were pervasive as the Democratic National Convention (DNC) convened in New York City. No unpleasant platform fights erupted and the only business at hand that carried an element of suspense was the selection of a vice-presidential running mate. The most serious contenders were three senators, Edmund Muskie of Maine, John Glenn of Ohio, and Walter Mondale of Minnesota. While the nation, awaited Carter's decision, a bit of drama unfolded as a group of delegates sought to promote their ideological causes as part of this seemingly straightforward process. According to time-honored party rules, all that was necessary to nominate an individual for the vice presidency was to collect fifty delegate signatures on a petition. Those favoring unconditional amnesty for draft evaders and military deserters planned to utilize the peculiar practice in order to advance their agenda, even though this stance was contrary to both the party's official platform and the stated position of the presidential nominee. The key individual in this scheme was Fritz Efaw.[47] Although Efaw's main reason for being in New

York City was to promote unconditional amnesty, he was also an alternate delegate for Americans Abroad, the roughly one million US citizens of voting age who lived in various countries around the world. The DNC, for the first time ever, had formally seated eleven delegates to represent the new party constituency Americans Abroad.[48]

Originally from Stillwater, Oklahoma, Efaw was a student at MIT when he left the United States in 1969 in protest of the draft and the war in Vietnam. He relocated to London and became the president of the Union of American Exiles in Britain. Returning to the United States in 1976 was risky; he was an indicted draft resister, but a New York court temporarily delayed his extradition to Oklahoma because he had official convention duties. Efaw was no lone wolf. He had consulted with Sarah Kovner, a director of the National Council for Universal and Unconditional Amnesty, and they worked together to have the exiled evader formally nominated for the vice presidency. At the time, Efaw was only twenty-nine years old and there was concern that his nomination would be ruled out of order; the Constitution required the president and vice-president to be thirty-five years of age. Nevertheless, he easily secured the fifty delegate signatures to meet the petition requirement. Complications arose, however, in recruiting someone to place his name before the convention. Actually, there were a number of high-profile Democrats willing to help, including Ramsey Clark. The former Johnson administration attorney general who gained notoriety when he publicly criticized American military aggression in Vietnam during a visit to Hanoi in 1971. Clark agreed to put Efaw's name before the convention, but Bella Abzug objected. The two antiwar liberals were competing against each other for a US Senate seat. Abzug feared that Clark might gain a political advantage over her if the media sensationalized his participation in the Efaw nomination. A disappointed Efaw turned elsewhere for help.[49]

Eventually, Efaw decided on Louise Ransom, who, like Kovner, held a leadership role with the National Council for Universal and Unconditional Amnesty. Her "credentials," as she herself asserted during her nominating speech, "had been earned in the hardest possible way." She was a Gold Star mother. Her oldest son had been killed in Vietnam on Mother's Day 1968. In endorsing Efaw for vice president, Ransom presented a message of healing, forgiveness, "peace and a new hope." She was not filled with bitterness. "The only way that we can give meaning to the lives of our sons and to guarantee that their deaths shall not be for nothing is to demonstrate that we have learned something from them and ensure that never again will there be another Vietnam," she declared. Her remedy: grant "total amnesty to over a million Americans, the largest portion of who are poor and black who still suffer serious consequences of their opposition to our military policies in Vietnam." Such an act, she appealed, would demonstrate that America was a nation "devoted to our founding principles of freedom of conscience, the right to dissent, and social justice for all our citizens." Ransom delivered a personal and deeply impassioned defense of unconditional amnesty for all.[50]

After a second to the nomination, Efaw finally took the stage, where he reminded the audience that he was still at risk of arrest and imprisonment. "The Democratic Party has come a long way in understanding this issue," he remarked in appreciation of Carter's pardon promise, "but we, too, have a long way to go." He spoke of his own decision to leave the country and that of his brother, who was "no less opposed to the War, couldn't go to college and couldn't get a job after high school," but was compelled to volunteer for the Navy in order to avoid being drafted into the Army and sent to the jungles of Vietnam. Efaw compared his brother to the hundreds of thousands of Vietnam deserters who lacked social and economic privileges because "the great majority" of them were poor and a disproportionate number were Black. He was not concerned that the 1 percent of Vietnam deserters had left their units on the field of battle because to punish the other 99 percent would be unconscionable in his opinion. Their unfavorable discharges had left them "virtually unemployable," and they were "still paying for opposition to a War that most members of this Party have come to realize was unjust." Efaw rejected a case-by-case review, as prescribed by the Democratic Party platform and by Carter, as being "provenly slow" and ineffectual, a contention he validated by pointing to the failure of President Ford's clemency program. "The wounds of that War can only be healed if President Carter proclaims an amnesty equal for all of the world's victims," he declared. It was a forceful antiwar speech, colored with anger, full of impatience, and demanding justice. In closing, Efaw "respectfully" declined the nomination for vice president, having been given the opportunity to make the case for unconditional amnesty he had accomplished his short-term mission.[51]

Efaw's speech and the dynamics of his nomination revealed a line of tension within the Democratic Party. There were certainly some Democrats who were offended by his appearance. Robert Strauss, the chairman of the DNC, desperately wanted to keep "that weirdo off the podium." Strauss feared any combustible situation that would ignite the convention in a manner reminiscent of 1968 and 1972. The one-time liberal presidential hopeful Morris ("Mo") Udall shunned Efaw as the activist began his speech. As Udall turned his back to leave the convention floor, Kovner, who had helped orchestrate the nomination, pleaded with him to stay. Rebuffed by Udall, she could only cry out, "Mo! Mo, I'm sorry I voted for you!"[52] This entire episode was an important reminder that even in an atmosphere of Democratic unity the Vietnam War still inflamed passionate responses. It also revealed that forces deeply committed to the principle of unconditional amnesty for both Vietnam draft evaders and military deserters were not afraid to push Carter's agenda beyond his stated positions. For the time being, their voices had been heard, and so they waited. The general election was the foremost battle, and success meant ending the Republicans' eight-year hold on the White House.

On the final day of the convention, Carter revealed his choice for vice president, Senator Walter Mondale. The Minnesotan was a popular choice among the party faithful and fit the mood of what some journalists were calling "the smoothest-running Democratic convention in a dozen years."[53] To close out the celebration, Carter delivered an acceptance speech that reiterated the major themes of his campaign. He did mention "the tragedy of Vietnam" as evidence of the need to plot a new course in American foreign policy. Carter, however, failed to discuss the pardon for draft evaders, the fate of military deserters, or, for that matter, any issue related to the veterans who had served in Vietnam.[54] With the nomination secured and a disruptive convention averted, Carter prepared to face the incumbent president. As he pressed forward, he sought occasions where he could use the Vietnam War and the plight of its veterans to draw a distinction between himself and his Republican opponent.

A Vietnam Veterans' Agenda

Vietnam was part of the Democratic primary, Vietnam was part of the Democratic National Convention, and Vietnam became part of the 1976 general election campaign. In late August, Carter began his final push for the White House with visits to key western and midwestern states. The most important of these took place in Seattle, Washington, where the Georgian addressed the annual convention of the American Legion. At the time, media coverage of the speech focused on Carter's reaffirmation of his campaign pledge to grant a presidential pardon to Vietnam draft evaders and the hostile response he received from that veterans organization. Scholars who have studied the 1976 presidential campaign have followed suit and consequently have missed the broader significance of the American Legion speech. In Seattle, Carter made a clear attempt to define himself as the candidate of the Vietnam veteran.

Although the bulk of the speech focused on developing an adequate military posture to face the prevailing threats to American national security, the Democratic candidate attacked previous Republican administrations for neglecting Vietnam veterans. Specifically, Carter accused presidents Nixon and Ford of underfunding veterans programs, understaffing VA hospitals, and of leaving a half-million Vietnam veterans unemployed. "The reason for this dismal record is clear. It is a failure of leadership," Carter charged, and "if I become President, the American veteran, of all ages, of all wars, is going to have a friend, a comrade and a firm ally in the White House." It was not until the end of the speech, and just briefly, that the candidate broached the subject of Vietnam War draft evaders.[55]

Carter repeated his earlier parsing of amnesty and pardon and stated that he would not extend a collective or blanket pardon to military deserters, leaving them subject to the prevailing "system of military justice." In addition, Carter sought common ground regarding Vietnam's divisive past. "We may not all be able to agree about what was the right course of action for the nation to take in 1966," he offered, "but we can now agree to respect those differences and to forget them. We can come together and seek a rebirth of patriotism in which all our citizens can join."[56] The Democratic nominee and some of his aides expected pushback on the pardon issue from the older veterans of the American Legion, but they hoped a political middle ground might avert a wholesale repudiation. They clearly misjudged the depth of opposing sentiment. When Carter confirmed that he would follow through with a blanket pardon for evaders, he was interrupted with boos and shouts of "No! No! No!" Although some in the audience followed the jeers with "energetic applause," journalist James T. Wooten was convinced "the strident chorus of disapproval seemed clearly to reflect the mood of the Legion's national convention."[57] With Republican vice presidential candidate Senator Robert Dole of Kansas speaking to the convention the following day, there was no chance that things would quiet down anytime soon.

Dole, a decorated World War II Army infantry officer who received permanently debilitating combat injuries, ridiculed Carter's distinction between a pardon and amnesty. He warned that the Democratic position "would signal weakness and generate strife" because it sent an insulting message to those who served that they were no more important than "those who turned their backs and scurried away." The vice presidential nominee defended Ford's clemency program, saying the president "had extended the hand of mercy" to draft evaders and military deserters by offering a chance at earned forgiveness; a few accepted the offer, but most did not. As to whether Ford might reconstitute the Presidential Clemency Board and inaugurate a new round of reviews, Dole bluntly stated that the matter was "finished." That remark drew loud applause from the audience. Interestingly, Dole did not respond to Carter's allegations that Republicans had neglected and failed to support Vietnam veterans.[58]

Roughly one month later, Carter and Ford sparred over these same issues during the first of three scheduled presidential debates. The presidential debates had been on hiatus since debuting in 1960, but in a tight race both men saw reasons to engage their challenger on a national stage.[59] Their initial exchange took place on September 23 in Philadelphia, Pennsylvania, and the focus that night was on domestic issues. Relatively early in the debate, one moderator, ABC News anchor Frank Reynolds, posed a question to Ford that conjoined the draft evaders, military deserters, and the pardon of Richard Nixon. For context, the moderator reviewed the president's clemency program, emphasizing that only a fraction of those eligible completed the process. He also repeated Ford's objective for pardoning Nixon, which was to promote national healing. Reynolds then asked, "Why does not the same rationale apply now, today, in our Bicentennial Year to the young men who resisted in Vietnam and many of them still in exile abroad?" The president did not see the respective cases as comparable and gave a curt reply to the question. "We gave them ample time" to take "advantage" of the earned reentry program, he stated. "I am against an across-the-board pardon of draft evaders or military deserters." He defended the Nixon pardon on the grounds that Watergate had so divided and distracted the nation that the government could not adequately address such problems as "high inflation, a growing recession," and the last stages of the war in Vietnam. Ford added that "Mr. Nixon had been penalized enough by his resignation in disgrace." Reynolds rejoined by asking if the president planned to reconsider and if the draft evaders, like Nixon, had "been punished enough?" Ford answered by reiterating his opposition to Carter's proposed course of action, and as far as he was concerned, the matter was closed.[60]

At this point the moderator invited Carter to express his views. The Democrat was eager to discuss the Nixon pardon. He emphasized the lack of fairness inherent in the two situations. Carter called the pardon of Nixon emblematic of a flawed criminal justice system where "the big shots who are rich, who are influential, very seldom go to jail," adding "those who are poor and who have no influence quite often are the ones who are punished." As for his own proposed pardon of the Vietnam draft evaders, he told the moderator, "I think that now is the time to heal our country after the Vietnam War. And I think that what the people are concerned about is not the pardon or the amnesty of those who evaded the draft, but whether or not our crime system is fair." This answer in no way honored antiwar resisters or validated their opposition to the war. Moreover, Carter tried to further insulate himself by slipping in an incredulous set of comments on Ford's clemency program. First, he referred to the strict alternative service option that the president had enacted as an "amnesty" program. Then, he claimed that "three times as many deserters were excused as were the ones who evaded the draft." Technically, Carter was correct on this point, but he failed to concede that there were twice as many deserters as evaders and that the deserters had a strong incentive to accept the offer because it carried the possibility of obtaining veterans' benefits. Finally, Carter failed to mention that his position as well as the party platform plank on military deserters essentially adhered to the status quo currently in place under President Ford. After the pardon-amnesty discussion, the debate shifted to new topics. With respect to Vietnam veterans' issues, moderators posed no questions to either candidate during the three presidential debates.[61]

Nevertheless, the plight and treatment of Vietnam veterans surfaced on several occasions during the general election. The impetus came from the Democratic Party and the Carter campaign team. The party's official platform included a plank that read, in part, "America's veterans have been rhetorically praised by the Nixon-Ford administration at the same time that they have been denied adequate medical, educational, pension and employment benefits." The plank singled out Vietnam veterans who had "borne the brunt of unemployment and economic mismanagement at home" and called for expanded job-training opportunities, counseling services, and educational assistance.[62] In all likelihood, this section on veterans originated from the efforts of Senator Vance Hartke because the Carter working platform proposal made no mention of veterans. Hartke, the chairman of the Senate's Committee on Veterans' Affairs, had testified before the DNC's Committee on Resolutions and Platform during the drafting phase. In his opening remarks, he stressed to party leaders that "our commitment must not be one of rhetorical praise, but rather adequate resources to meet veterans' needs." He provided several examples of the Republican propensity for rhetorical praise, such as Nixon's elaborate White House gala for the returning POWs, and he chronicled all the areas where the needs of veterans, including Vietnam veterans, had gone unmet. Without question, portions of that statement were adopted as the party's official position and as a basic framing of an agenda item.[63]

At some point during the general election, Carter's advisors drafted a lengthy memorandum titled "Vietnam Veterans Need Campaign Attention." The memorandum cited Charles Mohr's *New York Times* piece from May 21, when as a primary candidate the Georgian called Vietnam a racist war fought by men who were too poor or ignorant or not socially connected to avoid military service legally. The Carter camp was also sensitive to an op-ed written by James Webb that appeared in the *Washington Post*.[64] Webb, an Annapolis graduate and classmate of John McCain and Oliver North, served as a Marine Corps infantry officer in Vietnam, where he earned a Navy Cross. Receiving the 1976 Outstanding Veteran award from the Vietnam Veterans Civic Council enhanced Webb's reputation. The title of his op-ed was "The Invisible Vietnam Veteran." The roots of this unfortunate condition, Webb postulated, traced back a decade earlier, "when the veteran suffered the irony of having people, who directly opposed both his views and his acts, became [*sic*] accepted as his spokesmen." The former Marine refuted the notion that his entire generation shared a common view on Vietnam. Instead, he underscored the cultural differences among his peers and how his own voice had been muted in discussions on the war. "The cultures that fought Vietnam have traditionally lacked access to the media and power centers of this country," he maintained. "As a result, their views have gone unheard and it has been presumed that, on the whole 'youth' embraced the views of the anti-war action." Webb saw the championing of amnesty for war resisters as another example of perpetuating the invisibility of the Vietnam veteran. What frustrated him most was the elevation of "the ones who fled . . . to the level of prophets and moral purists." He looked disdainfully at their defenders who proclaimed that the evaders had "obeyed a higher law" of conscious while implying that men who went to Vietnam were foolishly obeying the "lower law" of conscience by answering their nation's call to arms. Webb was proud of his service and felt that Vietnam veterans had never been accorded the "dignity and respect" that they had "*always* deserved."[65]

Carter's campaign staff detected a disconcerting level of anger and alienation in Webb's words. Reading internal data that placed 50 percent of Vietnam veterans in the seven largest states and fearing retaliation at the polls, advisors developed a plan to cast Carter as the defender of Vietnam veterans.[66] The major problems faced by Vietnam veterans, as defined by the Carter camp, were an unemployment rate significantly higher than their civilian counterparts, an inequitable GI Bill that did not cover all educational costs, and the lack of psychiatric counseling. To address these challenges, the strategists recommended the following initiatives: First, the White House should "give proper recognition" to Vietnam veterans and establish a commission, similar to the one Carter had appointed as governor of Georgia. Second, the new administration should lobby Congress and educational institutions to resolve the inequities in the GI Bill. Third, with direction from the White House, the federal government should "set the tone for the rest of the nation" in employing Vietnam veterans. Finally, as president Carter should encourage the mental health and religious communities to work with government agencies to heal any "emotional" difficulties affecting veterans. In addition to a prescribed Vietnam veterans' agenda, the plan defined themes to be exploited politically during the final months of the election. For example, Carter could argue that "continuity" of neglect existed between the Nixon and Ford administrations because both claimed to care for Vietnam veterans but failed to deliver results. The Democratic challenger could point out that Ford had demonstrated a lack of concern for Vietnam veterans in 1974 when he vetoed a 23 percent increase in GI Bill benefits. Last, Carter could argue that Ford had "never" provided presidential leadership in developing a "national plan . . . to deal with the Vietnam veteran."[67]

In mid-October, when Carter's once double-digit lead in the polls had shrunk to just a few points, strategists put the candidate's Vietnam veterans' agenda on full display by announcing the formation of the National Committee of Veterans for Carter-Mondale. Through press releases and direct mailings to various veterans' organizations, Carter communicated his commitment to fulfilling the "historic covenant" between the government and military veterans. To Vietnam veterans, he made a special promise: "If I am elected, I will try to assure that . . . [you] are not forgotten but are given the same honor and benefits as those who fought in earlier wars." The campaign literature of the National Committee of Veterans for Carter-Mondale promoted the very same ideas that had been outlined in the "Vietnam Veterans Need Campaign Attention" memorandum.[68] The candidate also promised, while speaking in his hometown of Plains, Georgia, on Veterans Day 1976, to appoint Vietnam veterans "to policy making positions in the Veterans Administration."[69] The Carter camp was clearly raising expectations and trying to draw a contrast between the Democratic nominee and his Republican opponent.

If perceptions and messaging mattered, then Carter was making a better case than Ford that he was the candidate of the Vietnam veteran. In October the American Legion published the candidate responses to a formal questionnaire developed by the organization. There were five questions, of which three covered issues related to all veterans and their dependents. One covered the pardon of draft evaders and military deserters. The final question addressed who the American Legion called "the forgotten veterans . . . who served their country faithfully in Vietnam." Both politicians were asked how they intended "to rectify" the past mistreatment of this group, solve their employment woes, and increase their benefits. Ford disputed the very characterization of the neglected Vietnam veteran, maintaining, "These are not forgotten veterans and the Government has recognized and has tried to respond to their needs." Despite having vetoed a substantial GI Bill increase, he defended his administration's efforts to promote the hiring of Vietnam veterans and to improve the efficiency of the Veterans Administration (VA). Carter's answers revealed a much better understanding of the political dimensions of the question by agreeing with the American Legion's assertion that Vietnam veterans had been ignored and disregarded. In contrast to Ford, Carter called for more vigorous attempts to employ Vietnam veterans, an increase in the level of federal benefits, and an extension of the period of eligibility for the use of those benefits.[70] If nothing else, the Georgian was certainly following the campaign script and casting himself as the candidate of Vietnam veterans.

Just a few weeks before election day, *Playboy* magazine published an interview with the Democratic nominee. The backlash was immense. Carter lost significant ground with religious Americans and evangelical Christians.

The decision to even take part in the interview drew criticism from many quarters, and the candidate eventually admitted publicly that he had made a mistake by participating.⁷¹ The purpose of the interview, as explained by the editors and writers of the piece, was to offer a penetrating look at Carter as a person in order to shine a light on his perceived self-righteousness. Much, at the time and subsequently, has been written about Carter's confession to lusting after many women and to committing adultery in his heart. The obsession with Carter's peculiar morality has led to a general disregard for the content of the remainder of the interview. The *Playboy* interview took place at various times over the course of three months and was the single longest recorded interview with Carter during the entire campaign. It covered a wide array of topics, including Vietnam. Some of Carter's remarks help bring into sharper focus his handling of nearly every issue related to the war.⁷²

The conversation about Vietnam was prompted by a general question about whether there had been times in the past when Carter had been on the wrong side of an issue. He offered several examples of when he had, including his reluctance to not speak out against the war sooner. He dated his first call for a complete withdrawal to March 1971, ironically the same month as Lt. Calley's conviction for the My Lai massacre. He held fast to his previously stated interpretation of American Fighting Men's Day, denying in any way that he condoned Calley's actions. Carter explained American involvement in Vietnam in overtly partisan terms. He overlooked the extent of US support of the French during the Truman presidency while highlighting President Dwight D. Eisenhower's backing of South Vietnam following the Paris Peace Accords. He claimed that President Johnson's "motives were good" and that he sought peace even though the Texan escalated the war and deceived the American public about the lack of progress being made. Carter leveled his harshest criticism against President Nixon and Secretary of State Henry Kissinger, faulting them for widening the war into Cambodia and for unleashing an unrelenting bombing campaign that savaged most of Southeast Asia. The Georgian was as good at obfuscating the history of the war as he was at rewriting his own record on Vietnam. Finally, it took *Playboy* magazine to coax Carter into finally admitting that he used the word "pardon" instead of "amnesty" because it was less "emotionally charged" and a little more generally acceptable.⁷³

The *Playboy* interviewers also asked Carter about his son Jack's military service in Vietnam and whether he had any "qualms about it at the time."

The reply was revealing. "Well, yes, I had problems about my son fighting in the war, period. But I never make my sons' decisions for them," the candidate explained. "Jack went to war feeling it was foolish, a waste of time, much more deeply than I did. He also felt it would have been grossly unfair for him not to go when other, poorer kids had to."[74] This was not the first time the father had referenced his son's motives for military service in Vietnam. It had become part of his campaign stump speeches, and he had incorporated a similar version into his address on patriotism and national security to the American Legion in August. The candidate's explanation of his son's decision differed from the one offered by Jack in a 2003 interview, when he explained that his decision to volunteer for military service was prompted by a series of personal setbacks. After graduating from high school, Jack first enrolled at Georgia Tech. By his own admission he was "ill-prepared" academically for college, but he "got to be pretty good playing cards." His grades suffered and his poor academic performance resulted in a one-quarter suspension. He transferred to Emory University, where his past behaviors continued with similar results. Jack then entered his third college, Georgia Southwestern, an institution in his home county and one that both of his parents had attended. His grades improved and he returned to Emory. In what amounted to a fourth try, Jack finally admitted to himself, "me and college weren't on the same path." The tipping point came in early winter 1968 when he rolled his car in an accident. "I used it as an excuse to drop out of school, and then joined the Navy in April," he recalled. "My dad sort of suggested that I just sign up."[75]

Fortunately for Carter, he survived the political fallout from the *Playboy* interview. He won the 1976 presidential election with one of the slimmest margins of victory in modern history. He secured the popular vote by two percentage points, and his Electoral College advantage was the closest since 1916. In simple terms, he won because he convinced more voters that he could handle the economy and unemployment better than Ford. Carter also benefited from substantial backing from African Americans.[76] An election analysis conducted by George Gallup found that the biggest reason, by a considerable majority, that a voter supported Carter was because a change in administration was needed.[77]

Obviously, the presidential race had not hinged on the Vietnam War or the pardon of draft evaders and military deserters. Looking back, however, the 1976 Democratic primary, the Democratic platform debate, the Democratic convention, and the general election all confirmed the continuing relevance of the divisive conflict in American politics. Despite the time spent differentiating between amnesty and pardon, Carter remained steadfast throughout the entire campaign to his initial pledge to the draft evaders, a bold position that separated him from every viable Democratic opponent. He had been equally consistent on the fate of military deserters, to whom he offered no alternatives other than current policy. In addition, he defined himself as an advocate for Vietnam veterans by promising to address their unemployment problems, the inequities of the GI Bill, and a host of other issues. Collectively, these discussions and the promise of a full-scale Vietnam veterans' agenda raised expectations for new public policies. As governor of Georgia, Carter suffered no political consequences for how he handled the concerns of Vietnam veterans, but as he would soon discover, the national stage was far less forgiving. Indeed, he headed to the White House hoping to put the Vietnam War in the past but instead was forced to deal with its divisive legacies on a level that he had neither prepared for nor previously encountered.

3

The Vietnam Agenda

As the victory celebrations subsided, the Carter presidential transition team began the difficult work of converting position papers and campaign promises into an actionable agenda. Although team members compiled a list of pledges made by the candidate, Carter himself bore the responsibility of sorting through and establishing legislative priorities, a task he relished. His advisors cautioned him against attempting too much too quickly, but the Georgian prided himself on being a problem solver and he chose an ambitious early agenda.[1] Indeed, setting aside foreign policy matters, "the nucleus" of Carter's domestic agenda covered tax reforms, a reorganization of government, improving the American economy, energy and environmental programs, a new approach to health care, revising housing regulations, judicial reform, stricter rules for lobbyists, changes in the way elections were financed, and modifications to the voter registration process. The preliminary list of legislative goals filled a 100-page draft report, which, according to one Carter spokesperson, did not rule out "major additions."[2] Such an expansive legislative docket, as scholars have recognized, "would have taxed the political skills of any president, much less one as unfamiliar with Washington's modus operandi as Carter."[3] The inability to settle on a set of legislative priorities and articulate a political vision plagued Carter throughout his presidency.

Moving forward on multiple fronts, the president made Vietnam veterans part of his domestic agenda. On the afternoon of his inauguration, Carter had a five-minute meeting with fellow Georgian Max Cleland in which he asked the Vietnam veteran to head the Veterans Administration. The presidential transition team had already drafted proposals to address Vietnam veterans' unemployment, but omitted other parts of the Vietnam veterans' agenda that had been articulated during the final months of the presidential campaign. The presidential commission to review the readjustment status of Vietnam veterans had been shelved, and little attention was given to the mental health programs for those suffering from war-related psychological problems. Still, Carter's Vietnam veterans' legislative agenda was considerable and stood in stark contrast to the limited efforts of previous administrations. Nevertheless, important questions remained. Would Carter's selected priorities meet the high expectations that he created during the just completed campaign? Did he intend to expand or add to his stated intentions regarding Vietnam veterans? How would his administration handle any opposition to his Vietnam veterans' agenda? As for the matter of the pardon for draft evaders, Carter confronted that hurdle on his first full day in office, only to see old controversies reignited.

A Sham Pardon

On January 21, 1977, Carter issued a presidential proclamation and accompanying executive order granting a pardon to all Americans previously convicted, currently indicted, or under investigation for draft evasion during the Vietnam War. The White House, despite requests from reporters, declined to issue an estimate of the number of individuals affected by the order. The Justice Department, based on known cases, approximated 13,000 beneficiaries. An actual count was impossible to determine because there were unknown thousands who never registered with the Selective Service. They still were technically in violation of the law, but there were no records of their crimes. Even the unidentified were covered by the pardon.[4] Only those who had violated the Selective Service Act and had committed violent acts were excluded from the pardon.[5] Carter made no public appearance to mark the occasion and issued no statement to explain or justify his actions. The two directives, the proclamation and the executive order, merely stated who was eligible for the pardon and who was not. Perhaps after a lengthy debate during the campaign, the new president thought that no additional comment was needed. He had, after all, indicated in interviews that he would execute the pardon sometime during his first week in office in order to put the issue in the past as quickly as possible.[6] The White House's Media Liaison Office provided a background sheet with some basic "factual information" but left news outlets on their own to interpret the president's actions.[7] Now that the policy had been enacted, the entire effort, as the *Washington Post* editorialized, seemed a bit "spare and legalistic."[8] Nevertheless, Carter's actions sparked an immediate controversy.

Opponents of the pardon were quick to voice their displeasure and relentlessly bombarded the White House telephone lines. Janet Pleasant, who fielded the verbal onslaught, recollected that "90 percent of the calls were very negative, and there was much emotion, anger, and frustration involved."[9] A Louis Harris Poll indicated that a slight majority of Americans disapproved of the president's actions and found that it was prudent for Carter to have acted quickly because "with the passage of time, public opinion in this country is hardening against the draft evaders."[10] Members of Congress also expressed their opposition. Senator Barry Goldwater, the former presidential candidate and Arizona Republican, called the pardon "the most disgraceful thing that a President has ever done." He further argued that the executive order undermined military preparedness.[11] Such statements were commonplace throughout Congress. The new administration had anticipated some pushback, but the White House had not prepared for formal attempts by the legislature to oppose or even block the executive order.

Conservatives in the Senate immediately pushed a resolution condemning the blanket pardon for draft evaders. This first salvo failed to pass by seven votes, but the opposition was just getting started. The House of Representatives took up a more aggressive measure when John T. Myers (R-IN) introduced an amendment to the fiscal 1977 supplemental appropriations bill to prohibit the use of federal funds for processing and administering the pardon program. The amendment passed by a 220 to 186 margin. When the supplemental appropriations bill went to a joint legislative conference, the Senate conferees agreed to Myers's amendment, and the provision was added to the final supplemental appropriation bill. The restrictions applied only to the supplemental appropriation, but the government offices responsible for carrying out the pardon policy were not affected by the legislation; their existing budgets were sufficient to completing the task, thereby making the congressional contravention somewhat symbolic.[12] However, the collective reproach by Congress was an ominous sign. The November elections had afforded Democrats large majorities in both chambers, outnumbering

Republicans 292 to 193 in the House and 62 to 38 in the Senate. Despite the lopsided edge for the president, this first brush-up proved that the Vietnam War was still a politically toxic issue. Carter had intended for the pardon gesture to serve as an agent of healing and reconciliation, but it had the opposite effect. Fault lines were clearly apparent in Congress, but the pardon policy also raised the ire of draft evaders, proponents of unconditional amnesty, and their advocates in the media as well. Each faction believed that the president could have and should have done more.

American antiwar exiles from Sweden, France, and Canada reacted quickly to the pardon news and convened a conference in Toronto to discuss a formal response. That gathering, which included both draft evaders and military deserters, revealed a great festering bitterness among these groups. Describing themselves "as victims of an immoral war," the exiles accused the previous three presidential administrations of labeling them as "criminals," and they considered Carter's "limited pardon" of draft evaders as "too little, too late and a sham." The group scolded the president for making a "political mistake" by not including military deserters in the pardon proclamation. "The damage was already done politically for Carter," and the president would have suffered no additional consequences for pardoning the military deserters at the same time, explained Kevin Vrieze, a draft evader operating in the Toronto exile community. Amnesty activists at the conference also panned Carter for creating "two classes of war resisters." Draft evaders, they held, were "mostly white, middle-class youths" whereas the military deserters were more often "black, poor or otherwise disadvantaged."[13]

Prior attempts to offer some form of legal remission to draft evaders, such as George McGovern's amnesty proposal and Gerald Ford's clemency program, inspired passionate arguments about America's involvement in the Vietnam War. Carter's pardon of draft evaders conjured similar responses. In defending his pardon position Carter had once said he just wanted everyone to come home; everything would be forgiven, and the war would be in the past. Neither of these desires came true. By the end of March 1977, only 38 exiles had returned to the United States with the expressed intent of staying, and only 130 had returned on a temporary basis to visit their families. As for vanquishing the war, the Toronto organizers vowed to continue "to fight for universal, unconditional amnesty for all categories of war resisters and victims," signaling a future focus on the military deserters and the hundreds of thousands of veterans who had received less than honorable military discharges.[14]

Many in the media greeted Carter's pardon of the draft evaders with a mildly congratulatory tone, pointing out that the president's actions were the right and necessary thing to do and that he deserved credit for swiftly fulfilling a campaign promise.[15] However, as the *Washington Post* noted, the pardon was "a relatively limited and easy act" because it did not cover "the larger and thornier categories" of military deserters and Vietnam veterans with bad discharges. Although the *Washington Post* repeated the Toronto conference's call for a more expansive amnesty program, the newspaper was less critical of Carter and expressed tremendous optimism in his ability to handle these difficult questions.

We know that Mr. Carter has a generous and humane understanding of the catastrophe that the Vietnam war was for a substantial segment of a generation. He has displayed special sensitivity for the poor and unsophisticated youths—many of them black—who entered the armed forces, served loyally and, if they survived, often incurred physical or psychic wounds or legal disabilities (bad discharges) that left them at a disadvantage in rejoining the civilian mainstream. We feel confident, then, that Mr. Carter will go on to develop plans for servicemen who deserted or received bad discharges, and to care better for the health, education and employment needs of other Vietnam veterans.

Part of the editorial praise, whether a forthright affirmation of Carter or a vailed attempt to coax him into action, emanated from the president's recent decision to order the Pentagon to examine the review process for Vietnam veterans with bad discharges, but those instructions did not include military deserters.[16]

Politically speaking, Carter was walking a tight rope. On his very first day in office he granted a presidential pardon to those who illegally avoided military service and then opened the door to the possibility of upgrading the discharges of hundreds of thousands of Vietnam veterans who had been cashiered from military service for less than honorable conduct. Meanwhile, he had not really pressed forward with any part of his broader Vietnam veterans' agenda. These developments did not go unnoticed, which Carter learned firsthand when he received a stern message from a fellow Georgian during a nationally televised call-in show shortly after taking office. Ronald

Fouse of Centerville asked, "Now that you pardoned the draft evaders and you propose to pardon the junkies and deserters, do you propose to do anything for the veterans such as myself that served the country with loyalty?" Initially, Carter tried to deflect the criticism by suggesting that he expected a "friendlier question" by someone from his home state, but he did not shy away from defending his pardoning of the draft evaders. Moreover, he acknowledged he was considering upgraded discharges, but not for military deserters, and stated that his "preference" was to allow "the Defense Department [to] handle those cases by categories or by individual cases." Finally, the president praised the caller for being a "loyal and patriotic veteran" and took the opportunity to tout a recently announced jobs program as evidence of his commitment to all Vietnam veterans.[17] In just a short time, Carter had simultaneously raised expectations and opened old wounds across the political and cultural divides. For the next four years, the administration was left wondering if it could ever heal the national breach or satisfy either camp.

HIRE

In large measure, Carter had won the 1976 presidential election because voters believed he was the best candidate to fix the nation's troubled economy. The country had not fully recovered from the 1974–1975 recession, the worst recession of the post–World War II era. The annual rate of inflation stood just short of 6 percent, the unemployment rate was just above 7 percent, and the nation's total economic activity as measured by the gross national product (GNP) was continuing to decline.[18] On January 31, 1977, Carter presented his Economic Recovery Plan to Congress. The core components were a small tax rebate for the American people, the lowering of corporate taxes, increased federal expenditures on public infrastructure projects, and job-creation initiatives. The broad-based economic package also included something specifically for Vietnam veterans.[19]

When Carter took office, the unemployment rate for Vietnam veterans was 8.6 percent, slightly higher than the national rate. A wider discrepancy appeared in the 20 to 24 age group, where the unemployment rate for Vietnam veterans was 18 percent compared to 12.5 percent for nonveterans. The "hardest hit" of any demographic were disabled veterans and young Black veterans; the latter had an unemployment rate above 20 percent. There was an approximate total of 560,000 unemployed Vietnam veterans. Of that number, Carter intended to help 200,000, or slightly more than one-third, as part of his Economic Recovery Plan. Although all of the details had not yet been finalized and Congress would have to allocate funding, the Carter job proposal for Vietnam veterans relied on a combination of new federal programs and an expansion of existing ones. Regarding the latter, Carter asked Congress to fund and set aside 150,000 jobs for Vietnam veterans through the Comprehensive Employment Training Act (CETA). Enacted in 1973, CETA's purpose was to create public-sector jobs for minorities, women, and the poor in communities with high unemployment or underemployment. Under CETA, federal dollars flowed to "prime sponsors," most commonly state, county, and municipal agencies, who used the funds to create a variety of employment opportunities mainly in public works, transportation, and education. Meeting this target would have doubled the proportion of public-sector jobs currently held by Vietnam veterans. Carter also called for the establishment of a new federal program, Help through Industrial Retraining and Employment (HIRE). This incentive-based program offered federal reimbursement to large corporations to cover the cost of job training and job creation for Vietnam veterans. The initial goal of HIRE was to generate 50,000 to 60,000 new private-sector jobs for Vietnam veterans. Thus, the Carter administration looked to create 200,000 jobs for the approximately 560,000 unemployed Vietnam veterans, with nearly three-fourths being generated from the public sector. The estimated cost for the entire two-year Economic Recovery Program was $31.2 billion, with the Vietnam veteran employment portion accounting for $1.3 billion of the total.[20]

Secretary of Labor Ray Marshall spearheaded the administration's Vietnam veteran jobs programs. Before Carter made his big announcement as part of the national Economic Recovery Plan, Marshall had expressed his own "particular" concerns and ideas. He vowed to hire 2,500 disabled veterans immediately as part of a Department of Labor employment outreach service imitative with offices in the nation's 100 largest cities. The secretary also created a new position within his department, assistant secretary of labor for veteran affairs. Aside from his own projects, Marshall bore the primary responsibility for implementing the largest component of the president's comprehensive Vietnam veterans' job program. As part of the Economic Recovery Plan, the president requested that 35 percent of new CETA jobs be given to Vietnam veterans. This directive involved amending existing CETA guidelines, which meant that Marshall would need to lobby Congress to ensure that Vietnam veterans were given hiring preferences as part of CETA's funding appropriation. This assignment was crucial, as the president's proposal targeted 150,000 new public-sector jobs, roughly three-fourths of the promised total.[21]

The administration wanted the Vietnam veteran jobs program to be seen as a "serious" proposal and a "high priority" for the president. Chief domestic policy advisor Stuart Eizenstat encouraged the "early announcement" of the jobs program as a way to potentially "offset" some of the criticism that Carter had received for his pardoning of the draft evaders. As he explained in a White House discussion: "If we are to fully put the trauma of Vietnam behind us, we must not only be concerned with those who refused to serve out of conscience, we must be concerned with the plight of those who honorably served in the armed forces but have had difficulty obtaining employment." Amnesty had been the prime concern of the political left, so Eizenstat believed, but most Americans were more eager to help those who had actually gone to Vietnam.[22] Carter heard that exact perspective from fellow Georgian Ronald Fouse during the "Ask President Carter" television call-in show. Many members of Congress agreed.

Representative Mary Rose Oakar (D-OH) wrote to the president shortly after his inauguration, bluntly remarking, "Frankly, to grant a pardon to those who refused to serve without acting at the same time in behalf of the Vietnam veterans would, in my view, be a message to the veterans that what they did in serving their country was somehow wrong." Although she supported Carter's plan, Oakar informed the president that she intended to propose legislation that would create an additional 60,000 jobs for Vietnam veterans through public-sector hiring.[23] The president also received weighty advice from two members of the Senate Armed Services Committee, Sam Nunn (D-GA) and Henry "Scoop" Jackson (D-WA). The influential Democrats echoed Oakar's concern for balancing the treatment of those who served with that of "those who refused service." They believed that a failure to deliver a meaningful commitment to Vietnam veterans would intensify their disillusionment and, "most important," create complications and "difficulties in maintaining an effective military force."[24]

It should be noted that Carter's Vietnam veteran jobs program was not a knee-jerk reaction to combat any fallout over the pardon. The Vietnam veterans' agenda that he announced during the 1976 campaign promised job creation, and the presidential transition team had incorporated that promise into the early designs of the economic stimulus package.[25] Nevertheless, the administration recognized the political complexities that arose from the pardon of the draft evaders as well as the need to show appreciation to those who served. To navigate this sensitive political terrain, Carter employed the rhetoric of gratitude. In the official Economic Recovery Plan message that he sent to Congress, he maintained that "military veterans of the Vietnam-era deserve special attention, both because our Nation owes them a debt of gratitude for their service and because their employment problems are so severe."[26] These rhetorical choices asserted the unique severity of Vietnam veteran unemployment as well as a national obligation to those who served.

As the media poured over every facet of the Economic Recovery Plan, a few commentators concentrated on whether the stimulus package could realistically achieve the administration's goals with respect to full employment, a balanced budget, and lowering the misery index.[27] Others looked at the particular provisions that targeted Vietnam veterans. In the eyes of some, Carter's reference to a "debt of gratitude" owed to Vietnam veterans raised expectations and generated favorable impressions. James R. Dickenson of the *Washington Star* no doubt pleased domestic policy advisor Eizenstat when he wrote that the stimulus package proved that Vietnam veterans were a "top priority" with the new administration.[28] Even syndicated columnist Mary McGrory, who had been a harsh critic of Carter during the 1976 Democratic primary, offered the president tepid praise, calling the effort "a glimmer of light for Vietnam vets."[29] There were many details to be worked out, but there was a general optimism surrounding this first offering for Vietnam veterans. Just how much optimism was warranted remained to be seen.

Fulfilling a Promise

The jobs program was a significant step toward fulfilling Carter's agenda for Vietnam veterans, as was his nomination of Max Cleland to be the administrator of the Veterans Administration. Although the two men met on inauguration morning, the formal announcement of the appointment did not come until three weeks later. On that occasion, Carter praised Cleland for his military service in Vietnam and for his work on behalf of veterans during his two terms as a Georgia state senator. The president recognized Cleland's leadership of the Georgia Advisory Committee on Vietnam Veterans and alluded to his duties with the US Senate's Committee on Veterans' Affairs. Carter heralded his fellow Georgian, who was only thirty-four-years-old, as part of a "new generation" emerging from the ordeal of the Vietnam War.[30] Aside from the symbolism of the appointment, the nomination addressed a campaign promise to place Vietnam veterans in prominent leadership positions within the administration.

Although Cleland and Carter had a political relationship dating back to their days in Georgia, the two men were not particularly close. Cleland had interacted more with two of Carter's top gubernatorial aides, Hamilton Jordan and Jody Powell, both of whom followed Carter through the presidential campaign and into the White House. Cleland did on occasion appear with Carter on the campaign trail in 1976. The most conspicuous outing came when the Democratic nominee took the triple amputee with him to Seattle when he delivered his crucial address to the American Legion national convention. In addition to these connections, Cleland had the backing of influential members of the Senate's Veterans' Affairs Committee.[31] Carter's primary aim for the VA was improving the agency's effectiveness and efficiency. As he had earlier pledged, he wanted to install "competent, compassionate leadership" within the agency and, if warranted, an increase in pay for VA doctors and assistants in order to ensure the best possible health care for veterans.[32] Not much else beyond these basic prescriptions emerged as an administration priority from the work of the presidential transition team plan. Based on Cleland's confirmation testimony, his VA agenda seemed in sync with that of the president.

The confirmation hearing was a largely ceremonial affair because the outcome was never in doubt. On February 25, 1977, Cleland appeared before the Senate Committee on Veterans' Affairs. Senator Alan Cranston (D-CA) opened the hearing by delivering a fine tribute to Cleland. He saluted the nominee for his hard work, dedication, and "broad knowledge" of issues affecting veterans, and he described Cleland as an "extraordinary man" who was warm, compassionate, and "full of life." After this harmonious start, Cleland answered questions about his qualifications for the post, the problems the VA faced, and how he planned to guide the agency into the future. He envisioned three priorities for the VA. He wanted to finalize the implementation of an automated computer system capable of processing claims and dispensing benefits with maximum efficiency, to undertake a review of how the agency provided employment assistance to veterans, and to foster a VA culture that required its personnel to conduct themselves with compassion and sensitivity when interacting with veterans. The question-and-answer segment was rather perfunctory. Several senators who were obligated to attend other committee meetings cast their vote in favor of the nominee as they left the hearing before its completion. Perhaps the most interesting question fielded by Cleland came from Strom Thurmond. The South Carolina Republican asked the nominee if the Carter administration was "preoccupied with the problems of the Vietnam era veterans . . . to the detriment of the remainder of the veteran populations." Cleland assured Thurmond that while he would devote some attention to the special needs of the Vietnam generation, in areas such as "readjustment counseling and readjustment benefits," he "by no means" intended to favor "one class of veterans over the other."[33]

Popular and mainstream media responded to Cleland's selection in an overwhelmingly positive manner. "No appointment of Jimmy Carter's young Presidency seems as poignant—or as pointed—as that of Max Cleland to head the Veterans Administration," exuded *People* magazine.[34] From the *Arkansas Gazette* to the *Tampa Tribune-Times*, Cleland was celebrated as the youngest man as well as the first Vietnam veteran to lead the Veterans Administration. He was introduced to various readerships as patriotic and as a self-sacrificing soldier who had worked hard to overcome his catastrophic injuries. In addition to saluting his personal triumph over tragedy, the profiles reviewed Cleland's vision for the VA, focusing on his commitment to running the agency with compassion and efficiency and improving medical services.[35]

Some political constituencies and veterans organizations questioned the new administrator about his agenda more thoroughly than the Senate committee that approved his nomination. For example, representatives of the National League of Cities and US Conference of Mayors sat down with Cleland soon after his confirmation and delved into several major concerns. These urban political leaders were focused on unemployment. Cleland was careful to explain that job creation was the responsibility of the White House and the Department of Labor and that the ground work for Vietnam veteran job creation had been laid through HIRE and CETA when the president unveiled his Economic Recovery Plan. The VA's role was fairly small on the employment front, Cleland maintained, and limited to areas such as on-the-job training programs.[36] The American Legion, which conducted the very first interview with Cleland following his confirmation, wanted answers on an array of issues impacting the group's membership and posed several questions about how the interests of Vietnam veterans would be balanced against the needs of other veterans. Just as Cleland had assured Senator Thurmond during the recent confirmation hearing, he told the American Legion that while Vietnam veterans could count on him as "a friend" in their court, so could every other veteran. His personal ordeal with the VA had heightened his awareness of the frustrations experienced by many veterans, and his mission was to bring a "fresh attitude" to the agency and to take a "fresh look" at how it operated.[37] Cleland placed a great deal of faith in his ability to rehabilitate the VA's sullied reputation by emphasizing the need for courteous and respectful treatment for all those needing assistance and care. Without question, Cleland enjoyed a honeymoon period at the start of his tenure as the head of the VA. He formed his own transition team of advisors and began to tackle the group's most immediate concerns.[38] This work, however, was soon overshadowed when the president reached a decision on how he would handle the review process for those service members who had received less than honorable discharges.

"Bad Paper"

Throughout the 1976 campaign, Carter consistently stated that his intent was to only offer "a fair and thorough case-by-case review" to all who had received less than honorable discharges. He further added that he did not "believe that deserters should be entitled to all the rights and benefits earned by men and women who served their full tour of duty."[39] Unconditional amnesty activists tried to have draft evaders and military deserters treated equally under the Democratic Party platform, asserting that both groups were war resisters and that desertion had been both an act of defiance against onerous military regulations and a form of protest against the Vietnam War. The issue was complicated.[40] During the war there were five types of discharges granted: honorable, general, undesirable, bad conduct, and dishonorable. Anything other than an honorable discharge was often lumped under the label of a less than honorable discharge or a "bad paper" discharge. There were some 430,000 Vietnam veterans with less than honorable discharges. Some had competed full tours of duty in Vietnam. The vast majority of military deserters left their posts or base while in the United States. Saddled with the bad paper discharge, these veterans were denied automatic eligibility for VA benefits and were "blocked" from unemployment insurance and civil service hiring preferences. In addition, those with bad discharges carried a societal stigma that employers sometimes used to deny them employment. Advocates such as June A. Willenz, executive director of the American Veterans Committee, wrote that veterans with bad paper had "suffered cruel and unusual punishment" in jails, drug centers, and mental health facilities. Without decisive action on their behalf, these unfortunate "outcasts" remained "potential threats" to society, she maintained. Although procedures and guidelines existed for appeals, the military's Discharge Review Board could only adjudicate 10,000 cases annually, which created a backlog that left hundreds of thousands with bad paper discharges and no reasonable expectation for redress.[41] Throughout his campaign, Carter refused to link a pardon of draft evaders to the bad discharges cause, but following his November victory he listened to appeals that he reconsider his position.

Following those conversations, Charles Kirbo, a high-powered Atlanta attorney and an advisor to Carter since the early 1960s, constructed a broad outline for dealing with the controversial issue. He considered "summary upgrading of discharges" dramatically different from pardoning the draft evaders. Therefore, he urged caution and working closely with the Department of Defense (DoD), because it already had its hands full dealing with an "awkward" transition between two administrations as well as "serious existing personnel problems" associated with the arduous conversion to the All-Volunteer Force. Kirbo believed that after Carter was in office and had a clear idea of how he wanted to proceed, the DoD would be "helpful and resourceful" in accomplishing the administration's goals because it was "anxious to get Vietnam behind" them. His final recommendation was to make a formal announcement of a forthcoming study, in consultation with military officials, of a comprehensive overhaul of the appeals process or implementation of a new upgrade program. Kirbo had not calculated the financial costs of additional VA benefits for any changes to the status quo, though he was sure it was "considerable." In a final cautionary note, he added that he "would not fool with a commission until we try the military. It can be accomplished with less flack."[42] Although lacking in details, Kirbo's advice on what was clearly a controversial issue made working closely with the military an imperative, an admonition the administration largely ignored.

To be sure, the domestic policy staff examined key concerns and anticipated some political headwinds. For example, it foresaw that the addition of 175,000 "new eligibles" to the VA rolls would create "a significant budgetary impact" and prompt a serious pushback from veterans organizations and congressional committees with oversight of veterans' affairs. These groups "see veterans benefits as a reward for honorable service rather than social welfare programs," the domestic policy staff informed the White House Counsel's Office in a detailed memorandum. The administration expected congressional opponents to introduce legislation to limit any new benefits granted under an upgraded discharge.[43] The Justice Department also envisioned difficulties. Attorney General Griffin Bell was most concerned about whether "we are protected from having to pay retroactive benefits in the event of an upgraded discharge either in individual suits or in class actions." He discussed the matter with Cleland and was led to believe that they were protected by US statute. Bell, however, argued against proceeding "until we have resolved this question." The attorney general and Cleland also discussed the idea of making the upgrade "more palatable" by including non–Vietnam era veterans with undesirable discharges. In theory, the inclusion of all veterans would combat charges that Vietnam veterans were being singled out for special or preferred treatment.

The domestic policy staff considered ways to sell the presidential discharge upgrade in order to quell any misperceptions, the reaction to Carter's pardon of the draft evaders still fresh on their minds. One strategy was to call into question the fairness of the entire military discharge process. As the war ground to a halt, military discipline deteriorated in the services and court-martial calendars were inundated. This administrative burden occurred at a time when the military's manpower needs had been greatly reduced. To alleviate both of these pressures, commanding officers presented offenders, often without trial or counsel, a variety of unfavorable discharge options that service members accepted rather than face military punishment or possible court-martial. Another tactic the domestic policy staff considered was "to point out that only an unknown fraction" of bad paper veterans "had any political motive for their actions." Some studies had shown that most offenders had broken regulations because of family or personal issues, not in order to protest the war. These studies also maintained that the offenders were young and typically came from disadvantaged backgrounds, lacked the social maturity and intellectual acumen necessary to succeed in the military, and should have never been inducted in the first place. By stressing these lines of contention, Carter could show that he was offering "compassion" to young American victims of the war without having to condone any antiwar activism.[44] Having identified a number of potential hazards but without determining any real contingency plans, the administration made a bold decision.[45]

In late March 1977, the White House sent the Department of Defense a framework for granting a blanket upgrade to individuals who met one of six criteria. The criteria for the Carter Special Discharge Review Process were: (1) having been awarded a military decoration, (2) having been wounded in combat, (3) completion of a tour of duty in Southeast Asia, (4) completion of alternative service under the Ford clemency program, (5) having received an honorable discharge from a previous tour of military service, and (6) completion of twenty-four months of military service with a satisfactory record prior to discharge. Veterans who did not meet these standards could still make an individual appeal for an upgrade. For deserters still at-large, they had to "return to military control" and complete processing before they could become eligible for the program. The 30,000 former service members who received dishonorable or bad conduct discharges were still not eligible for upgrades, nor were those who deserted in a combat zone or whose separation from service involved "violence, criminal intent or the use of force."[46]

Perhaps hoping to divert direct questioning, the Carter administration did not release its discharge review policy through a formal White House announcement; rather, the guidelines were sent directly to the Department of Defense. Over the course of the following week, details about the president's plan began circulating in the press. It was not known how many of the 433,000 former service members would automatically qualify for an upgrade, but the Pentagon placed the number around 60,000.[47]

Reaction to the news was swift. The Reverend Barry Lynn of the National Council for Universal and Unconditional Amnesty called Carter's program "significant" because it was a tacit admission that "the military discharge system was so bad that they have to come up with something" to compensate for the arbitrary and discriminatory handling of these cases. Nevertheless, he and other amnesty groups considered the proposal "a few slices of the loaf." The entire loaf was a blanket pardon and full reinstatement of veterans' benefits for the nearly one-half million veterans holding bad paper discharges.[48] A *Washington Post* editorial called the president's combined decisions of pardoning the draft evaders, the VA's pledge to improve service, the just-announced jobs programs, and the discharge upgrade proposal "a major effort" and "an impressive performance." The upgrade plan in particular, the newspaper admitted, "took some courage." There were caveats, however, to the approbation. The *Post* wondered whether these efforts were "impressive enough" given that "a great toll of human wreckage has been wrought upon the community of veterans not only by the war but by their country's post-war neglect. For many, too much damage has been done and too much time has passed for any government program, no matter how compassionately conceived and effectively executed, to offer adequate relief." In addition to this somber reflection, the editorial pointed to the limitations of Carter's program, namely that it provided "no assurance that discharges will be upgraded to the only level (honorable) truly free of civil disability and moral stigma," and that "the great majority" are not guaranteed rectification. The *Washington Post* also delivered a rather ominous warning, promising to "keep a clear eye on the administration of the program" and to hold the president accountable to "broaden" his authorization if necessary. Anything less would fail to achieve the president's goal to "get the Vietnamese war over with."[49]

A *New York Times* editorial viewed the discharge upgrade plan as evidence of Carter's "earlier promise to close the book" on that "unhappy period" in American history. Although acknowledging that the executive authorization "still leaves up in the air the future of many former servicemen who clashed with military authority," the *Times* credited Carter for fostering a "spirit of forgiveness and compassion." Expressing concerns similar to the *Washington Post,* the *New York Times* reminded the White House that it had "a special responsibility to keep a watchful eye on the review boards" and to ensure that "a martial mentality and bureaucratic delay" did not undermine the objectives of the upgrade plan.[50]

Interestingly, the *New York Times*'s White House correspondent, Charles Mohr—the same journalist who accused Carter of making false and misleading statements about his Vietnam War positions during the 1976 Democratic primary—wrote two generally positive pieces on what the president was attempting to do. "The scope," he wrote, was "much broader" than was generally assumed based on the case-by-case position offered during the campaign. "Its practical effect seems likely to go a long way toward ending official recriminations against those who resisted the Vietnam War," Mohr concluded. The journalist contrasted this new directive with the earlier pardoning of the draft evaders, pointing out that a "predominately white middle-class and relatively well-educated" group benefited from the pardon whereas the discharge upgrade mostly applied to former service members who "are black, poor or ill-educated." Mohr emphasized that the military discharge review boards still yielded a lot of control even under the new guidelines, and "only time will tell how lenient" those boards would be in complying with the president's desires. For now, the White House correspondent felt that "Mr. Carter spoke softly [and] effectively" on the matter of bad discharges.[51] Not everyone in the media was so complimentary of the president.

Syndicated columnist Jack Anderson speculated that the White House had stopped short of a more sweeping plan late in the decision-making process because of certain political considerations. He suggested that "the cost of compassion . . . could be high for Carter" if he was seen "as soft on military discipline" by showing favoritism to men who received bad discharges for alcohol and drug abuse. Anderson even dropped a not so subtle hint that the president wanted to shield his Vietnam-veteran son from closer media scrutiny.[52] Jack Carter spent a month in a makeshift military stockade in San Francisco for admitting use of marijuana, LSD, and THC. The Navy then cashiered him, giving him a general discharge, whereas other service members typically received undesirable discharges for similar infractions. Jack's expulsion from the military, as he recalled, was "about the time Dad was getting elected governor."[53] To ward off any allegations of favoritism, especially in light of Anderson's column, Jack appeared on *ABC's Good Morning America* television program to explain why he would not be applying for a discharge upgrade. "The first and most obvious reason," he told viewers, "is that my father is President, he's the one that kind of authorized this, and I don't want people to think he did that for me, because he didn't." Jack also candidly confessed that he did not need the upgrade because he had not encountered "the problems many other people have had who got out of the Navy with less than honorable discharges." By this time, he had graduated law school and passed the Georgia bar exam.[54]

As embarrassing as the family revelations may have been, the president faced much more serious obstacles to his discharge upgrade program from opponents in Congress. Back when the White House was formulating the upgrade guidelines, the president received a letter from Senator Cranston. The Californian conveyed strong disagreement with a "wholesale granting of general discharges" if automatic eligibility for veterans' benefits was included. That a Democrat and the chair of the Committee on Veterans' Affairs expressed this opinion was a foreboding message.[55] Soon a bipartisan coalition formed in Congress to block the president's discharge upgrade program.[56] The complaints against Carter's Vietnam veterans' agenda multiplied as reports surfaced over slow progress on another front.

Mounting Frustrations

"Back in January, the Carter administration got a lot of big headlines for proclaiming new jobs programs for unemployed Vietnam veterans," William Greider wrote in the *Washington Post*, "but those early promises have already soured on many veterans' organizations." It had been roughly three months since the president submitted his Economic Recovery Plan to Congress with its promise of 200,000 jobs for Vietnam veterans, but little had actually been achieved in the intervening period. Based on the original announcement, the bulk of the new jobs, nearly 150,000, were to come from an expansion of CETA. However, the Department of Labor drafted "vague" guidelines that "merely encouraged" prime sponsors to provide jobs to Vietnam veterans and then stood by as the House of Representatives, during the legislative authorization phase, granted discretionary powers over CETA hires to state and local governments, preferring "to keep the jobs money free of categorical guarantees for any specific group." Thus, the federal guidelines that Congress eventually adopted did not guarantee that Vietnam veterans would receive the newly budgeted public-sector jobs. Compounding this setback was the fact that the private-sector component of the president's job program had not been launched. The White House had neither appointed a HIRE advisory board nor tapped a coordinator for the program.[57]

In developing his report, Greider had contacted representatives from several veterans' organizations for on-the-record comments. Their statements were damning. "Our high hopes have now turned to frustration and cynicism," explained Lawrence W. Roufee Jr. of Paralyzed Veterans of America (PVA). "In our opinion, the way the programs have been developed there is little chance of making any significant reduction in the unemployment rate." Ronald W. Drach of the Disabled American Veterans (DAV) accused the Carter administration of being more concerned about draft evaders than making a "concerted effort to assist all disabled veterans who served their country honorably." The foot-dragging convinced Thomas J. Wincek, veterans coordinator at the University of Minnesota, that the administration only promoted a message "that the veteran is No. 1." In reality, veterans "aren't that important and programs to help them can be dropped or neglected."[58] One after another veterans' activists accused the Carter administration of feigning concern for Vietnam veterans and of showing a greater commitment to draft evaders and military deserters. The PVA and the DAV were frustrated particularly with the performance of Secretary of Labor Marshall. Back in January, he promised to hire 2,500 disabled veterans to act as employment outreach specialists, but only one-fifth of the positions had been filled. These criticisms, some warranted, by Vietnam veterans' groups and their allies in the press illustrated that by formally launching an agenda, the president had raised expectations. Moreover, this vocal alliance expected the administration to deliver results.

On February 7, just one week after unveiling the Economic Recovery Plan, domestic policy advisors had initiated conversations about launching the HIRE program, but to no avail.[59] Perhaps the White House had been overwhelmed by the flurry of activity surrounding the president's first 100 days in office. To mark that ceremonial occasion, Eizenstat compiled a list of accomplishments for the president's personal perusal. The nine-page memorandum covered ninety-four specific items. Eizenstat mentioned the pardon of draft evaders and efforts to begin work on America's missing in action (MIAs) in Vietnam, but not the jobs program for Vietnam veterans.[60] Whatever the causes or reasons, the administration had lost momentum on the first major initiative for the war's veterans, and nearly five months passed before it gained any traction on the jobs plan.

On June 14, the president convened the White House conference on HIRE. He spoke in a public ceremony from the East Room and in his remarks characterized the typical Vietnam draftee in a manner that elicited sympathy and respect. "There has been in our country, and still is, unfortunately," the president reflected, "a sense among some that the young men and women who did go to Vietnam are somehow not to be admired, but despised and not to be appreciated, but castigated." This notion about the unpopularity of the war animated Carter's speech. In justifying the HIRE program, he asserted that the nation owed Vietnam veterans a debt of gratitude, and he called on all Americans, in the spirit of national "healing,' to support his endeavor. Although Carter told those assembled that he felt a personal responsibility to help Vietnam veterans, he did not seem particularly troubled that Congress had ignored his original instructions on guaranteeing them new jobs through the expansion of CETA. In response to this rebuff, Carter remarked, "we believe . . . that local officials, state officials will try to give places and opportunities for those young veterans." The president expressed satisfaction with the work that he, his staff, and Secretary Marshall had done thus far with the HIRE program, but he recognized the need to compensate for the lost momentum and the changes that Congress made to his plan. To that end, Carter announced that the private sector would now generate 140,000 jobs, a sizeable increase from the initial figure of 50,000. Because the success of the HIRE program now depended largely on employers and business executives, he encouraged them to be generous, "even in a slightly sacrificial way."[61]

To head the president's committee on HIRE, Carter selected G. William Miller, the chairman of the board and chief executive officer of Textron Incorporated. Miller, who was active in Democratic politics, was also the incoming president of the National Alliance of Businessmen (NAB), an association that provided "jobs and job training in private industry for the nation's disadvantaged men and women."[62] Having been shunned by the Nixon and Ford administrations, the NAB "was pleased to be welcomed back to the White House" after a seven-year absence. Miller and the NAB's primary tasks were to manage the two private-sector components of HIRE. The first was a reimbursement option where companies received federal funding to provide job training for Vietnam veterans. In return for the subsidy, the companies were required to offer permanent employment to the newly trained Vietnam veterans without displacing anyone else who was part of its current workforce. The second was a voluntary option that lacked any federal monetary incentive. Under this option, the NAB, motivated by its own mandate as well as the president's national campaign of gratitude, simply had to recruit or lobby companies to hire Vietnam veterans.[63]

The HIRE committee began its work shortly after being constituted. It mailed pledge cards and robo letters from the president to hundreds of companies across the country. Carter gave the committee a goal of 5,000 pledges for the first month. In his first official report, Miller happily informed the president that the committee had exceeded its goal, receiving 7,800 pledges from such companies as American Standard, General Electric, Goodyear Tire and Rubber, and Sears Roebuck. By August 15 the number of pledges totaled 12,550, with more than thirty businesses participating.[64]

Despite this promising start, the White House did not receive credit for the progress.[65] In fact, some media outlets were cynical of the president's overall commitment to a Vietnam veterans' agenda. The mounting frustration boiled over during the first Memorial Day observance of the Carter presidency. The *Washington Post* used that occasion to chide the administration for not doing enough to deal with the "needs and entitlements of Vietnam veterans." The newspaper gave two examples of the long neglect of Vietnam veterans. The first was an inadequate GI Bill, which failed to provide the level of financial assistance necessary for most veterans to attend school and complete their education. The second was the lack of a federal commitment to study and treat the widespread "emotional problems" that burdened many veterans. Believing that solutions were obtainable, the *Washington Post* argued that it was "the responsibility" of the president to articulate a "coherent national policy for dealing with the problems of returned service personnel."[66]

Coinciding with this public dressing-down, the Carter administration undertook a self-assessment of its veterans' policies. How much of this decision was driven by media criticism remains unanswered, but the White House instructed VA administrator Cleland to review all of the actions he had taken to date and identify any problems that he had encountered or anticipated. Cleland reported that trouble was brewing in Congress on several fronts. The Democratic majority in the legislature craved a greater share of the "spoils" now that a new administration was in place, he explained, and wanted to increase spending for veterans' benefits. Congress was also upset over the VA's cost-saving "crackdown" on educational overpayments that were expended through the GI Bill. Finally, the president learned that authorizing committees in Congress were moving forward with plans to block his proposal for upgrading bad discharges. Cleland further warned that the staff shortages at VA hospitals were straining the quality of care offered to veterans and further eroded morale among the agency's health-care providers. Most notably, Cleland informed the president that high unemployment rates constituted "a potential liability" for the administration. He reminded Carter that the Department of Labor and the White House, and not his agency, had the "principal" responsibility for moving the job programs forward. In concluding his summary, Cleland communicated that the VA was "actively participating" in the president's broader plans for reorganizing government, which was to streamline the totality of the federal bureaucracy in order to eliminate duplication of services and, just as important, to reduce costs across the board. To those ends, Cleland placed severe restrictions on first-class air travel for VA employees and eliminated the position of chauffeur to the administrator. He also reported that the VA was in compliance with a presidential directive that all agencies reduce the number of consulting firms hired for service contracts.[67]

Within a few days of receiving Cleland's memorandum, the president responded with handwritten comments in the margins identifying what areas and items that he considered priorities. He instructed Cleland to "continue crackdown" on educational overpayments and to "support my position" on the discharge upgrades. With respect to improving VA medical care, solving staff shortages, and addressing stagnant wages for the agency's health-care workforce, Carter simply noted, "see Bert when necessary," an order to coordinate with the director of the Office of Management and Budget. As for Cleland's approach to the administration's plans for the reorganization of government, the president pressed the young Georgian to "be strict" in curtailing first-class air travel for VA employees and to "eliminate all possible" contracts with consulting firms.[68]

By any standard of measurement, Carter had in the first months of his presidency put Vietnam veterans on the national agenda. Even his critics in the media called the pardon of the draft evaders, the rehabilitation of the VA, the jobs program, and the discharge upgrade proposal, which was not an original element of his campaign agenda, an impressive start. Yet, these same critics wanted more from Carter, both in the form of leadership and policy scale. Ironically, the *Washington Post* contemplated whether any amount of effort or activity could compensate veterans for the tragedy of Vietnam. This insatiable appetite for more raised expectations at a time when Max Cleland warned a fight was brewing in Congress over the president's discharge upgrade plan and that compromise might be necessary.

Making Compromises

In the summer of 1977, as some feared and others invited, Congress erupted into a raging battle over the question of bad paper discharges. Representative Robin Beard (R-TN), an active duty officer in the Marine Corps Reserve, led the charge against the president. He introduced a rider to an appropriations bill denying the use of Veterans Administration benefits to anyone receiving an upgrade under the president's Special Discharge Review Program. In defending his measure, the Tennessean made clear that he was not trying to halt the existing case-by-case upgrade review process. Instead, he objected to the "automatic" component of the Carter proposal, which carried with it the restoration of all forms of veterans' benefits. Beard was especially irritated by the provisions to assist deserters, calling the changes "a slap in the face to the thousands who have lived up to their full military commitments with honor."[69] To counter this opposition, the White House needed help.

One of the most compelling defenders of the president's plan was John Murtha (D-PA). A Marine combat officer in Vietnam, Murtha did not hold back any punches and made the debate personal. He told the chamber the story of a veteran from his district who served thirteen months in Vietnam, was severely wounded, but upon returning home to the states had in fact deserted. The former Marine officer understood the violation in its "technical sense," but he wanted his colleagues to appreciate the context of the young man's decision. He had "only" thirty days left to complete his enlistment, Murtha explained, but quit the military in order to care for his father, who was dying of cancer. Men of this sort with bad discharges were not war resisters in Murtha's mind. Rather "they worked, they fought" and in the end they were overwhelmed by it all. Murtha had much more respect for a fellow war veteran whose unfortunate circumstances triggered a bad decision than he did for those who claimed to support the war but "went to college and avoided it [Vietnam] because their parents had a lot of money."[70]

Beard and Murtha were emblematic of the sensibilities on both sides of this issue. In summing up the opening debate on the House floor, an exasperated Frank Evans (D-CO) exclaimed, "How many years has it been since we concluded the Vietnam War, and yet, a subject like this still tears our guts out." Although passion ran high, a majority clearly opposed the president and Murtha. Beard's rider passed in the House by a 273 to 136 vote and was included in an appropriations bill sent to the Senate.[71]

The Beard-led revolt transpired just a few days before the House was set to hold formal hearings on the discharge upgrade program. In the lead-up to that crucial moment, the *Washington Post* weighed in on the issue. The newspaper faulted the White House for "apparently [being] caught off guard by the opposition" in Congress and urged the administration to use the hearings as "the time and place" to make a strong case for the program.[72] Secretary of the Army Clifford Alexander and his deputy assistant Paul D. Phillips appeared before the House Veterans' Affairs Committee, ostensibly to defend the Special Discharge Review Program, but as journalist Lee Lescaze reported, "Time and time again the congressmen asked why Vietnam-era veterans should be treated differently," and Alexander and Phillips "waffled" repeatedly. The testimony of the secretary of the Army stood out in particular as he "declined to criticize the discharge procedures used during the Vietnam period, even though Carter administration officials have called those procedures capricious."[73] Without a stronger defense of the program coming from the White House, opponents in the Senate sensed an advantage. In fact, Senator Robert Dole, the former vice presidential candidate who had sparred with Carter on the amnesty issue during the 1976 campaign, made the first move by introducing the Beard amendment in the upper chamber. However, he withdrew it at the behest of a colleague who had an alternative amendment to block the administration proposal. That colleague was the Democratic chair of the Veterans' Affairs Committee, Senator Alan Cranston.

In a display of bipartisan opposition to the Carter Special Discharge Review Policy, Senators Cranston and Thurmond cosponsored S. 1307, an amendment to the House-passed appropriations bill. Commonly referred to as Cranston-Thurmond, S. 1307 voided the automatic upgrade criteria and accompanying entitlement to veterans' benefits in its entirety and substituted a requirement that a military discharge review board evaluate cases individually and weigh "all the evidence and factors in the case under uniform standards and procedures generally applicable to all persons." In its original form, S. 1307 totally undercut the core purpose of the president's plan, but it was more flexible than the House-approved measure. The Cranston-Thurmond option allowed military review boards to upgrade discharges and confer veterans' benefits when the evidence revealed that an individual had been subjected to arbitrary or discriminatory standards or procedures. It also allowed for discharge upgrades without the conferring of veterans' benefits, a minimal attempt to remove the societal and psychological stigma of having bad paper. The Veterans' Affairs Committee reported out S. 1307 with little delay, but the debate was far from over as the Senate considered several alternative amendments.[74]

On September 22, after more than two months of deliberations, the Senate voted 87–2 to pass an amended version of Cranston-Thurmond. In its final form, the bill invalidated the Carter program and required a new set of discharge review criteria for upgrades and opened eligibility to all veterans, not just Vietnam veterans. The rules were to be applied on a case-by-case basis. Veterans who were disabled as a result of combat-related injuries were entitled to VA medical care provided they were not cashiered under a bad conduct discharge. On the crucial issue of access to veterans' benefits, deserters—those being AWOL for 180 days or more—were still denied access, although the VA administrator had the power to reinstate benefits if extenuating circumstances existed. On September 23 the House agreed to the Senate bill by a staggering 321–75 margin. The measure was then presented to the president.[75]

Between the passage of the Beard amendment in mid-June and the passage of Cranston-Thurmond in late September, Carter had over three months to defend and advocate for his upgrade plan. Despite being warned by the *Washington Post* and the *New York Times* that it might become necessary for him to demonstrate leadership on the matter, the president sat on the sidelines as Congress dismembered his program. Indeed, as the White House Counsel's Office noted, "the only substantive special feature of the discharge review program—automatic upgrading" had been gutted. Moreover, by opening the process to all veterans, the legislation "does away with the compassion and forgiveness aspects" of the president's original proposal that was directed specifically toward Vietnam veterans.[76] As a result, the president was left with few choices. He either had to sign or veto the legislation.

Carter's chief of the domestic policy staff, Stuart Eizenstat, laid out the pros and cons as well as the political consequences associated with each course of action. A veto "would indicate the strength of your commitment to the Program and your unwillingness to allow Congress to change that Program in any respect," reasoned Eizenstat, and would be supported by pro-amnesty groups and liberal members of Congress, who believe "you have an obligation" to fulfill your promise to Vietnam veterans with bad paper discharges. He also explained to the president that the press was "watching the issue closely," and the failure to veto the legislation would "unleash a series of stories" about his "refusal to stand tough with Congress." Finally, a veto afforded the president an opportunity to work out a better solution before the current session of Congress ended, even if it were another compromise solution.[77] There were, however, political ramifications to consider if Carter decided to veto the bill. Eizenstat explained that most members of Congress found it easy to vote against the "automatic granting" of veterans' benefits, and "it therefore seems unlikely that a veto could be sustained." Carter had not yet exercised a presidential veto. Conventional wisdom within administration circles favored using that executive authority on an issue that had "wide public appeal," which the discharge program lacked. In addition, Carter needed to project "strength" as another battle with Congress was looming over something he was deeply invested in and committed to: his energy policy. To have a veto overridden would come at an inopportune time and would be an indication of weakness, a domestic policy staff memorandum detailed.[78]

The broader political consequences deeply concerned the White House. "The House [Democratic] leadership will be extremely upset and embarrassed by a veto," Eizenstat told the president. "I do not think the changes this bill makes . . . warrant so impairing relations with the leadership, especially at a time when its help is needed on so many major matters." Additional support for signing the bill came from Frank Moore, the administration's congressional liaison, and Cleland, who felt that at a minimum the current bill was an improvement over the rigid Beard amendment, which denied veterans' benefits to any special discharge upgrade cases. Cleland also saw congressional intransigence against the awarding of automatic benefits as too formidable to overcome. The case had been made that the bill was the best the president could hope for at the time, and a veto posed too great a risk to Carter's already tenuous relationship with Congress.[79]

On October 8, Carter signed S.1307. He defended his decision in an official statement declaring, "Nothing in this bill detracts from the impact of the Presidential pardon [of draft evaders] or the Special Discharge Review Program in helping to wipe the records of these veterans clean." He highlighted what the bill accomplished, stressing that now for the first time veterans of all eras could undergo a discharge review process with the same "uniform" standards. The president emphasized that veterans with less than honorable discharges who suffered service-related injuries were entitled to VA healthcare benefits. Carter noted that the bill denied benefits to deserters who had been AWOL for more than 180 days, and he pledged to submit legislation the following year to correct some of the bill's defects.[80] Given that Congress had altered the intent and scope of Carter's original plan by a veto-proof majority, the president's comments confirmed his resignation to compromise on this particular issue.

The *Washington Post* expressed considerable disappointment with the president's handling of this issue. Although allowing that "some of the blame" for the outcome rested with "mean-minded" members of Congress, the paper editorialized, the administration was culpable "for its failure to explain its intentions." As a result, "the one group that was especially vulnerable: the poor, the uneducated, the unemployed and those who were pressed into service despite their being unfit for military life," had been deprived of passion and forgiveness. For these victims of the war, "upgrading and benefits represent a last-chance shot at rehabilitation and a useful life," the *Washington Post* mourned. The editorial also speculated that "with disillusionment already high among Vietnam veterans . . . the President's decision is likely to increase the feeling of being forgotten." Amid its lamenting, the *Post* held out hope that all was not lost, clinging to the president's promise of proposing new legislation in the coming year to correct the shortcomings of the bill he signed.[81] Liberal commentators in the media were not nearly as conciliatory toward the president.

For example, Mary McGrory assailed both Carter and Congress for the bad-paper discharge debacle. Carter had caved-in to the opposition in a "lame and specious" display of presidential leadership, she wrote. Moreover, McGrory called into question both his sincerity and commitment to Vietnam veterans.

Liberals have been freshly reminded that the President never shared their outrage over Viet Nam. The pardon for Viet Nam draft-evaders was extracted from him as a minimal condition for nomination. . . . A veto of the Special Discharge upgrade would have done Carter—and the veterans—good. It would have said that he really cares about what he once defined as his special constituency, the defenseless and unrepresented in our society. By signing, all he said was that he is not responsible when his good intentions get mangled elsewhere.[82]

Congress, however, was also part of the problem. They were "not interested in rehabilitating Viet Nam veterans," the liberal journalist alleged, "but . . . are obsessed with rehabilitating the Viet Nam war."[83]

The bad-paper discharge debate marked the first serious setback in Carter's Vietnam veterans' agenda. This situation also demonstrated that the upgrade program did not take precedence over other aspects of his Vietnam veterans' agenda or his broader domestic priorities. Too, the episode showed the growing politicization of Vietnam veterans' issues and how much power Congress had in shaping and controlling that agenda.

The Vietnam GI Bill

On October 24, 1977, Carter laid a wreath at the Tomb of the Unknown Soldier and delivered his first Veterans Day address as president. In some ways, his remarks were similar to those given by previous commander in chiefs. Carter reflected on the country's martial past beginning with its birth in the American Revolution, and he celebrated the bravery of those who had answered the call for military service throughout the intervening centuries. He included his family's martial heritage as part of this celebration. Notably, the president used the national day of commemoration to remind Americans of the "special debt of gratitude" still owed to Vietnam veterans. He applauded his own work on that score, pointing to increases in VA compensation and pensions as well as the jobs program created by his Economic Recovery Plan. In Carter's mind, his administration had made Vietnam veterans a top priority.[84] Not everyone, however, accepted his laudatory self-narrative. The *Washington Post*, for example, responded to Carter's Veterans Day speech with an editorial that rejected the president's claims of success and called into question his commitment to repaying that "special debt of gratitude" owed to Vietnam veterans. If the president was serious about this obligation, the *Post* opined, then he would throw his executive "weight" behind a congressional proposal to increase GI Bill educational benefits for Vietnam veterans.[85]

During the summer of 1977, Congress began deliberation on a cost-of-living increase to the educational benefits portion of the GI Bill. The discussions immediately triggered claims from some quarters about the inequity of the Vietnam Veterans GI Bill. Both Carter and Cleland had been down this road before during Georgia's free college tuition debate. The fundamental problem was that GI Bill education benefits were not keeping pace with either skyrocketing tuition costs or higher inflation. The stipend, in dollar terms, was higher for Vietnam veterans than the stipend granted to Korean War and World War II veterans. Nevertheless, the amount awarded to Vietnam veterans, in contrast to previous generations of veterans, did not cover all of the financial needs of a student-veteran. The problem was particularly acute in Eastern and Midwestern states. By 1977, studies had shown that 80 percent of eligible veterans in Pennsylvania, Indiana, and Vermont had not used their GI educational benefits. Despite a vigorous effort by more than one hundred members of the House of Representatives to enhance education benefits, the Veterans' Affairs Committee blocked all of their proposals. The committee was satisfied that a 6.6 percent cost-of-living increase, slightly more than the 5 percent proposed by the White House, was adequate for Vietnam veterans. The committee argued that Vietnam veterans had access to an array of federal and state educational programs that were not available to earlier generations of veterans. These additional or supplemental benefits made an increase to the GI Bill unnecessary. With only an all-or-nothing choice, the lower chamber voted unanimously to pass the bill.[86]

Meanwhile, the Senate debate over education benefits unfolded more favorably for Vietnam veterans. The Veterans' Affairs Committee heard proposals that went beyond the basic 6.6 percent cost-of-living increase and ultimately endorsed an accelerated payment plan. Under the current system, most veterans only collected thirty-six of an available forty-five monthly payments while completing a four-year undergraduate degree. The committee wanted to grant early access or accelerated access to available benefits to Vietnam veterans who lived in areas where tuition costs were high. The full Senate made some slight modifications to the committee's proposal but passed by a 91–0 margin a version of an accelerated payments plan along with a 6.6 percent cost-of-living increase. There were now two competing measures, a House version and a more generous Senate version, but neither was sent to a joint conference committee. Instead, members and staffers of the two Veterans' Affairs Committees hammered out a compromise bill. The 6.6 percent cost-of-living increase was not altered, but the accelerated payment plan was dropped and replaced with a proposal that authorized the Veterans Administration to forgive a portion of any VA education loans if the state where the veteran resided matched the forgiveness amount. This compromise, known as the GI Bill Improvement Act, passed both the House and Senate by voice vote.[87]

The domestic policy staff reacted favorably to the passage of the GI

Improvement Act and offered no substantive reasons for vetoing the measure. In recommending that the president sign the legislation, Stuart Eizenstat pointed out that although the cost-of-living increase was "slightly more generous than our proposal,' the overall budgetary impact was minimal and represented a "reasonable compromise" between the opposing positions. That factor, in his estimation, made it "far better than the original Senate proposal and can legitimately be said to be a response to the problems of Vietnam veterans." Moreover, he maintained that the provisions to help veterans in areas with high-cost schools was "particularly welcomed by the mid-western and eastern states." The Office of Management and Budget, the Veterans Administration, and the Civil Service Commission all recommended signing the bill as well.[88]

On November 23 the president signed the GI Bill Improvement Act. The Thanksgiving holiday prevented an elaborate signing ceremony, but the White House did release an official statement from the president. Carter was "pleased" that the legislation "expanded" benefits for approximately 1.7 million Vietnam veterans. He also highlighted the loan forgiveness program as one of the bill's achievements and sounded a note of triumphalism by pointing out that 65 percent of Vietnam veterans had utilized some aspect of GI Bill education benefits, a rate that "far exceeds the final participation" figures of the World War II generations. In signing the legislation, the president conveyed the message that a meaningful part of the special debt owed to Vietnam veterans was being paid under his watch.[89]

The Liberal Critique

With respect to Vietnam veterans' issues, the first year of the Carter presidency ended in extreme disappointment for the *Washington Post* and such journalists such as Mary McGrory and Colman McCarthy, who had consistently called for bigger and more expensive programs for Vietnam veterans.[90] Speaking unofficially for the group, McCarthy remarked, "The Carter administration committed itself to stand with the newest and worst-treated veterans—Vietnam's" and compared it to "the policy of indifference that the Nixon and Ford administration inflicted. . . . Vietnam veterans may be better treated now. But not much better." The employment picture for Vietnam veterans continued to "darken" under Carter, he maintained, and the chance to convey "forgiveness and compassion" to those who held bad paper discharges ended shamefully, as the president refused to veto a measure that clearly undercut his original intentions. It was still early in the Carter presidency, but these liberal critics were sounding the alarm of "the continuing neglect" of Vietnam veterans.[91]

In a dour assessment, McCarthy offered two explanations for the "disarray and failure" of Carter's Vietnam veterans' agenda. First, there was no one inside the White House "working full time on veterans policy." The domestic policy staff, which had coordinated the early policy efforts of the president's Vietnam veterans' agenda, was also tasked with other time-consuming and politically volatile issues such as welfare reform, Social Security, and energy policy. Second, Carter's aloofness toward members of Congress and his failure to provide leadership prompted more than one politician to remark, "A lot of us who are willing to support him aren't really sure what he wants. If he isn't sure, how can his friends be?"[92] In many respects, this second criticism could have been applied to Carter's entire presidency. Opinion polls confirmed his struggles: his approval rating declined dramatically from when he first assumed office. More and more people were uncertain that the president could deliver on his campaign promises.[93] But all was not lost despite the obvious headwinds. As seasoned political correspondent David Broder wrote, "Carter will have a real opportunity to show he has his priorities straight" when he delivered his first State of the Union address and submitted his first budget at the start of his second year in office.[94]

The president believed that he had already delivered on many of the promises that he made to Vietnam veterans during the 1976 presidential campaign. In his first year in office, he launched a jobs program, he initiated a new discharge review program for veterans, and he signed the first increase to the GI Bill since the Nixon administration. Although Carter was not always successful in obtaining his objectives and sometimes conceded the outcome to Congress, Vietnam veterans' issues was becoming a national agenda item. This consequential accomplishment, however, failed to satisfy the promoters of the narrative of victimhood, whose incessant critiques of Carter's Vietnam veterans' policies were meant as a perpetual reminder of the abject lessons and legacies of America's disastrous military intervention in Vietnam.

Entering the second year of his presidency, Carter faced the growing fear that "Vietnam veterans were becoming a lost generation."[95] The sense of urgency had been heightened by an ABC televised documentary entitled *The*

Class That Went to War. The program chronicled the story of twenty young men from Chatham High School in New Jersey who served in Vietnam. Not all of them returned home, but those who did faced a variety of challenges. The key message of the documentary was that for Vietnam veterans, their struggles did not end with their military service; for too many, their problems were just beginning. The *Washington Post* used the broadcast of *The Class That Went to War* to deliver yet another scornful reminder to those who seemed unaware of the extent of the pain and suffering of so many Vietnam veterans. "The message of the program . . . doesn't seem to be that hard to grasp," the *Post* editorialized, "and yet the Carter administration and a majority of Congress still don't seem able to grasp it fully—or at least not nearly as fully as those at ABC who put together the documentary."[96]

Interestingly, Max Cleland had been overlooked in the routinized assessments of Carter's veterans' policy. Appointing Vietnam veterans to positions of influence in the Veterans Administration had been a 1976 campaign promise. Cleland's appointment had been widely applauded, but he had not played a critical role in the development of Vietnam veterans' policy during the first year of the Carter administration. His primary concern was on improving the bed-side manner, so to speak, of the VA: making the agency more compassionate, sensitive, and efficient in dealing with the nation's veterans. Moreover, he had spent a great deal of his tenure outside of the nation's capital, having traveled 60,000 miles while visiting and inspecting over five hundred facilities under the VA's jurisdiction. Cleland sat in an awkward position between Congress and the president. He had a deep loyalty toward the two congressional Veterans' Affairs Committees—and especially to Senator Cranston, dating back to his days as a staffer. As time progressed, he became a more visible figure in the debates regarding Vietnam veterans' policy.[97]

4

Battling Expectations

In explaining the general public's growing disillusionment with Jimmy Carter, journalist Kenneth Crawford suggested that the Georgian had not mastered the transition from campaigner to president. As a candidate, Crawford wrote, he attempted to "be almost all things to almost all men," but "once in office his efforts to satisfy all his various constituencies made him seem loyal to none."[1] Others in the journalistic community pointed to different political shortcomings. For example, the *Washington Post* editorialized that "Mr. Carter thinks that virtue and reason speak for themselves" and that he demonstrated an unfortunate habit of announcing new initiatives with "rain-hail-and-thunder speeches," only to turn his back and move on to "other things."[2] The *New York Times* rendered a similar verdict opining that Carter "is a soothing flatterer and a sensible President, but not yet a leader."[3] Elements of the Vietnam veterans' activist network had leveled similar pronouncements against the president during his first year in office. Whether any of these admonitions concerned Carter or not, he began the second year of his presidency with the obvious intention of limiting expectations.

On January 19, 1978, Carter delivered his State of the Union address. He set the tone early in the speech when he declared, "Those of us who govern can sometimes inspire, and we can identify needs and marshal resources, but we simply cannot be the managers of everything and everybody." The president added, "We need patience and good will, but we really need to realize that there is a limit to the role and the function of government. Government cannot solve our problems." It was not necessary or feasible to greatly expand existing programs or implement new ones, Carter explained; the federal government simply needed to be more efficient.⁴ "By conventional standards it was a dull speech," the *Washington Post* editorialized, "because it contained very little in the way of thrilling new ventures and bugle calls to action."⁵

Although Carter had stressed the limits of government and the need to practice fiscal restraint, there were a number of issues he intended to engage. The administration was determined to get a version of its energy program passed. Carter also targeted reform measures in the areas of welfare, labor law, lobbying, and consumer protection. And passage of the Panama Canal Treaty was a consequential foreign policy objective.⁶ Members of Congress had their own preoccupations in year two with the upcoming midterm elections approaching and a looming docket of such politically sensitive issues as federally funded abortions, financial bailouts for New York City, tax cuts, and an ethics probe involving Korean influence peddling.⁷

Answering the Critics

As he fought the battle of expectations at the start of his second year in office, Carter's Vietnam veterans' agenda seemed poised for progress. After a slow start, the HIRE program began to pick up steam. In January 1978, chairman G. William Miller announced that the cumulative total of pledged jobs had reached 70,000, with 360 companies participating. Recent additions to the mix included such firms as ConAgra, Honeywell, Pillsbury, and Twentieth Century Fox Films.⁸ The following month, which was the initiative's halfway point, Miller confirmed an additional 7,600 pledges and reported that 145 companies had made 21,200 actual hires. Based on these figures, the chairman predicted that the September 1978 goal of 100,000 new jobs would be met.⁹ The president congratulated Miller for the "excellent" work. Confident in HIRE's eventual success, Carter felt comfortable making some personnel changes. He rewarded Miller by naming him chairman of the board of governors of the Federal Reserve System.¹⁰ Rueben Mettler, the incoming chairman of the National Alliance of Businessmen (NAB), assumed responsibility for leading HIRE.¹¹ From the White House's perspective, everything seemed on track with respect to the Vietnam veterans' job program. The president was making good on an earlier promise, and HIRE validated Carter's penchant for private-sector solutions to social and economic concerns. However, the administration soon found itself on the receiving end of a series of rebukes.

With invective, the *Washington Post* proclaimed that Carter's Vietnam veterans' job program was "a dismal failure." Citing unnamed sources in the Department of Labor and a soon-to-be released Government Accounting Office (GAO) report, the paper alleged that HIRE had only produced 200 of the 100,000 jobs promised to Vietnam veterans. The reasons for HIRE's failure were numerous, according to the *Washington Post*, but the most regrettable were that the program had been poorly "conceived" and that the Department of Labor had "avoided any effective consultation with the business community." To illustrate the program's many "flaws," the paper highlighted one original regulation that required employers to hire a minimum of 100 workers in order to qualify for the federal reimbursement provision. As the *Washington Post* sardonically remarked, "how often do many companies, even major corporations, hire 100 workers in one sweep?" Conceding that "some improvement" in the employment figures for Vietnam veterans had occurred since Carter took office, the *Washington Post* argued that valuable time had been wasted and substantial federal money remained unspent as a result of poor execution, adding "still another burden . . . [to] a group that already has more burdens than it needs." For HIRE to fulfill its goal of 100,000 jobs, the newspaper recommended that the Department of Labor "be more open to taking the advice of the business community" and that the administration provide new guidelines to "at least correct the mistakes of last year." The fundamental criticism leveled against the administration was that it lacked a forthright commitment to its Vietnam veterans' agenda.[12]

The charges directed against the HIRE program struck a nerve with the administration and caused an immediate reaction. The same day the editorial appeared in print, the president discussed the matter in a Cabinet meeting at the White House, and Secretary of Labor Marshall emerged as the administration's point person "to set the record straight."[13] Soon Marshall sent a rebuttal to the *Washington Post*. Interestingly, the op-ed did not appear in print until several weeks later.[14]

The secretary of labor directly challenged the severely "misleading and largely inaccurate" assertions made by the *Washington Post*. He pointed out correctly that the editorial covered only the reimbursable option of HIRE and neglected to mention that 76,000 jobs had been pledged and 21,000 actual hires had been completed under the voluntary component. Marshall maintained that instead of only 200 hires, the reimbursable option had contracted 8,000 positions, with pledges for an additional 4,000 more jobs. He also explained that a "dramatic" improvement in the employment picture for Vietnam veterans had occurred over the preceding five months, coinciding with a general improvement in the nation's economy. The unemployment rate for Vietnam veterans aged 20 to 34 had fallen below that of nonveterans in the same bracket. He deigned the *Washington Post*'s lack of appreciation for all of the progress as "unfortunate." There was still room for improvement, Marshall admitted, particularly among African Americans and "other minorities," who continued to encounter "serious and unique unemployment problems." Feeling that he had defended successfully the president's record, Marshall clarified the mechanics of the HIRE program, including revisions to the program, and the administration's strategy moving forward. He acknowledged that HIRE had not been "free of problems" but implied that unreasonable expectations had created biases against a fair assessment of the program. Marshall attributed some of the slow start of the program to Congress's delay in passing the enabling legislation, and he excused the "few administrative errors" that had been committed as a function of the administration's "eagerness to get the program underway." As for the requirement that businesses hire a minimum number of workers to receive federal reimbursement, the secretary expected that revised guidelines would eliminate that provision entirely. In addition, the administration was in the process of devising a plan to shift the roughly $120 million in unused HIRE funds to CETA in order to generate more public-sector jobs for Vietnam veterans. Finally, Marshall flatly rejected the claim that anyone in the administration had failed to consult the business community by highlighting the administration's close working relationship with the National Alliance of Businessmen and by giving the organization "much of the credit" for the progress thus far. It was a forceful defense of HIRE and the president's Vietnam veterans' job program.[15]

Perhaps the delay in publishing Marshall's rebuttal, two full weeks after he submitted it, had been intentional. Indeed, on the same day that Marshall's op-ed appeared, the *Washington Post* included a rejoinder. The newspaper did not deny that some positive employment trends had occurred, but it stood by its original assessment of HIRE and called for "a full and vigorous commitment from the administration."[16] Marshall's response did not stem the tide of criticism being leveled against the White House over the president's Vietnam veterans' agenda. As one wave crested, another began to form.

In late March, the *Washington Star* ran a series of articles calling into question the administration's level of commitment to the troubled Vietnam veteran. The first installment was entitled, "Vietnam Vets: Is Help Coming 10 Years Too Late?" Journalist Donia Mills argued that a decade after the Tet Offensive and five years after America's withdrawal from the war, "government officials have not dealt with the social, moral and psychological damage suffered by the men who fought" in Vietnam. She concluded that they had "not been deliberately neglected so much as simply set on a back burner with low priority, in budget after budget, year after year, all the way down the line." As part of her reporting, she solicited input from members of the Carter administration, allowing them to defend the president's record and his commitment to Vietnam veterans. Frank Raines, a member of the domestic policy staff, hit back hard against all of the criticism that the administration had received. "The White House feels no more concern over veterans right now than over other areas," Raines remarked. "We spend a lot of money on vets—about $20 billion a year. Our main concern is that the money is being properly utilized. But there is no crisis in veterans programs at this time."[17] Raines's statement, combined with the exchange between Secretary of Labor Marshall and the *Washington Post*, suggested that the Carter administration had finally decided to aggressively answer its critics. The new posture coincided with Max Cleland's one-year anniversary as the head of the Veterans Administration.

To mark that occasion, Cleland granted numerous interviews to a variety of news outlets.[18] During the media blitz, the question everyone seemingly wanted answered was whether Vietnam veterans had received a "raw deal" in comparison to returnees of other wars. "There's a grain of truth to it," Cleland admitted in a lengthy exchange with *U.S. News & World Report*, "stemming mostly from the fact that the country cannot separate the war from the warrior." The Vietnam veteran has been "perceived by his own society as a stranger: something different from the young kid on the block whom we sent to Vietnam." These perceptions caused serious readjustment problems for former service members. But Cleland was careful to point out that the vast majority of Vietnam veterans had readjusted quite well. By his estimation 80 percent of Vietnam veterans were "better employed" and earned a higher income than their generational counterparts who did not serve. In comparison to veterans of earlier periods, Vietnam veterans had cashed in on GI Bill benefits "in greater proportion" than any prior group of veterans. "What you've got in your average Vietnam-era veteran is a guy who's really tougher and stronger and probably ultimately more motivated and more capable" than his civilian peers, Cleland extolled. He labeled this achievement the "untold story," one that deserved much greater attention over the more prevalent portrayals of the Vietnam veteran as "a potential drug user, potential killer, potential weirdo."[19]

There still remained, however, a cross-section of Vietnam veterans with significant problems, according to Cleland. Their readjustment difficulties were "not necessarily" greater than those faced by earlier generations of returning veterans, but their problems were different and in some cases unique and therefore required a "tailored" approach. When asked by *U.S. News & World Report* what all of that meant in practical terms, the head of the VA identified psychological counseling and alcohol treatment as two of the most pressing concerns. As for the next steps forward, Cleland said the Carter administration intended to focus on the 20 percent of Vietnam veterans who "somewhere along the line missed the boat" and had "been unable to adjust." These were the "hard core" cases who needed special attention.[20]

During the first half of 1978, members of the administration navigated the politics of the president's Vietnam veterans' agenda by pushing a narrative that most of the war's veterans had readjusted successfully. The president's policies, they maintained, had aided that difficult transition. If the administration thought that it had gained an advantage in the contest to control expectations, then it was mistaken. In fact, lingering questions over the president's jobs program served as an indication of the political challenges on the administration's horizon.

A Public Relations Battle

Monthly reports of the HIRE program indicated that the initiative was routinely meeting or exceeding its goals. By March 1978 over 550 companies were participating and had pledged a collective 82,000 jobs, of which 22,210 had already resulted in hires. The success was almost exclusively in the volunteer component of HIRE. At that time, the reimbursable component had still not made meaningful headway, having obligated only 15 percent of its allocated funds and having netted only 285 actual hires. This feeble performance stood in stark contrast to the torrid pace of the volunteer option. For its part, the NAB remained "confident" that it could deliver 100,000 hires by September 1978.[21] Good news continued to come in, and by early May the NAB was less than 10,000 pledges short of the ultimate target, with actual hires continuing to increase.[22] Although the NAB was on pace to fulfill the president's promise on private-sector job creation, influential members of Congress raised questions about efforts to provide public-sector jobs to Vietnam veterans.[23] In addition, a recent poll revealed that roughly fifty members of Congress felt that the government was "failing to fulfil its obligations to veterans of the Vietnam War, especially the disabled."[24] Granted, only one-fifth of the members of Congress responded to the survey, but of that number fewer than fifteen legislators considered the president's job program a success.[25] To counter the discontent, the White House called on the National Alliance of Businessmen to address the concerns.

On May 3, 1978, Charles P. Collins III, the NAB's vice president of veterans' programs, testified before the Subcommittee on Employment and Training of the House Committee on Veteran Affairs. Not to be overlooked, Collins was a Vietnam veteran, having served three tours of duty in Southeast Asia. He presented an overview of the NAB and a detailed report on the organization's involvement with the president's HIRE program. As he explained, the NAB had been working for the past seven years to provide "job opportunities for Vietnam-era veterans in private sector companies." Collins reminded the committee that while the organization had in the past received "resources" from the Department of Labor, the NAB had willingly accepted "the additional assignment" of running HIRE "without any additional funding assistance from the federal government." It had marshalled the necessary "manpower and resources" for the task on its own. He assured the committee that the NAB would "meet and indeed surpass" the numerical goals given to the organization by the president.[26]

After this informative but hardly controversial testimony, Collins addressed the "considerable amount of attention" that had been given to the reimbursable component of HIRE and the fact that a small portion of the $140 million allocation had been utilized. He and the NAB were not pleased with the inferences made by the media to an oft-cited GAO report: "In our opinion, such evaluations are incomplete and very limited in scope. They do not address the important success we have had in obtaining commitments to voluntarily hire veterans. We are chagrined that those involved in the program would hang the failure sign on a program because it isn't going to cost $140 million while meeting or surpassing its goal." Having presented his case, Collins's final thoughts seemed to imply that government bureaucrats and elected officials were the ones primarily responsible for any disappointing outcomes. "With properly engineered tools of the trade—that is, with well-designed and constructed federal programs for human resource initiatives—we can achieve the goal to get as many unemployed veterans trained and in private sector jobs as possible," he told the committee in his closing statement.[27]

Despite the laudable work of the NAB, Carter's program was still falling short of the original promise to generate a total of 200,000 new jobs for Vietnam veterans. The expectation, at that time, was that the bulk of the new jobs would be created in the public sector through the expansion of CETA, something that never materialized because Congress failed to provide the hiring guidelines as recommended by the administration. Although the sizeable $140 million allocation for HIRE had not been well utilized, the administration was planning to shift most of the HIRE money to CETA. Success, however, required the cooperation of Congress to ensure that federal guidelines guaranteed that Vietnam veterans received the public-sector jobs.[28] At the heart of the growing negativity in the media was the perception that Carter needed to demonstrate presidential leadership.

In what was becoming something of a common reprise, using martial-inspired national holidays as a platform for launching attacks about inadequate veterans' policies, syndicated columnist Jack Anderson used Memorial Day 1978 to join the ranks of those criticizing the president. The theme of Anderson's piece was easily discernable in its title, "Carter, and U.S., Forget Vietnam Vets." He spared no one in his national lampoon, faulting the government "that drafted them . . . the neighbors who sent them off . . . [and] the troubled society that failed to welcome them back." But Anderson directed his utmost contempt to "a peanut farmer named Jimmy Carter" who enthusiastically promised to help Vietnam veterans, but once he reached the White House "forgot them too." The columnist brazenly accused the president of merely going "through the motions" with his jobs program for Vietnam veterans, and he assailed the Department of Labor for covering up the failures. There was a litany of specific accusations, with the most serious being that the administration had cooked the unemployment numbers so that it appeared to be effectively dealing with that problem. Anderson also contended that the administration had mismanaged the jobs program.[29]

As a syndicated columnist with a muckraker's flair, Anderson's broadside shook the White House. An obviously vexed Carter reached out to his secretary of labor on how to counter the charges leveled by the columnist. Marshall doubted another op-ed in the *Washington Post* would do much "to remedy" the situation given that Anderson's syndication placed him in hundreds of newspapers all across the country and with a larger and more diverse readership than the *Washington Post*. Therefore, the secretary proposed a lunch meeting with the columnist, hoping that he could convince Anderson "to run some kind of correction in the context of a second column highlighting the Administration's major accomplishment of reducing Vietnam-era unemployment." Marshall gave the president a preview of his talking points. What was clear from the communication between Carter and the secretary of labor was that the administration firmly believed its policies had lowered considerably the unemployment rate for Vietnam veterans and that it wanted credit for fulfilling its promises on job creation.[30]

Unfortunately for the administration, the Marshall-Anderson meeting did not produce the desired retraction. In fact, the syndicated columnist wrote a follow-up piece that expanded upon his earlier criticisms and specifically mentioned how unpersuasive the secretary of labor had been during their get-together. Taken collectively, in two columns, Anderson made the following claims: First, he faulted the administration for not ensuring the adoption of regulations protecting Vietnam veteran hiring preferences as part of the expansion of CETA. Second, Anderson reported that the administration had "lost track" of the program to hire 2,000 disabled veterans as part of a larger job placement initiative. Third, he explained that the administration had created a "ridiculous new definition" of the Vietnam veteran as someone who had been discharged from the armed forces within the past four years, which according to Anderson had been done because "it lowers the veterans' jobless rate and reduces President Carter's embarrassment."[31]

Bitterness colored the dispute between Anderson and administration officials. For example, Marshall asserted that 2,000 disabled Vietnam veterans had been hired in his department's employment services offices. They found work for an additional 26,000 disabled veterans and expected to find work for 14,000 more disabled veterans. Anderson refused to believe these assertions and dismissed Marshall's evidence as "a smorgasbord of statistics."[32]

Notwithstanding the acrimony, there were broader implications at play. Anderson had created a score card upon which to judge the administration's record of successes and failures on the important issue of Vietnam veteran job creation. Exposing the flawed CETA regulations was a valid complaint, and the administration had no answer except to say, "We tried and failed to get a 35-percent veterans' goal written into the law."[33] It offered a similarly weak response to Anderson's charge that Vietnam veteran unemployment figures had been manipulated. Marshall could only quip that in his estimation the GAO "could be unreliable." The most persistent question, and one that went unanswered, was why so little of the $140 million allocated to HIRE had been spent.[34]

Meanwhile, the National Alliance for Businessmen concluded its work on the HIRE project in impressive fashion. By the end of September, Chairman Mettler reported that through the voluntary option 878 participating corporations had made 114,000 actual hires and had pledges to make 21,000 additional hires, all at a minimal cost to taxpayers. In addition, under the reimbursable segment nearly 200 firms had signed agreements to provide 23,700 on-the-job training positions at a cost of $40 million. Through actual placements and pledges, the NAB had delivered 158,700 jobs for Vietnam veterans. However, the failure to generate enough public-sector jobs through CETA left the president a good bit short of the 200,000 jobs that he had promised in January 1977 when he unveiled his Economic Recovery Plan. But the administration was satisfied with HIRE's results and the overall level of economic improvement for Vietnam veterans. Nationally the unemployment rate for all Americans had fallen 1.5 percent between the time Carter took office and the second quarter of 1978. During the same period, Vietnam veteran unemployment fell at an even greater pace to a figure below civilian percentages, at least according to the administration estimates. In addition, there was talk of transferring the $90 million leftover from the original HIRE allocation to 300 CETA prime sponsors as part of a new program called HIRE II. But there was no stated plan guaranteeing the adoption of regulations ensuring Vietnam veteran hiring preferences.[35]

The administration deserved more credit for its Vietnam veteran job program than it received from its critics. The National Alliance of Businessmen had served the president well, producing a substantial number of jobs in a relatively short period of time. Conversely, Congress ignored the administration's directives regarding veterans' hiring preferences for public-sector jobs in order to serve other constituencies. Still, the naysayers were not willing to overlook the fact that Carter had promised more jobs than he delivered. Privately, members of the administration admitted that it lacked a coordinated and disciplined approach to its Vietnam veterans' agenda. To these ends, the domestic policy staff sought to improve the administration's approach and handling of Vietnam veterans' policy. In fact, they had been working on a plan to that end since January 1978, but the task was proving more difficult than expected.

Vietnam Veterans PRM

In January 1978 the written version of the State of the Union address presented to Congress contained a proposal for a comprehensive executive-level study of Vietnam veterans.[36] The idea came from the domestic policy staff. "I consider this a high priority item," Frank Raines explained to his boss, Stuart Eizenstat, "because we have received a great deal of undeserved criticism because our initiatives have not been coordinated and highlighted." He added: "It is important that . . . the President's policy of giving special consideration to these veterans . . . [be] packaged in a form that we get the credit that we are due." To tackle the public relations battle and better coordinate the administration's Vietnam veterans' agenda, Raines recommended a Presidential Review Memorandum (PRM).[37] The PRM traced its origins to "strong-minded presidential assistants" such as McGeorge Bundy, Walt Rostow, and Henry Kissinger who sought to expand their influence in the realm of national security. Carter's National Security advisor, Zbigniew Brzezinski, adopted the practice at the start of his tenure, and Eizenstat turned to the PRM after the president suffered early setbacks on his energy, economic, and health-care proposals.[38] In theory, the PRM represented an opportunity for the domestic policy staff to more clearly define, coordinate, and implement a Vietnam veterans' agenda.

Eizenstat first sent an Issue Definition Memorandum (IDM) to seven Cabinet offices and relevant government agencies. As the domestic policy staff director explained, the main objective was to determine "the current status of Vietnam-era veterans in terms of education, employment, health, family life and form of service discharge." The evaluation was to include a judgment on the successes and/or failures of current programs and investigate whether "reforms, improvements or modifications" were warranted. In addition, the review was to determine the feasibility of "new programs or initiatives." He sought feedback from each of the invested parties, although even at this initial stage the broad parameters were set and he reiterated the need for speed.[39] If Eizenstat received any feedback, then little was incorporated into the report that he submitted to the president six weeks later.

Eizenstat had not involved Carter in framing the Vietnam Veterans PRM. Therefore, he and Raines included a short explanation of their work when they submitted the authorization memorandum. The president's handwritten comments on the authorization memorandum revealed his displeasure. When told that the version of the State of the Union address that was submitted to Congress included a promise to enact a "government-wide review of the status of Vietnam veterans," Carter wrote tellingly, "I don't recall this." He further admonished his domestic policy staff to "minimize p.r. [public relations] & do not raise unwarranted expectations of new programs, etc," and added that they should "be reticent about studies of this kind" in the future. Somewhat reluctantly, the president consented to proceed.[40] It should be noted that the PRM discussion overlapped Secretary Marshall's public relations battles with the media over the HIRE program. Sensitive to the incessant criticism of his Vietnam veterans' agenda, Carter's desire to manage expectations was understandable. But in giving his approval for the Presidential Review Memorandum, Carter elevated Vietnam veterans' issues as a national agenda item.

After a short delay, Eizenstat completed the PRM's preliminary report. In summary, the key conclusions were that Vietnam veterans were "on the whole better off than their non-veteran counterparts." They had "benefitted from more generous programs than previous veterans." Minority and disabled veterans continued to have "serious problems." Although Vietnam veterans' programs were "numerous," many suffered from "a lack of coordination between agencies," particularly those within the Department of Labor and the Veterans Administration. These findings, particularly the one that Vietnam veterans had already received more federal assistance that any generation of veterans, were certain to be countered by the president's critics.[41]

After a month of evaluations, Eizenstat forwarded the PRM background papers, policy considerations, and recommendations to Carter, informing him that there was "consensus" and "no controversies" among the participating agencies. The Veterans Administration, Department of Labor,

Defense Department, Office of Management and Budget, and the Department of Health, Education and Welfare were in general agreement on the study's primary conclusion, which advocated "improving existing programs and avoiding, wherever possible, significant requests for additional funds." The president was no doubt pleased upon hearing this news, given that his original instructions were to keep expectations low and budget outlays to a minimum. Moreover, the recommendations meshed with one of Carter's core political principles: efficiency in government. The PRM, however, did not simply recommend doing nothing. Based on the accumulated information, Eizenstat identified five major areas where special problems existed or improvements were needed. The list included: (1) high unemployment rates among disabled and minority veterans, (2) GI Bill services and benefits, (3) the bad discharge review and upgrade process, (4) the problem of incarcerated veterans, and (5) promoting public recognition of and appreciation for Vietnam veterans. These areas of concern gave new definition and structure to Carter's Vietnam veterans' agenda. Accordingly, the domestic policy staff included policy options that required the president's approval. Finally, to better coordinate and better implement the administration's Vietnam veterans' agenda, Eizenstat favored "the establishment of an interagency Veterans Federal Coordinating Committee."[42] While Carter weighed his options, Eizenstat and his staff began to consider another challenge: how to formally release the study's findings.

A major consideration in the "public presentation" of the Presidential Review Memorandum was securing the support of Representative David Bonior and the Vietnam Veterans in Congress (VVC) caucus. This bipartisan group of thirteen representatives and senators had formed in March 1978 because, as Bonior explained, "There's just not enough sensitivity to the needs of Vietnam era veterans. . . . Economically and psychologically they're still victims of the war. It's our job, our responsibility, to help them." Not all of the caucus members had served in Southeast Asia or in combat. Bonior, who conceived the idea of the caucus and led the group, spent his four years of active duty in the continental United States as an enlisted man in the Air Force.[43] The small caucus included Representative Les Aspin (D-WI), Representative Albert Gore Jr. (D-TN), Senator Thomas Harkin (D-IA), Representative Leon Panetta (D-CA), and Representative John Murtha, the Marine combat officer from Pennsylvania who had previously given an impassioned defense of Carter's bad discharge upgrade policy. The lone

Republican of the founding members was Senator John Heinz of Pennsylvania. Obviously, they were all relatively new to Congress and lacked seniority on legislative committees, but as was the case with Murtha, they brought a unique credibility to the debates on Vietnam veterans' policy. The group had its own ideas and outlined an agenda that was distinct from the president's. The VVC prioritized three issues: the education allowance of the GI Bill, expanding psychological counseling and drug treatment programs, and helping unemployed and underemployed Vietnam veterans achieve a greater quality of life.[44]

On August 1, just a day after he received the FRM background papers, Carter met with the VVC.[45] He gained a tacit agreement from the caucus to work with the administration on Vietnam veteran issues. The caucus, which had not yet exerted any real political influence, received accolades from the *Washington Post* for conferring with the president about the continued neglect of Vietnam veterans.[46] Following the positive encounter, the president signaled his desire for an "expedited" public presentation of the Vietnam Veterans PRM. Bill Spring, Ellen Goldstein, and Kitty Higgins of the domestic policy staff developed a plan to accomplish that request. The trio of staffers were cognizant that various Vietnam veteran activist groups had been "anxiously" awaiting for several months the release of the PRM. With so much pent-up anticipation, they recommended that the president hold a news conference and host a reception for veterans' groups, Vietnam War Medal of Honor recipients, and key congressional representatives and their staffs. Such a visible demonstration by the president, the staffers argued, would convey a spirit of "gratitude" toward Vietnam veterans and help allay "criticism of Administration policies." They also encouraged Carter to take part in a forthcoming entombment ceremony for an unknown Vietnam soldier at Arlington National Cemetery.[47]

For the president to participate in such high-profile events required the approval of Gerald Rafshoon. An Atlanta advertising executive and a long-time Carter advisor, Rafshoon came to the White House in the summer of 1978 under the official title of assistant for communications. He received his appointment at a time when the president's "political fortunes" and "popular support" were in decline. Indeed, in late April an NBC–Associated Press poll saw Carter with a 25 percent positive rating, a dismal number that remained unchanged through August, when an ABC-Harris poll resurveyed the American people and reported the same results. Rafshoon, according to two Carter scholars, bore the responsibility of "changing the public's perception of the president."[48] After reviewing the proposal by the domestic policy staff, Rafshoon bluntly told the president, "I have serious concerns about doing this." He pointed out that the PRM promised "no new money or programs," and therefore outspoken activists such as Robert Muller and Stuart Feldman of the Council of Vietnam Veterans as well as others who embraced their "movement" could not "be counted on to respond favorably to the PRM." Rafshoon warned, "If they left a meeting expressing disappointment the effect would be worse than no announcement at all."[49] His worries were well-founded.

Muller was one of the most recognizable figures in the Vietnam veteran activist community. A paraplegic as a result of combat injuries sustained in Vietnam, the former Marine first appeared on the activist stage in 1970 as part of a *Life* magazine exposé. The story focused on his Bronx VA Hospital ward, which was depicted as a medical slum that drove his best friend to commit suicide. Muller later joined Vietnam Veterans Against the War, attended Hofstra University's law school, and settled into a position as the legislative director of the Eastern Paralyzed Veterans Association. In 1976 he and lawyer Stuart Feldman formed the Council of Vietnam Veterans (CVV).[50] The fledgling operation received an endorsement from the *Washington Post* in the summer of 1978 when the newspaper published several articles by Muller and Feldman as well as a companion editorial entitled, "Giving Vietnam Veterans a Break."[51] The common theme in the pieces was that the Vietnam veteran was a neglected victim. Feldman summarized the sentiment of everyone when he wrote, "Although presidential recognition of Vietnam veterans is crucial any response requires a substantive effort to reshape and improve a number of government programs related directly to the problems of Vietnam veterans . . . [which] may require the expenditures of significant amounts of money as well as symbolic gestures by the president."[52] Among the journalists explicitly supporting this sentiment and the CVV was Colman McCarthy, an editorial writer with the *Washington Post* and an avowed pacifist who had been an outspoken critic of the Vietnam War. McCarthy had picked up the mantle of the victimized Vietnam veteran at the beginning of the Carter presidency, because, as he explained, "Vietnam isn't over. . . . The veterans are back now, and for me it's as much a principle of pacifism to work to eliminate the brutal aftermath of a war as against the insane reasons to start one."[53] Without question, this vocal alliance intended to place the

Presidential Review Memorandum on the Status of Vietnam Veterans under intense scrutiny.

In addition to these concerns, Rafshoon reminded Carter that the late summer and early fall was a crucial time for his presidency. On the docket were the Camp David Summit with Egypt and Israel, "a possible inflation announcement, and a full plate of legislative action." These matters took precedent and could not be jeopardized by potential negative fallout from the release of the PRM. Rafshoon, recognizing "the need to do something public" for Vietnam veterans, strongly preferred limiting Carter's participation to a Veterans Day ceremony for a Vietnam soldier at the Tomb of the Unknown Soldier. "It would be more interesting, receive better coverage, and be less controversial," he advised. "I don't see any need for doing two events on this issue." With respect to a public announcement to accompany the release of the PRM, Rafshoon felt that either Vice President Mondale or Cleland could handle that responsibility at a press conference, or they could do it in tandem.[54] Before Carter made up his mind on whether to participate in the rollout of the PRM, he sought out Cleland's opinion through intermediaries.[55] Carter learned that his VA administrator thought it was "very important that the President of the United States personally thank the Veterans of the Vietnam War for their sacrifice and service" as part of the PRM announcement.[56] Cleland's words were not persuasive. Carter in a handwritten note on a White House memorandum informed Eizenstat of his decision, "Let V.P. do it if he wishes."[57] The president's decision testified to his desire to manage expectations as well as to disagreements within the administration over how best to handle the Vietnam veterans' agenda.

Deploying the Rhetoric of Gratitude

On October 10, Vice President Mondale and VA administrator Cleland held a press conference at the White House to reveal the key recommendations of the Vietnam Veterans PRM. "Despite the shattering nature of the war, the great majority of veterans have in fact made a successful transition to civil life," the vice president reported. He cited evidence that Vietnam veteran employment and income trends compared favorably to their civilian counterparts, and he hailed the widespread usage of GI Bill benefits. Mondale did mention the unemployment woes of Black and disabled Vietnam veterans and those former service members who continued to face an assortment of "readjustment problems." Following these prefatory remarks, Mondale and Cleland announced that Carter had authorized a $250 million package to cover the most urgent needs of the approximately one out of five Vietnam veterans who warranted some type of special assistance. Just over half of the funding was earmarked for Department of Labor on-the-job training programs. Other measures included extending from ten years after discharge to twelve years the time frame for Vietnam veterans to utilize the educational benefits of the GI Bill. The administration also pledged to expand public-service employment opportunities for Vietnam veterans through CETA and to revisit the bad-discharge review process. Money was set aside for drug, alcohol, and psychological treatment programs and for an outreach program to advise incarcerated Vietnam veterans of "their rights and of benefits for which they may be eligible." Finally, Mondale and Cleland reported the creation of the White House Veterans Federal Coordinating Committee.[58] These priorities now constituted the core of Carter's Vietnam veterans' agenda.

On the day that Mondale and Cleland outlined the administration's next steps forward, the president submitted a formal written message to Congress. The statement signified the administration's dedication to a new narrative that emphasized the need to recognize "the courage and patriotism of those who served in Vietnam." He stressed that it was vitally important for the nation to cease confusing "the war with the warrior." Healing, Carter maintained, required moving beyond the divisiveness of the war in order to convey the "full measure of honor and respect" that was deserved and "earned" by those who answered the call to serve. As part of the adoption of the Presidential Review Memorandum, Carter intensified his use of the rhetoric of gratitude and his public recognition of Vietnam veterans.[59]

Muller and other activists in the media, true to Rafshoon's prediction, disparaged the PRM, characterizing Carter's efforts as "too little and too late." Finding nothing "new" or "innovative" or "bold" in the proposed policies,[60] the disabled Marine charged that the problems faced by Vietnam veterans were "far greater" than portrayed by the White House.[61] Muller said that the administration had "glossed over the huge numbers of low income earners, those who never completed their courses, the imprisoned, and the haunted."[62] He felt betrayed. "During Vietnam, it was suggested that we leave Southeast Asia and declare ourselves victors," he reflected. "That appears to be the administration's policy regarding the Vietnam veteran: Let's look on the bright side of things and say that the veteran is in fine shape."[63] Muller rejected the president's prescription and called for an across-the-board expansion of programs. Among his demands were tax credits and vouchers "to spur employment," an increase in the education benefits under the GI Bill to cover the high cost of college tuition, and funding for private psychiatric counseling and other treatment programs not currently provided by the Veterans Administration. The total estimated cost for Muller's wish list was $1 billion, roughly four times what the Carter administration had approved.

Rafshoon's prediction had come true. Critics lined up to lambast the president. National Council of Churches director William Thompson, whose organization operated an Incarcerated Veterans Program, commented that Carter's plan amounted to about $4 per prisoner [64] David F. Addleston, director of a military discharge project for the American Civil Liberties Union, saw the president's solution to addressing the punitive backlog of bad discharge cases as more of the same.[55] There was also harsh commentary from old antagonists McCarthy and McGrory. McCarthy questioned the timing of the release, four days before the scheduled adjournment of Congress, labeling the decision a symbolic message from the administration that "as Vietnam fades from memory, the warriors who still suffer its effects also can be allowed to fade from view." Borrowing from Muller's messaging, McCarthy challenged the administration to choose between being "content" with the fictive spin that Vietnam veterans had readjusted successfully or making "a solemn commitment to deal more vigorously with the dark side—the less visible grievances that have yet to be resolved."[66] McGrory made a similar case, arguing that the recommendations set forth in the PRM indicated that the administration was declaring "that for Vietnam veterans the war is finally over" because the majority had readjusted successfully back into society. As for "the near-voiceless Vietnam veterans" who continued to suffer, Carter and Congress preferred to keep them "at arm's length," she wrote, accusing the president of ducking an opportunity to lead a national discussion on "the whole miserable business of the war and its consequences."[67] Once again, the victimized veteran served as the object lesson and lingering legacy of the liberal critique of the Vietnam War.

Nearing the midpoint of his presidency, Carter had no intention of leading a national reckoning over the Vietnam War. Instead, he decided to employ the rhetoric of gratitude to rehabilitate the image of the Vietnam veteran and to follow the policy prescriptions outlined in the PRM in order to validate his Vietnam veterans' agenda. This approach was clearly on display during Veterans Day services at Arlington National Cemetery. On November 11, 1978, Carter appeared with Cleland at the amphitheater of the Tomb of the Unknown Soldier to speak and to unveil a plaque honoring all Vietnam veterans. In his remarks, the president noted the sixtieth anniversary of the armistice ending World War I and reflected on the preceding generations of American soldiers, who had fought for and in some cases died for "the great goal of a permanently peaceful world." Most of the president's speech focused on the place of the Vietnam veteran in the nation's recent past. He called Vietnam veterans "unknown soldiers" because individually and as a group their service "has not been adequately realized." They have too often been "ignored" because "their presence among us" has functioned as "an awkward reminder to the anguish that accompanied that war at home." In some ways Vietnam veterans were like veterans of other wars, Carter reasoned, because they knew "the same pain . . . the same loss when they returned home without a leg or an arm or were unable to see the land or the familiar faces they had known." What made Vietnam veterans different was in the way the nation perceived them. "They have been criticized and rebutted because they answered the call of duty," Carter contended, and "were further wounded by the attitude of those who stayed behind." Collectively, the national "response to their heroism hurt more than their wounds." The president called on the country to acknowledge that Vietnam veterans had "paid a bitter price not asked of the veterans of any other war." For all of these reasons, he believed they were owed "a special debt."[68]

In what was a highly emotional moment, the president paused his Veterans Day address and turned to Cleland, who was at his side. Carter "threw his arms around Cleland in a warm embrace" and gently lifted his fellow Georgian from his wheelchair. As tears filled Cleland's eyes, the president told the crowd: "He personifies the dedication and sacrifice of those who served in Vietnam."[69]

Carter's Veterans Day address had separated the war from the warrior. In measured tones, he alluded to the tragedy of Vietnam, but he offered no praise for those who opposed the war or for those who he had pardoned. These rhetorical strategies are what scholar Roger Stahl defines as "deflection and dissociation." Deflection "directs civic attention away from the question of whether the particular war policy is just" in order to focus attention onto the "struggle to save the soldier." Dissociation, Stahl explains, relies on a support-the-troops rhetoric that constructs "a war that needs no justification." Carter's deployment of the rhetoric of gratitude used deflection and dissociation to avoid the question of why the United States had fought in Vietnam and allowed him to separate the soldier from the protestor and to imply that those who opposed the war were "hostile" to those who served.[70] In addition to smearing the antiwar movement, Carter appeared to apologize for the anguish caused by those who opposed the war. Moving forward, commemorating the patriotism, valor, and sacrifice of those who served became the cornerstone of Carter's Vietnam veterans' agenda.[71] The president's critics, however, demanded more than what they considered to be simple expressions of gratitude.

The Battle Rages

In late 1978 Carter signed the Veterans and Survivors Pension Improvement Act. The legislation provided for as much as an 82 percent increase in the pensions of indigent veterans with non-service-connected disabilities. Current guidelines considered any veteran aged 65 or older to be 100 percent disabled. The budget impact of the increased pensions was considerable, adding an estimated $30 billion in the first five years. Although the original measure was altered at various points, a substantial increase in veterans' pensions was never in jeopardy; the House agreed to the final conference report by a 387 to 1 vote.[72] Despite its popularity in Congress, the Veterans and Survivors Pension Improvement Act was maligned by such news outlets as *Fortune* magazine, the *Wall Street Journal*, the *Washington Post*, and the *Boston Globe*. Fiscal conservatives such as George Will ridiculed the president for signing the legislation, especially after the administration just a few days before had announced its determination to reduce federal spending as part of the fight against rising inflation.[73] The *Washington Post* also noted this policy contradiction but admonished the president for not being more aware of a "much more important" need, compensating those who had "been injured in active military service." Carter, in the paper's estimation, had privileged a group of veterans whose only disability was "simply age."[74]

The loudest condemnation came from the spokesmen of such organizations as Paralyzed Veterans of American (PVA) and the CVV. Larry Roffee, executive director of PVA, charged that the legislation left "the seriously disabled veteran worse off than before" because there were no provisions to assist disabled veterans who were looking for employment. "A job is incredibly important to a disabled veteran who is trying to regain his sense of independence and value," Roffee maintained.[75] Robert Muller was upset with what he termed the "empty promises" of the Carter administration and the general "lack of commitment" by Congress to Vietnam veterans. On the one hand, it approved a multi-billion-dollar pension deal for veterans without service-related disabilities. On the other hand, Congress was hesitant, in a separate measure, to consider a $12 million appropriation for psychological counseling for Vietnam veterans. This attitude was just the latest example of the continuing neglect of Vietnam veterans, Muller protested. "How can the administration just look on the bright side of things. . . . We all put our trust in this country."[76] Of all of the criticisms leveled against the president for signing the veterans' pension bill, the domestic policy staff was primarily concerned with the "distortions" painted by the Council of Vietnam Veterans. As staff advisors explained to the Office of the Assistant for Public Outreach, "The resulting media attention to Bob Muller's and Stuart Feldman's claims have turned into an attack against the administration's anti-inflation program as well as our commitment to service-connected disabled veterans. The issue is not going away; Muller and Feldman are beating the drums for an inflationary disability bill next year that is not necessary nor desirable."[77]

By the end of Carter's second year in office, a battle raged over his Vietnam veterans' policies, a testament to the ever-growing salience of this national agenda item. Both the *New York Times* and the *Washington Post* ran year-end pieces connecting broader questions about presidential leadership to Carter's new image maker Gerald Rafshoon. The papers recounted the tug-of-war between Eizenstat and Rafshoon over the president's participation in the release of the Vietnam veterans Presidential Review Memorandum. On-the-record remarks indicated that Eizenstat felt strongly that the president needed "to show his sensitivity to an important group of veterans" whereas Rafshoon saw personal involvement as pointless given the likelihood that the CVV would "immediately denounce the program." In the end, *Times* reporter Terrence Smith summarized, "Mr. Carter agreed with his media adviser."[78] The *Washington Post* ran a similar account by Martin Schram, Washington bureau chief for *Newsday*, that called the conflict over how to announce the PRM "an intra-White House battle."[79] These revelations demonstrated how much politics had become infused in Carter's Vietnam veterans' agenda. The domestic policy staff had originally hoped that the memorandum would generate positive press for the president and help him receive credit for delivering on his campaign promises. What it had not counted on was a widening network of critics of the president's Vietnam veterans' policies. Muller and Feldman were gaining supporters—and not just in the media. The CVV had added several prominent individuals to its advisory board, including National Urban League president Vernon E. Jordan Jr., former chief of naval operations Admiral Elmo Zumwalt, and perhaps most importantly, Rep. Bonior, the head of Vietnam Veterans in Congress. Bonior had clearly broken with the president on Vietnam veterans' issues, and the VVC was planning a major legislative push when Congress convened in January 1979.[80] As Bonior explained, "Anyone claiming that the Vietnam vet has been adequately cared for by this Administration simply ignores the facts. . . . In many respects, the veterans are the last victims of the war. They're buried in the silence of the war."[81]

5

Losing Control of the Agenda

Carter entered the third year of his presidency with only four in ten Americans rating him better than his Republican predecessor, Gerald Ford.[1] At a crossroads, the Georgian needed to demonstrate clearly his ability to lead the nation. "New departures have to be taken, often on uncharted seas," counseled journalist Joseph Kraft. "The real Jimmy Carter will have to stand up."[2] For some time, Carter's advisors had been calling for him to adopt a theme for his presidency similar to John Kennedy's New Frontier or Lyndon Johnson's Great Society. He finally relented and in his State of the Union address issued a call for "a new foundation" upon which to build "a peaceful and prosperous world." The domestic priorities of Carter's New Foundation included regulatory reform, battling inflation, and keeping the budget deficit in check. His foreign policy priorities concerned bringing to fruition an Egyptian-Israeli peace agreement, continuing détente with China, and negotiating the SALT II arms treaty with the Soviet Union.[3] Despite the promise of a New Foundation, what the State of the Union address actually signified to Congress, according to historian Charles O. Jones, was that the essential form of the Carter domestic program remained the same.[4] The commitment to a continuum became apparent just a few days after the address when a reporter posed a question about the adoption of the New Foundation theme and the president responded, "We are not trying to establish this as a permanent slogan."[5]

Fiscal policy continued to concern Carter. As such, he proposed a "lean and austere" budget. He refused, however, to make "major reductions" in areas of national importance, which he identified as maintaining "a strong defense," a comprehensive energy plan, and assisting "people in need." For Carter, those Americans most in need of federal assistance were low-income and "medically-underserved" women, minorities, and youth.[6] There was no mention of veterans, in either the delivered or the written version of the State of the Union address, the "budget message," or in the president's first nationally broadcast press conference of the year.[7] The president was satisfied with his policy prescriptions for Vietnam veterans. HIRE, despite some disappointment, provided a significant number of new jobs for Vietnam veterans. Moreover, the administration had concluded that most Vietnam veterans were doing quite well considering their low unemployment numbers, positive income trends, and by virtue of their historical rate of usage of the GI Bill. Going forward, the initiatives encapsulated in the Presidential Review Memorandum were sufficient for assisting those individuals who had failed to readjust successfully. In order to defend its record, the White House relied increasingly on the rhetoric of gratitude. However, a broadening public debate over the national obligation to Vietnam veterans unfolded during the third year of the Carter presidency. At times, it seemed as if the direction of Vietnam veterans' policies was beyond the administration's control, especially when the president's policies were at odds with Vietnam Veterans in Congress as well as with the Council of Vietnam Veterans. Working together, they were prepared to push an agenda of their own.

Vietnam Veterans Week

"America is taking a fresh and sympathetic look at the forgotten victims of the Vietnam War," *U.S. News & World Report* editorialized in January 1979. "Passions have cooled to the point that the warriors no longer are blamed for the war . . . [and] attempts at understanding now replace the indifference or hostility that awaited many veterans." The newsweekly characterized the nature of the "public acceptance" of Vietnam veterans as "tentative, yet growing." Nevertheless, in concluding a candid reflection on the readjustment journey of former service members, *U.S. News & World Report* looked optimistically to a forthcoming observance called Vietnam Veterans Week.[8]

The idea for a national outpouring of gratitude for those who had served in Vietnam had a multi-sourced history. Stuart Feldman, prior to joining Muller and the CVV, had written to Vice President-elect Mondale during the Carter administration's transitional phase. He urged Carter to give Vietnam veterans a formal "thank you for a job well done" in conjunction with the planned pardoning of the draft evaders.⁹ Over time, the general idea of a thank you gained wider support. By the summer of 1978 the White House weighed the possibility of some type of special "recognition" that might counter negative perceptions of Vietnam veterans, but stopped short of developing specific plans.¹⁰ The catalyst that made Vietnam Veterans Week a reality came not from the White House but from Congress. On October 4, 1978, Rep. Bonior introduced a resolution requesting that a seven-day period be designated as Vietnam Veterans Week. The measure quickly passed the House and the Senate, and President Carter signed a joint resolution just three weeks after Bonior first introduced the proposal. The event was scheduled for May 28 to June 3, 1979. The joint resolution empowered the president to issue a proclamation expressing gratitude to Vietnam veterans, to "initiate and coordinate ceremonies and activities," and to call on all Americans to participate in the observances.¹¹

Sensitive to the political implications for the administration, the domestic policy staff intended to "zero in on the people who served . . . rather than the conflict itself." It designed a programming strategy based on three themes: (1) showing appreciation to Vietnam veterans for their military service and highlighting their "civilian achievements" in their local communities and to society at-large, (2) explaining the readjustment status of Vietnam veterans, and (3) using the weeklong focus to tout the administration's record of accomplishment and to advertise the many programs available to Vietnam veterans. The domestic policy staff envisioned a significant role for the White House, including hosting a reception, designating a representative to place a Memorial Day wreath at the Vietnam veterans plaque at Arlington National Cemetery, and inviting state and local governments to join the administration in sponsoring a recognition program that awarded certificates "for achievement and contributions to the community."¹²

There was no shortage of ideas for Vietnam Veterans Week, and the White House received advice from various groups. For example, chairman William E. Lawson of the American Association of Minority Veterans Programs Administrators (AAMVPA) expressed concern that the traditional outreach techniques utilized by various federal agencies were not effective. "Setting up tables in shopping malls or appearing on radio talk shows," he insisted, did not appeal to veterans with "no job, no skill, [or a] bad discharge," to the incarcerated, or to someone with "drug or alcohol addiction, [or] psychological instability." Through his work with AAMVPA, Lawson was well aware that many Vietnam veterans who suffered from these conditions or situations were reluctant to seek help directly from the federal government, an attitude that only compounded and prolonged their problems. What was needed, he felt, was a greater emphasis on Vietnam veterans reaching out to and counseling one another. To facilitate his own idea, Lawson provided a list of individuals to contact—including Vietnam veterans who were professional athletes, such as Rocky Bleier (Pittsburg Steelers), Roger Staubach (Dallas Cowboys), Charlie Johnson (Philadelphia Eagles,) and Greg Maddox (Philadelphia Phillies).[13]

The American Legion, the nation's largest veterans' organization, with some 2.7 million members, threw its support behind Vietnam Veterans Week. It wanted to see Vietnam veterans properly thanked and praised for their service and sacrifices. The American Legion had a very specific proposal on how to make the observance "a positive experience" for the war's veterans. In a letter to the president, national commander John M. Carey identified unemployment as "the most pressing need" of Vietnam veterans and advocated that the White House coordinate a national jobs telethon. Carey volunteered the members of the American Legion to help staff the phone lines and turn the event "into a community affair."[14] Notwithstanding the administration's claims that Vietnam veterans had outgained their civilian counterparts in terms of employment success and income levels, making a jobs telethon the centerpiece of the White House's efforts opened up a Pandora's box of problems for the domestic policy staff. Communications between staffers revealed that the American Legion had "touted" the telethon proposal "all over" and that representatives of the organization were "essentially daring" the administration to back down. The telethon did not appeal to the administration for a variety of reasons. It favored something "smaller scaled" and worried about the precedent of conducting a telethon for one group, knowing that at some point in the future it would have to say no to a request by another constituency.[15] As the start of the observance approached, the domestic policy staff still had many details to work out, but the most serious problem to arise happened when the president indicated that he would not participate personally in Vietnam Veterans Week.

The previous fall Carter declined to participate in the public release of the Presidential Review Memorandum. His image consultant had warned—presciently, it turned out—of political fallout from disaffected activists and their supporters in the media. Perceptions of Carter's handling of Vietnam veterans' issues had worsened since then, and the administration faced new ardor emanating from the very public and contentious reassignment of Department of Labor employee David A. Christian. In January 1979 the department demoted Christian from his high-level DC-based position and offered him a lesser position in the department's Philadelphia field office. Adding to the Christian drama was the fact that he was a highly decorated Vietnam War veteran who had received two Silver Stars and seven Purple Hearts while serving multiple tours. A front-page story in the *New York Times* speculated that Christian had been "purged" because administration officials were upset that in public speeches he had urged Vietnam veterans to organize politically and to demand better programs and expanded opportunities. Not willing to go down without a fight, Christian appealed his case through the media, including an appearance on NBC's *Today Show*.[16] Against this tumultuous backdrop, the president and Gerald Rafshoon faced a conundrum. They expected negative press coverage of the president's handling of Vietnam veterans' policies to continue unabated, but they were aware that Carter's absence from Vietnam Veterans Week would merely add more fuel to the fire. The domestic policy staff shared these concerns, worrying that no matter how "impressive" an array of events it planned, without the president's "visible support and participation" the administration risked being "sharply criticized" by "the media, local public officials, and most traditional and non-traditional veterans organizations."[17] At a momentary impasse, both Max Cleland and Stuart Eizenstat intervened.

"Speaking frankly," the VA administrator told Carter that some nine million former service members were anxiously looking to him for "leadership" and that his "lack of participation would be considered an affront," adding that the president's present intransigence placed his prior accomplishments in jeopardy. To curry receptiveness to his entreaty, Cleland flattered his fellow Georgian by praising him for having already "gone to great lengths" to support Vietnam veterans through his Presidential Review Memorandum and reminded the president of his "memorable" Veterans Day address at Arlington National Cemetery the previous November. Cleland asked Carter for only a minimal commitment, suggesting a White House reception comprised of a carefully "selected group" of attendees and a modest obligation of a brief statement during "a Presidential drop-by."[18] The head of the domestic policy staff made the case that the president's involvement was necessary on several fronts. The overarching purpose of the weeklong tribute, Eizenstat reasoned, was to recast the negative image of Vietnam veterans and confer a "long overdue" national expression of gratitude. He reminded Carter that he had "highlighted" these very issues during his presidential campaign and at various times during his presidency, making his leadership in this endeavor critically important. Furthermore, there were serious political ramifications to consider. If the president refused to be a participant, then his absence, Eizenstat contended, would "lend credence to charges that the Administration does not really care about Vietnam Veterans." Furthermore, Carter risked alienating key veteran constituencies whose "support on major Administration initiatives" was needed.[19] In the end, Carter acquiesced to the forceful arguments of his senior advisors, agreeing to be part of an intimate White House event. The domestic policy staff had averted one politically sensitive problem, but as Vietnam Veterans Week drew near, another problem developed that proved much harder to manage.

Vietnam Veterans of America

In late 1978, not long after the release of the Presidential Review Memorandum, Robert Muller met with *Washington Post* editor Philip L. Geyelin to discuss ways of improving the political influence of the Council of Vietnam Veterans. Frustrated that official Washington had dismissed himself and Feldman "as two guys with a mimeograph machine," Muller was open to transformative solutions. Geyelin recommended converting the CVV from a small lobbying team into a national membership organization whereby they could draw from the large number of disaffected Vietnam veterans.[20] The counsel was taken to heart. In spring 1979 Muller announced the formation of a new organization, Vietnam Veterans of America (VVA). Sympathetic journalists rushed to affirm the retooling and rebranding, hailing VVA as "the first nationwide group specifically designed for Vietnam veterans."[21]

Ward Sinclair, writing in the *Washington Post*, explained that many Vietnam veterans felt "abandoned" by a president who two years earlier "held out hope and promise of reconciliation and special help for a special kind of veteran." To illustrate the disillusionment, the journalist reached out to several individuals who were disgruntled with Carter. Deflecting criticism that his new organization was only looking for government handouts, Muller spoke about the need to get the entire country to change its attitude toward Vietnam veterans and to see them as "a resource to society, not a burden." He expressed cautious optimism that the nation was ready "to come to terms" with what the Vietnam War "meant" to those who had served. For that to occur, Muller stated, "I don't know if the remedy really is in Congress. That's why I am upset with Jimmy Carter.... He could have done something different, but his first official act as president was to honor those who did not serve by announcing his draft pardons." Making a similar accusation of failed leadership was Joseph C. Zengerle, a Washington attorney, Vietnam veteran, and a member of the newly constituted governing council of VVA. "Last fall, Carter came up with these legislative proposals, and Vice President Mondale was sent out to announce them. Why not the president?," Zengerle asked. Another complaint leveled by Zengerle was that of the top seven hundred administrative appointments made by the president, only five had gone to Vietnam veterans. The lack of representation in the face of an out-ranking "of people from other movements—civil rights, environment, antiwar, antipoverty, consumer, [and] feminist . . . who were not in the armed services and who shared an anti-war spirit" made it difficult for the administration to understand "the thoughts and problems of Vietnam veterans," Zengerle maintained.[22] Interestingly, neither Muller nor Zengerle acknowledged any ideological or cultural kinship with the draft evaders.

Aside from calling attention to the creation of Vietnam Veterans of America, Sinclair portrayed the president as phony in his treatment of Vietnam veterans. To illustrate his point, he offered an "insider's view" from two former administration officials, Roland Mora and David Christian. Mora had been the second-highest-ranking Vietnam veteran in the administration, receiving an appointment to the specially created position of assistant secretary of labor in charge of veterans' employment. Lasting only a year on the job before resigning, Mora had remained quiet, but his silence had been predicated on the continued employment of four Vietnam veterans he had placed on his staff. They were all gone now. Christian had been the last to leave. With no one left to protect, Mora broke his silence, lashing out angrily. "Dave's strong advocacy" and call to action brought unwanted attention onto the administration and resulted in his termination, Mora told Sinclair. "The Christian case is only symbolic of what is happening generally to Vietnam-era veterans." To round out his attack on the Carter White House, Sinclair turned to Rep. Bonior, a leading voice in Congress on Vietnam veteran issues. "One of the problems is that Vietnam veterans have a low priority with the administration," the Michigander remarked. While "the president has some sensitivity to the problem . . . they are a long ways from resolving this." He dismissed the administration's touting of the Presidential Review Memorandum, deriding it as "little more than administrative reform." Bonier raised the stakes by proposing a "package of legislation" known as the Vietnam Veterans Act, which promised large budgetary outlays to cover such issues as unemployment, education, psychological counseling, and drug- and alcohol-abuse treatment. The impatient caucus knew that its proposal faced significant headwinds in Congress and certainly was not supported by the president, but its decision to sponsor the legislation illustrated just how far apart the parties were on the core issues of the agenda.[23] The administration had faced public-relations battles before, but what made this collection of testimonials problematic was the timing in which they were delivered. Only a month remained until Vietnam Veterans Week. Furthermore, a coordinated alliance between Muller and the VVA and Bonior and the VVC was taking shape.

Members of the domestic policy staff fumed over Sinclair's piece, calling it "an unfair portrayal of the Administration's response to Vietnam veteran issues" and "typical" of press reporting on the subject. Staffers questioned Sinclair's objectivity because he had ignored information that they had provided to him, sarcastically commenting that he had "relied upon Bob Muller, our old friend from the pension assault last fall, and his 'network' of critics." The accusation that the White House had painted an excessively "rosy picture" of the number of Vietnam veterans who were as successful, or more successful, than their nonveteran peers perturbed staffers. "This is a fact," they noted in a memorandum. "It would be a disservice to these former soldiers to deny it." They also decried Sinclair's disregard of the appointment of Vietnam War veteran William Lawson as director of the White House Veterans Federal Coordinating Committee, despite direct communication between the domestic policy staff and the journalist on the very topic. This omission frustrated staffers and exposed the activist nature of the reporting. Early in the Carter presidency, the press complained that no one in the White House was working full-time on veterans' issues. Subsequently, the PRM created a new administrative position, and the president appointed someone attuned to the experiences of those who fought in the Vietnam War. Yet, the White

House did not receive any credit for its efforts. In total, the domestic policy staff identified nearly a dozen "specific problems" with the *Washington Post* piece and accused Sinclair of spreading falsehoods, although it did admit to vulnerabilities on several items.[24]

The White House staff knew they had taken "too long to replace Mora." The position remained vacant for more than nine months, which left the White House open to criticism. As for the number of Vietnam veterans appointed by the administration, no one among the domestic policy staff knew the answer; subsequently, the Office of Personnel Management was asked to conduct a survey. To counteract the onslaught of misrepresentations and looming challenges, the domestic policy staff notified White House press secretary Jody Powell that a strategy was being developed, and concluded with an ominous forecast: "The Vietnam veteran issue is essentially unwinnable for the time being, but we must attempt, in the next few weeks, to better communicate what we have done and are doing."[25]

Seemingly on cue and just one day before the start of Vietnam Veterans Week, Bernard Weinraub published a piece in the *New York Times Magazine* that added to the onslaught of misrepresentations. Weinraub maintained that while the national observance had broad support, there were many individuals who deemed it a largely symbolic move by an administration that "had so far failed in any real way" to meet the needs of Vietnam veterans. He recirculated the story about the intra–White House battle between Rafshoon and Eizenstat over Carter's decision not to be part of the release of the Presidential Review Memorandum and repeated some of the criticisms leveled by Sinclair a month earlier, including the allegation that there was no one at the White House working full-time on veterans' issues. Most of the article, however, was an impassioned description of the current effort by Vietnam veterans "to organize, to assert themselves for the first time, [and] to come to terms with an experience that many of them had sought to erase." To personalize this movement, Weinraub profiled three Vietnam veterans: Muller, Zengerle, and Christian. He covered a good bit of the same ground as Sinclair, but where he differed was in his much more elaborate explanation of what the war's veterans wanted from the country and the president. Here, Muller laid out the case. They demanded a full "accounting" of the Vietnam War and an explanation "for everything that happened," including the lives lost, the sacrifices made, and the money spent. They sought an answer to the most basic of all questions, "Why did Vietnam happen?" Beyond this, as

Zengerle reflected, they desired "some degree of self-acceptance" and an opportunity to be recognized by the American people as something other than "evil or stupid" for having fought in Vietnam. Christian too saw the importance of removing the stigma and accompanying burden of guilt associated with their military service. "We're a very patriotic group," he confessed. "We still believe in symbols, in the flag, in America. I'm against anyone that tries to taint that for us."[26]

We Love You

Given the waves of criticisms against the administration in the weeks leading up to Vietnam Veterans Week, the events planned by the White House and the president's participation were closely watched. Although the jobs telethon favored by the American Legion did not materialize, the honoring of the war's veterans included the issuance of a presidential proclamation, the unveiling of a commemorative postage stamp, and the distribution of the Presidential Certificates for Outstanding Community Achievement. In addition, Cleland delivered a special Memorial Day address at Arlington National Cemetery. Nothing, however, attracted more of the media's attention than remarks delivered by the president at a reception in the East Room of the White House.[27] On May 30 Carter addressed approximately four hundred people, including members of Congress and, of course, Vietnam veterans. During his address he took credit for being someone who "saw very clearly that the Vietnam war was different." What made the war different, in his estimation, was the nation's lack of commitment to the US military effort. The American people and their elected officials had failed to support those sent to fight. This failure, Carter maintained, required of those who served "an extra measure of patriotism and sacrifice," and they suffered under a cloud of indignity when they returned home and there were no victory parades to welcome them back or to thank them. Despite their mistreatment, most Vietnam veterans "have almost miraculously been able to assimilate themselves back into civilian life and to further service of our country," the president declared. He was mindful, however, of the stigma imposed on them by the opponents of the war. The antiwar opposition, he asserted, caused many veterans to be seen "as an unfortunate or embarrassing reminder of the divisiveness of the war itself." These men "were disadvantaged to begin with," the president said, and they now carried additional burdens from an unpopular war.[28]

Throughout his remarks, Carter praised Vietnam veterans for both their military service and their successful readjustment to civilian life. He faulted the nation for its lack of support, and he blamed antiwar sentiment for causing "additional hardship" for those who had served. However, Carter's use of the rhetoric of gratitude on this commemorative occasion also functioned as a way to defend his Vietnam veterans' agenda. He called his appointment of Cleland to head the Veterans Administration "the most significant action" that he had taken to demonstrate his commitment to Vietnam veterans. He spoke too of all the pending legislation recommended by his Presidential Review Memorandum, and he enjoined Congress to act swiftly in support of his agenda. In closing his remarks, Carter read a lengthy passage from Philip Caputo's *Rumor of War* and then offered the following paraphrased benediction: "I would like to say, as president, on behalf of 220 million people in our country, we love you for what you were and what you stood for; and we love you for what you are and for what you stand for."[29]

Journalists recognized the solemnness of the atmosphere at the White House reception and described the president's remarks as "an emotional speech" that drew moments of "sustained applause."[30] The *New York Times* suggested that "people are learning to distinguish between a war they resent and the soldiers who fought it," touting the week of tribute as a long-awaited welcome home.[31] *Time* magazine echoed this sentiment, detecting a "new view of the Viet Nam vet." Nevertheless, as the newsweekly editorialized, "Welcome as they are, warm words alone will not satisfy the vets."[32] Indeed, as Tyrone Bailey, a Vietnam veteran and employee of the National Park Service, put it, "Just one little ceremony and a 20-minute speech doesn't do it."[33]

Others, such as Otto Lukert, vice president of the National Association of Concerned Veterans, seized the moment to renew attacks on the Carter administration.[34] Senator Larry Pressler (D-SD), a member of Vietnam Veterans in Congress, wrote personally to the president and urged him to back legislation sponsored by the caucus.[35] One of the dominant themes to emerge from the media coverage of the week of tribute was that Vietnam veterans were on the precipice of becoming "a political force." As long-time Carter critic Colman McCarthy opined, "What is new this week, and deserves to be noticed, is the veterans' relations with themselves. A spirit that is caring, positive and self-confident has been created. The struggle now is to nurture it."[36]

Heading into Vietnam Veterans Week, Carter's domestic policy staff doubted whether the public relations battle over Vietnam veterans' issues was winnable in the short term. The seven days of tribute did not alter that calculus. As McCarthy noted, the activist landscape was changing. There was a newfound energy among disaffected Vietnam veterans. Similarly, Vietnam Veterans in Congress, which had grown to nineteen members, was becoming more visible and more assertive. Furthermore, the issue of psychological counseling for Vietnam veterans had reached a tipping point. In fact, Jack McCloskey, a disabled Vietnam War veteran, confronted the president on this matter at the White House reception, telling him, "If you want to honor me" then you must "implement programs that realistically deal with a lot of the problems that Vietnam combat veterans still suffer from."[37] Shortly after the conclusion of Vietnam Veterans Week, the president got a chance to help McCloskey and fulfill a campaign promise at the same time.

Congress and the Vietnam Agenda

For some time, Congress had been considering legislation to expand psychological counseling and drug and alcohol treatment programs for Vietnam veterans. Under existing Veterans Administration guidelines, veterans could not receive counseling unless they formally checked into a VA psychiatric ward for evaluation. Few veterans needing psychological help wanted the experience of a VA psychiatric ward or the accompanying label of having a mental illness. As early as 1971, Senator Alan Cranston proposed changes allowing the VA to conduct outpatient evaluations and requested funding for veteran treatment at community-based non-VA programs. The Senate approved a Cranston bill on three separate occasions, but the House failed to follow suit. Neither the Nixon nor Ford administrations had supported the senator's efforts. However, in the weeks leading up to Vietnam Veterans Week, Cranston represented the legislation. This time VVC members Bonior, Pressler, and Heinz joined the fight, and Cleland lent his assistance by testifying before Congress in favor of the programs. Equally important, the president, unlike his predecessors, signaled his approval and indicated his willingness to sign the legislation.[38]

Despite the new momentum afforded by the backing of the VVC, Cleland, and the president, there remained entrenched opposition to Cranston's reforms. Some members of the House objected to the bill because it permitted care "to be conducted outside of the VA." Others simply felt that Vietnam veterans did not have special needs and thus did not merit special programs. Yet, these reasons do not explain the full story. At the heart of the debate was an intra-congressional struggle for power. Specifically, the Senate Appropriations Committee held the legislative authority under current rules to approve or block construction projects for VA hospitals and other medical facilities. In exchange for approving the Cranston bill, the House demanded that authorizing authority on VA construction projects be shared by the House and Senate Veterans' Affairs committees. After a complicated and controversial negotiation process, a joint congressional conference committee produced a compromise measure known as the Veterans Health Care Amendments of 1979. Carter signed the legislation a week after Vietnam Veterans Week ended. The Veterans Health Care Amendments required the VA to provide outpatient counseling and mental health services to veterans and members of their families. It authorized the VA to conduct a pilot program using halfway houses and community-based centers to treat veterans with drug and alcohol problems. The measure also enabled federal departments to hire "rehabilitated veterans" who had completed drug and alcohol abuse programs. The political price extracted by the House for passage of the Veterans Health Care Amendments was a rule change establishing the House and Senate Veterans' Affairs committees as the authorizing committees for VA construction projects costing more than $2 million.[39]

An international humanitarian crisis, one involving Vietnamese war refugees, overshadowed the signing of the Veterans Health Care Amendments. Consequently, few journalists covered the veterans' health-care story. Those who did focused as much on the embarrassing spectacle of pork-barrel politics as they did on the legislation itself. Columnist David Broder expressed a sobering assessment when he wrote, "Next to tipping over a wheelchair, it is hard to imagine a shabbier way for Congress to mark Vietnam Veterans Week."[40] Colman McCarthy used the spectacle as a case study of how not just Congress but also the White House viewed and treated Vietnam veterans. "The legislation is useful," he opined, "but no one should get breathless in praise of it. It took eight years to pass and no one really knows whether it can be made to work, whether veterans will risk exposing themselves to the government and just how ardent a commitment the VA is willing to make." All in all, he saw "nothing new in the government's relations with Vietnam veterans." Moreover, he called the $16 million first-year price tag of the Veterans Health Care Amendments "a flicker of a program." McCarthy spread generously the blame for this latest disappointment, but he pinned the lion's share on the White House, accusing Carter of delivering nothing more to Vietnam veterans than "presidential pieties" on special occasions such as Memorial Day and Veterans Day, and at White House receptions.[41]

No doubt the White House felt the goal post kept moving, as administration officials continued to engage members of the press over its record of achievement on Vietnam veterans' policies with no signs of success. Notwithstanding Cranston's undeniable leadership, Carter made psychological counseling one of the priorities of his original Vietnam veterans' agenda. And now that he had delivered on his promise, critics refused to give him any credit. In truth, Congress was now driving most of what was being attempted on behalf of Vietnam veterans. Vietnam Veterans Week had originated with Rep. Bonior and the Vietnam Veterans in Congress caucus. Moreover, the passage of the Veterans Health Care Amendments came down to the House's ability to wrestle power away from the Senate.

Looking under the surface, it was clear that Carter himself could not afford to invest deeper into his Vietnam veterans' agenda. By the summer of 1979, his poll numbers were abysmal. His entire presidency was in turmoil. An attempt to right the ship in a nationally televised address, subsequently dubbed the "malaise speech," only made matters worse. There were now serious doubts about whether the president could win a second term, and with Senator Ted Kennedy outpolling the president by a 2-to-1 margin, even the Democratic nomination seemed in doubt.[42] In a fight for his presidential life, Carter still faced mounting pressure to advance a more comprehensive Vietnam veterans' agenda.

New Challenges

In late September 1979, Bernard Weinraub and Ward Sinclair questioned the credibility of the White House regarding its commitment to Vietnam veterans, thereby raising the political stakes even higher. They based their challenge on what Weinraub dubbed "the first Government-sponsored study of Vietnam veterans." His reference was to a VA-funded review conducted by the Center for Policy Research (CPR) on how successfully Vietnam veterans had reintegrated into civilian life. During the summer of 1979, Cleland received two working papers from the CPR. These findings covered a tiny sample group of 190 veterans from three New York City communities: Bridgeport, Brooklyn, and Westchester. Weinraub and Sinclair obtained copies of the working papers. Despite knowing that a completed study was not due for another year, the journalists rushed to publicize two premature but unsettling discoveries: First, that 60 percent of Vietnam veterans "returned home with nightmares, physical wounds, diseases, nervous conditions and alcohol and drug abuse."[43] Second, that Vietnam veterans lagged "somewhat behind veterans of the same period who did not serve in Vietnam and far behind non-veterans of similar age" in terms of education and employment success. The revelations contradicted the narrative of success that the Carter administration had been pushing for more than a year and provided ammunition to critics who had maintained that Vietnam veterans' readjustment problems ran "considerably deeper" than the administration acknowledged. Moreover, both journalists raised concerns about the VA's willingness to release the CPR's findings. They reported that Muller of the VVA had been forced to file a freedom-of-information request in order to obtain the working papers and then enlisted Bonior and Heinz's help to provide copies to the press.[44]

Despite the implication of hiding evidence, the attack did not come as a complete surprise to members of the president's team. In fact, Cleland began interpreting the working papers as soon as he received them. Shortly thereafter, he provided copies of the working papers and his impressions of the data to Sen. Cranston, which occurred several weeks before the press broke the story.[45] In prior instances, the administration typically responded to criticism of the president's handling of Vietnam veteran issues in the form of an op-ed, and usually without much success. This time around, the administration pursued a different tack and allowed Cranston to do its bidding. On September 28, just two days after the damaging stories appeared in the *New York Times* and *Washington Post*, the chair of the Veterans' Affairs Committee delivered remarks from the Senate floor. He stated that he had received the documents from Cleland two weeks earlier as part of routine communications. Cranston was concerned that Sinclair had mislead readers by not giving an "adequate account of the very tentative nature of the study." He called the preliminary findings statistically unreliable because of "the very small sample" group and the "very limited geographical" coverage of the studies. He also pointed out that the authors of the working papers cautioned against making "categorical statements about the effects of military service during the Vietnam War until we have analyzed thoroughly the data on our respondents' early life experiences and how these affect present day adjustment." Here Cranston's intent was to warn his colleagues against prematurely jumping to larger conclusions. After questioning the veracity of Sinclair and Weinberg's reporting, Cranston reminded his colleagues of how Congress, the VA, and the White House had worked together on behalf of Vietnam veterans. He cited the recently passed counseling and treatment programs and referenced pending legislation to provide Vietnam veterans with more educational benefits and job training—initiatives, he reiterated, "first proposed" by Carter as part of his Presidential Review Memorandum. In closing, Cranston reaffirmed his "total commitment to Vietnam veterans who had not made a successful transition" back into civilian life.[46]

Cranston's defense of the administration's commitment to Vietnam veterans failed to persuade those who were already convinced otherwise. Commenting on the Center for Policy Research's working papers, McCarthy wrote, "The findings are devastating enough, but they surface at least a decade after they were obvious to anyone—psychiatrists, family members, social workers—who took the time to listen to the veterans."[47] Muller echoed this sentiment when he declared, "The V.A. historically has denied that the Vietnam veteran has had readjustment problems, and, now, a major governmentally sponsored study recognizes those problems."[48] Both Rep. Bonior and Sen. Heinz ignored Cranston's call for patience.[49] They used the incomplete report to sound the alarm and reintroduced the Vietnam Veterans Act. This version included a massive expansion of educational benefits as well as compensation for veterans and their families "who suffered health problems after exposure to Agent Orange." In total, the estimated first-year cost of the Vietnam Veterans Act was $464 million, with an increase to $892 million for the second year, prompting Heinz to refer to the measure as "the most comprehensive veterans assistance legislation since the G.I. Bill." Although all nineteen members of the bipartisan VVC backed the plan, as did such key legislators as Senator Daniel Patrick Moynihan (D-NY) and Representative Margaret Heckler (R-MA), co-chair of the Congresswomen's Caucus, congressional aides admitted privately that "enactment of the package was uncertain."[50]

For some time, a difference of opinion existed between the administration and its activist critics regarding the extent of the veterans' problems, how many were affected, and how much government response was necessary. During this most recent clash, the *New York Times* again sided against Carter, presenting the Center for Policy Research working papers as definitive and hailing the Vietnam Veterans Act as "a modern version of the G.I. Bill." The handwritten comments on a photocopy of the editorial by a member of the domestic policy staff revealed the dismay over losing control over the Vietnam veterans' agenda. The most obvious example involved the *New York Times*'s suggestion that the Vietnam Veterans Act would provide compensation to victims of Agent Orange poisoning, to which a staffer scribbled a question mark.[51] Some of the frustration was merited. However, the reaction to the Agent Orange issue signified a certain degree of denial. The domestic policy staff had recognized six months earlier that Agent Orange was a looming "controversy."[52] In actuality, the controversy had been brewing throughout the Carter presidency and had been a decade in the making.

Agent Orange

The US Air Force sprayed more than nineteen million gallons of herbicides during the Vietnam War as part of a nine-year defoliation campaign to expose enemy troop positions and to diminish food sources for Communist forces. Agent Orange, the most commonly used defoliant, was a compound mixture of two herbicides, 2,4-D and 2,4,5-T. Improperly manufactured 2,4,5-T produced highly toxic dioxins. During the 1960s, herbicides containing 2,4,5-T were widely used throughout the United States by ranchers and farmers. The National Forest Service alone sprayed 4.1 million acres of public lands with such herbicides annually. In 1969 a National Cancer Institute study found that laboratory animals exposed to 2,4,5-T developed different types of cancer and reproduced offspring with birth defects. The following year these concerns led the Departments of Agriculture, Interior, and Health, Education and Welfare (HEW) to ban the use of Agent Orange domestically. The Department of Defense followed suit and suspended the use of Agent Orange in Vietnam. Its decision coincided with anecdotal reports that civilians in defoliation zones had been stricken with serious health problems. These reports were also part of an international debate over violations of the Geneva Protocols on Chemical Weapons. Curtailing the use of Agent Orange, however, did not stem the concerns of a looming health crisis.[53]

In 1977 Vietnam veterans moved to the forefront of the Agent Orange controversy. Maude DeVictor, a benefits counselor at the Chicago regional office of the Veterans Administration, served as a catalyst. She received calls from Vietnam veterans who believed their serious health problems were attributable to Agent Orange exposure. DeVictor investigated their claims, but higher-ups in the VA instructed her to cease her inquiries, at which point she reached out to and shared her case files with Bill Kurtis, a reporter with Chicago's CBS affiliate. On March 23, 1978, the documentary *Agent Orange: Vietnam's Deadly Fog* aired. Kurtis's documentary recounted the use of herbicides in Vietnam and told the stories of a number of Vietnam veterans who believed they had been victimized by their exposure to Agent Orange. Doctors and scientists spoke on camera of anecdotal studies of Vietnamese civilians that linked dioxins to grave medical conditions and birth deformities. Kurtis also explored the health tragedies of ordinary Americans exposed to Agent Orange through industrial accidents or domestic applications. At the time, there was no epidemiological data regarding the health effects of Agent Orange on humans, a fact that Kurtis conceded in his documentary. Nevertheless, he did make the implication of a connection, and he advocated that all Vietnam veterans exposed to Agent Orange be tested for dioxin poisoning and recommended that the VA immediately provide medical treatment and disability compensation to Agent Orange claimants. As historian Edwin Martini has written, *Vietnam's Deadly Fog* "completely changed the political landscape of veterans' allegations about their exposure to Agent Orange."[54]

By October 1978, five hundred veterans had filed exposure disability claims with the VA based on such ailments as "skin lesions, nausea, diarrhea, fatigue, headaches, backaches and lack of sex drive." Without admitting a correlation, the VA approved only eight cases. The military followed a similar pattern of denial. The deputy surgeon general of the Air Force told a House Veterans' Affairs subcommittee that illnesses related to herbicide or dioxin exposure were temporary and that all patients eventually recovered. His testimony reflected the official policy of the Veterans Administration.[55] Cleland had instructed VA personnel to "avoid premature commitment to any diagnosis of defoliant poisoning," and he had ordered that medical records omit causal statements linking a veteran's illness to defoliant exposure "unless unequivocal confirmation has been established."[56] These efforts to deny culpability proved futile.

The work of DeVictor, including her appearance in Kurtis's documentary, caught the attention of Vietnam veteran Paul Reutershan. He had served as a crew chief on a resupply helicopter during the war and had been recently diagnosed with terminal abdominal cancer. The diagnosis came as a shock to Reutershan because he prided himself on living an exceptionally healthy lifestyle. In light of the news stories and the nature of his military service, he concluded that his sickness stemmed from his exposure to Agent Orange. In addition to the cancer, he had chloracne, the only accepted symptom of dioxin exposure. Gravely ill, he appealed to the VA for treatment. Despite confirming the cancer and chloracne, the VA refused his claim. Feeling angry and betrayed and facing mounting medical expenses, Reutershan hired a personal injury lawyer and filed suit against Dow Chemical Corporation and two other manufacturers of Agent Orange. With his time fleeting, but determined to draw greater attention to the Agent Orange issue, Reutershan founded Agent Orange Victims International (AOVI), an advocacy group composed of a handful of veterans, friends, and family members. On December 14, 1978, six months after he filed the lawsuit, Reutershan died. Among those closest to Reutershan was fellow Vietnam veteran Frank McCarthy, who had served with the First Infantry Division, earning a Bronze Star and Purple Heart. Although McCarthy personally made no claim to Agent Orange exposure, Reutershan tapped him to lead the AOVI upon his death. Prepared to fight, McCarthy wasted little time moving forward, obtaining the services of a new lawyer, Victor J. Yannacone Jr. On January 8, 1979, Yannacone amended the original Reutershan complaint and filed a class-action lawsuit on behalf of all Vietnam veterans, naming Dow, Monsanto, and three other manufacturers of Agent Orange as the defendants. The AOVI hoped that a ruling in its favor would compel the federal government to provide additional medical, disability, and death benefits to the veterans and their families.[57]

A class-action lawsuit of this magnitude faced serious legal obstacles, but the Agent Orange saga galvanized Vietnam veterans' groups and their media allies. In the week leading up to Vietnam Veterans Week, the *New York Times* published a three-part series on the herbicidal victims of Agent Orange.[58] The newspaper also published an editorial punctuating the plight of those who believed they were sick from exposure to Agent Orange. This gathering storm pulled the Carter administration into the Agent Orange controversy and became part of Vietnam Veterans Week.[59]

When the guests assembled for the highly anticipated White House reception, Frank McCarthy was among those in attendance. Before the president concluded his remarks, McCarthy stood up and interrupted him, defiantly asking, "What about the Agent Orange victims?" Caught completely off guard, Carter responded, "What about what?" McCarthy unloaded, "Twice as many men are dying here in the States as died in the war. Agent Orange contains dioxins, the most toxic substance known to mankind. Dow Chemical Company lied to this country, lied to the Government when it said it wasn't toxic." At this point, the confrontation evolved into a short exchange between the two men, with McCarthy pleading with the president to initiate epidemiological studies to determine the effects of Agent Orange on Vietnam veterans and to do whatever was necessary to help them and their families. Carter agreed that studies were needed and pledged to work with his VA head toward that end.[60] Before Vietnam Veterans Week concluded, Cleland confirmed that the Air Force would begin conducting the sought-after research.[61] It soon became apparent that the Agent Orange controversy was much different from the previous debates regarding the nation's obligation to Vietnam veterans.

On June 26, 1979, during a congressional hearing, a new chapter unfolded in what journalist Margot Hornblower called "the history of sinister allegations against Agent Orange." The Subcommittee on Investigations and Oversight of the House Commerce Committee heard testimony from Vietnam veterans Michael Ryan and John Woods as well as members of their respective families. Muller also appeared on behalf of the VVA. Without question, the most compelling witness was Kerry Ryan, the eight-year-old daughter of Michael. She was born with eighteen birth defects, including "missing bones, twisted limbs, a hole in her heart, deformed intestines, a partial spine, shrunken fingers, [and] no rectum.' Her father, who also suffered a variety of ailments, attributed both of their conditions to his exposure to Agent Orange. Kerry Ryan's presence raised the haunting specter, Hornblower wrote, that the herbicide may have even victimized the children of Vietnam veterans, making this "sinister drama" worse than already imagined. Members of the subcommittee were moved by the emotional testimony and castigated the administration for moving too slowly in response to the mounting revelations. Representative Andrew Maguire (D-NJ) berated the Veterans Administration for continuing "to ignore the data." Representative Martin A. Russo (D-IL) saw the government's dodging of the problem as an attempt "to wipe out the thought of the whole war." The chair of the subcommittee, Bob Eckhardt (D-TX), judged the administration's inaction "a national disgrace." Interestingly, the subcommittee did not invite anyone from the White House, the VA, or the Department of Defense to testify at the hearing.[62]

"The public embarrassment of the hearings" provoked editorials from the nation's leading newspapers. "How sad that such prods are necessary to remind a Government of its most elementary obligation," the *New York Times* retorted, "but regardless of their findings, the damage to the Government's credibility has been done."[63] The *Washington Post* recognized that the health effects of Agent Orange remained "a fiercely debated issue." Nevertheless, the *Post* opined, "whatever the truth of that matter, simple justice demands that the veterans not be held hostage to its resolution."[64] The administration's perceived lack of urgency prompted bitter reactions. "It would appear at this point that the only thing in high gear now is the Government's publicity program," commented Frank McCarthy. Attention shifted to the previously announced Air Force study. A month after Cleland made the formal announcement, the Air Force had not commenced its work, and it estimated a six-year time frame to complete the study.[65] Taking six years to complete an epidemiological study was too long to wait, a *Washington Post* editorial reasoned, and the military's leadership of any investigative research presented the appearance of a "conflict of interest."[66] Rep. Eckhardt wanted the Department of Housing, Education and Welfare to be the lead government agency investigating Agent Orange, and he called for the National Institutes of Health and the Centers for Disease Control to conduct independent studies because he questioned the impartiality of the Department of Defense.[67]

The Agent Orange controversy created new alliances. In mid-July "Vietnam veterans, joined by scientists, public interest lawyers and church organizations," formed the National Veterans' Task Force on Agent Orange. Their "first order of business" was to assist the American Health Foundation in conducting an epidemiological study of Vietnam veterans. Among the task force signatories was the National Council of Churches, which counted among its members Louise Ransom, the Gold Star mother who had nominated Fritz Efaw for vice president as part of the unconditional amnesty crusade for Vietnam veterans during the 1976 Democratic National Convention.[68] Not waiting for any studies to be completed by the government, the National Veterans Law Center filed a lawsuit against the Veterans Administration asking a US District Court to overturn agency guidelines that denied disability benefits to Agent Orange claimants.⁶⁹ The lawsuits and coalition building revealed a sense of urgency, resolve, and a high level of distrust of government.

Yet, the Department of Defense doubled down on its strategy of denial. In addition to claiming that Agent Orange posed no long-term health risks to humans, the DoD stated that US troops had limited exposure to the herbicide because they remained outside of spray zones for six weeks following a defoliation operation. The Government Accounting Office officially disputed this contention in a report released two months later, a story covered by Bernard Weinraub of the *New York Times*. Using records covering only the northern one-fifth of South Vietnam, the GAO found that thousands of Marines were actually in the spray zones during or just after the defoliation missions, and thousands more had entered the areas sooner than the DoD previously maintained. Members of Congress reacted to this news with disgust. "I do not understand," railed Senator Charles H. Percy (R-IL), "how it was possible for the Defense Department to be in the dark about what G.A.O. has no trouble finding in the department's own records." Percy, who had initially requested the GAO investigation, strongly criticized the government's handling of all aspects of the Agent Orange issue. "Those veterans who now claim debilitating illness as a result of exposure to Agent Orange have been viewed with suspicion, mistrust and what is as bad, apathy and lack of concern," he wrote in a letter to the secretary of defense, "almost as tragic as the physical suffering has been the anguish of uncertainty. Thousands of veterans now live in the shadow of fear, and wonder if they, too, will suddenly be struck by the host of illnesses that other veterans have reported."⁷⁰ In less than a year, the number of service members seeking treatment from the VA for presumed Agent Orange–related illnesses had risen from five hundred to five thousand. Of that number, 750 filed compensation claims, but only two individuals had been awarded compensatory benefits.⁷¹

Recognizing the need to appear more responsive, the White House in mid-December created an interagency working group "to oversee all Federal and non-government research on the suspect herbicides and their toxic contaminant dioxin." A domestic policy staff memorandum explained all of the factors that necessitated this policy decision. First, the "controversial" nature of the subject was causing "great concerns" among Vietnam veterans. Second, the delays in the Air Force study, coupled with its six-year completion schedule, led several members of Congress to propose canceling the study all together in favor of one directed by HEW. Third, the GAO report requested by Sen. Percy had led to allegations of a coverup, which "further complicated" matters by undermining the administration's credibility on the issue. To address all of these concerns, the White House placed the working group under the direction of the Department of Housing, Education and Welfare, a move reflective of the need to create transparency and impartiality.[72]

During the third year of the Carter presidency, the White House lost control of the focal points of the Vietnam veterans' agenda. The well-publicized tragedies of Paul Reutershan and eight-year-old Kerry Ryan as well as the release of *Vietnam's Deadly Fog* transformed the dioxin exposure debate into a highly charged political issue. Congress, activist groups, and the media were now framing and driving the agenda. The administration was merely responding. The VA's refusal to grant benefits to claimants placed the White House on the defensive. Despite the need for exacting attention, the third year of the Carter presidency ended in a manner that temporarily relegated veterans' issues to the political margins. Between November and December 1979 a sequence of events occurred that soon consumed the White House. Two of those events occurred concurrently, during the first week of November. First, a group of Islamic radicals seized the US embassy in Tehran, Iran, taking sixty-six American hostages. Second, Ted Kennedy announced he was seeking the Democratic Party nomination for president. Then, in mid-December Soviet troops invaded Afghanistan, and by Christmas Day they had entered the capital city of Kabul.

6

The Revolt of the Veterans

Carter spent the final year of his presidency managing crises. In his own words, "1980 was pure hell—the Kennedy challenge, Afghanistan, having to put the SALT Treaty on the shelf, the recession, Ronald Reagan, and the hostages . . . always the hostages! It was one crisis after another."[1] The nation heard these concerns when he devoted more than three-fourths of his State of the Union address to foreign policy matters.[2] He set the tone for his last year in office, most notably, by outlining what became known as the Carter Doctrine, a declaration that the United States would use "any means necessary, including military force" to defend its vital interests in the Middle East.[3] Although Carter's State of the Union address identified a five-point plan for strengthening the nation's economy, most observers characterized his domestic agenda as containing "few new initiatives and no surprises." Even the seventy-five page written version of the address resembled a "political defense" of the administration and "perhaps was more noteworthy for what it did not contain than for what it did," according to journalist Kenneth A. Weiss.[4] By his own admission, the president's budget emphasized "restraint" and focused on increased defense spending, energy solutions, youth programs, and "making Government work better."[5]

Congressional priorities, one journalist explained, were "written in pencil and subject to rapid change." The consensus view held that Congress planned to act on the president's energy package and supported increased defense spending. Because of their own pending reelection bids, members of Congress were likely "to find ways of maintaining or increasing federal services and—if possible—approving

[121]

new benefits." In addition, the national campaign made them less inclined to vote on "controversial issues" such as the SALT II Treaty or the president's health-care proposals.[6] With so much uncertainty swirling in a critical election year, neither Congress nor the president anticipated major legislative developments on the Vietnam veterans front.

Carter's position on Vietnam veterans, since the announcement of the Presidential Review Memorandum in October 1978, was that he had fulfilled his campaign promises of 1976. He believed that the majority of that war's veterans had readjusted successfully. However, he did feel, as he expressed in his written State of the Union, that Vietnam veterans had not yet been "accorded the full honor bestowed upon veterans of past wars." With respect to the "special needs" of the remainder of the war's veterans, the president was willing to allow Congress the prerogative in shaping these legislative debates.[7] The Iranian hostage crisis, the Kennedy primary challenge, and the Soviet invasion of Afghanistan had become Carter's agenda. The one crisis that he did not foresee coming in 1980 was the revolt of the veterans.

Battling a Congressional Agenda

In the months following the airing of *Agent Orange: Vietnam's Deadly Fog* and the House Subcommittee on Investigations and Oversight hearings, the number of individuals claiming they were victims of Agent Orange exposure grew steadily. The claimants faced "a legal-scientific quagmire" and a slew of bureaucratic hurdles. At the time little was known about the relationship between environmental contaminants and the origins of cancers and birth defects. The development of these medical conditions could arise from multiple causes over the course of a long period of time. Tort law as well as VA benefit regulations required strict cause-and-effect proof for medical or disability payments, which meant that the Vietnam veteran had to prove his health condition stemmed directly from his military service and had not been precipitated or developed subsequently by other factors. Moreover, compensating "an unknown number of victims" for a wide variety of illnesses and "possibly even the lifetime earning losses of their children born with defects" carried a multi-billion-dollar price tag. Neither the federal government nor private industry was eager "to assume such a burden." A foremost concern for Vietnam veterans was to force the VA to adopt "a much looser standard" of proof, such as a presumptive finding, which would allow the agency to award benefits and provide care. The Vietnam Veterans in Congress caucus had asked for such a ruling the previous year as part of the Vietnam Veterans Act. Senator Alan Cranston, however, blocked the measure, calling it "totally inappropriate." He feared that the adoption of the lesser standard of proof might set "a very harmful precedent." The Carter administration endorsed Cranston's position.[8] Complicating matters was the fact that the VA already recognized "over 40 diseases" under the lesser burden of proof. The coalition of Vietnam veteran activists were determined to use these precedents in their pursuit of a presumptive determination for the casualties of Agent Orange.[9]

Against this backdrop, the House Subcommittee on Medical Facilities and Benefits of the Committee on Veterans' Affairs convened a hearing to address the ongoing Agent Orange controversy. On February 25, 1980, chairman David E. Satterfield III (D-VA) plainly spelled out the parameters of the hearing in his opening statement. "The express and sole purpose" of the hearing, Satterfield explained, was to determine "what has been done and what has been learned" by the government agencies tasked with resolving the Agent Orange issue. Accordingly, the chairman limited testimony to representatives of the Veterans Administration, the Department of Defense, and the Department of Health, Education and Welfare. Aware that Vietnam veteran activists and civilian Agent Orange claimants had inquired about testifying at this hearing, Satterfield held open the probability in the near future for a second hearing to give voice to their concerns. He cautioned that his subcommittee lacked the authority and the jurisdiction to render a verdict as to whether dioxin exposure caused certain health problems or to rule which veterans were eligible for VA benefits and care. For now, the committee's intention was to establish some level of accountability over the Carter administration's efforts. Max Cleland appeared as the primary spokesperson for the administration.[10]

Referencing his own military service, Cleland asserted that he had "a personal stake in the outcome of the questions surrounding Agent Orange." He had been in Vietnam during the "peak spraying years" and was exposed to the defoliant on two occasions. Consequently, he told the subcommittee, he was as committed as anyone to learning "the truth," although he was equally committed to a "thorough valid and objective scientific inquiry." Having explained his personal stake and concerns, Cleland summarized the investigative review process undertaken by his agency. The actions included the formation of an advisory committee and the development and dispersion of "informational and instructional materials" to medical staff. In addition, the VA constructed "a data base on the potential health effects of Agent Orange." Finally, the agency conducted a study of dioxin levels in the fat tissue of veterans known to have been exposed to Agent Orange and compared those samples to individuals "with no known exposure." Cleland informed the subcommittee that the VA lacked scientific proof of a "delayed syndrome of toxicity" regarding Agent Orange, meaning there was no evidence that a person developed serious health issues in the years following exposure to the defoliant. He also revealed that the VA lacked "precise data on U.S. ground troop movements in Vietnam during the time when spraying" occurred. As a result, Cleland confidently concluded, "There is not now any proof that a definitive Agent Orange syndrome exists in our Vietnam veterans."[11]

Cleland's testimony drew the ire of Representative Thomas A. Daschle (D-SD), a former Air Force intelligence officer who had assumed the leadership of Vietnam Veterans in Congress. "I can't help but sit here and be very frustrated with this discussion, and I can understand the frustration of so many of the Vietnam veterans," the South Dakotan charged. "I think we are putting Vietnam veterans in the role of a plaintiff and the VA in the role of a defendant and a judge." Daschle argued that out of ten thousand cases presented to the VA, only two individuals had met the agency's stringent criteria for proof of Agent Orange–induced illness. The congressman accused the VA of requiring a standard of proof from Agent Orange claimants that was much higher than any standard set for other veterans seeking benefits or compensation. He further alleged that the agency designed its various studies in order to prove the "nonculpability" of the federal government. Daschle in effect suggested that the VA was purposefully discriminating against Agent Orange claimants. From this point on, Daschle and Cleland engaged in a testy exchange that included some fiery rhetoric. "I am trying not to take a side here," the VA administrator interjected. "I have a personal interest in the outcome" due to wartime exposure, but "we are not trying to prejudge." Daschle dismissed the claim of impartiality, maintaining that the agency had "more flexibility than a court of law in determining culpability." He wagered "that in a court of law, out of 10,000 cases, that there would be better than two wins," especially given the available information on dioxin toxicity. Cleland countered that the toxicity of dioxin was not the key question but rather "what level of exposure is harmful and what that means later in life." An irritated Daschle replied, "I would argue with you very strongly that it isn't scientific evidence, it is legal culpability, that you are concerned about."[12]

The acrimony was palpable, but "the defensiveness" of Cleland perplexed the ranking minority member of the subcommittee, John Paul Hammerschmidt (R-AR). "There should be no such thing as 'sides' on a question such as this," he remarked. Hammerschmidt saw the entire federal government as having "a sworn and serious duty" to do everything in its power "to determine whether or not a causal nexus existed between the use of Agent Orange and the difficulties our veterans are talking about." And if a link existed, then "we must provide for our countrymen who trusted us and did their duty"; anything less "dishonors and cheapens the notion of combat service to the United States of America," the congressman exhorted.[13] The purpose of the hearing, as defined by Chairman Satterfield, was to ascertain what the government's principal actors had learned and done to address the health concerns surrounding Agent Orange exposure. Based on the reactions of various members of the subcommittee, they felt the administration was failing. In particular, Congressman Daschle rejected Cleland's contention that he and the VA were doing all they could to address the Agent Orange issue, and he even accused the administrator and the agency of turning their collective backs on veterans rather than admit to some level of government culpability in the apparent health crisis. Segments of the media seized onto the Agent Orange saga to dramatize the historical mistreatment of Vietnam veterans.

"One of the bitterest legacies of the Vietnam War has been the generally shoddy treatment accorded its veterans by the government they served and by the general public to whom the veterans—some jobless, drug-addicted, maimed—are a painful reminder of a time they would rather forget," the *Washington Post* editorialized. The newest tragedy impacting the war's veterans was "the uncertainty over what health damage they may have suffered from exposure to the wartime defoliant Agent Orange." Conceding that dioxin was "a highly toxic but still mysterious chemical," the newspaper considered the mounting evidence of catastrophic health consequences associated with Agent Orange exposure as sufficient to necessitate a more robust response from the Carter administration. "Instead," the editors opined, "for more than two years the VA has offered only steady resistance and the confident assertion that Agent Orange led to nothing more serious than a skin rash." Moreover, the *Post* charged that "every one of the limited steps that have been taken was the result of fierce pressure from veterans groups and, more recently, from Congress." The editorial painted a picture of an incompetent federal approach composed of an Air Force study with an unreasonable six-year completion period, a HEW study that did not include veterans, and a VA study already behind schedule. The administration's embarrassing failure created a situation in which many Vietnam veterans "had understandably lost hope" in the VA and had consequently turned to raising "money from foundations for an independent epidemiological study." The *Washington Post* termed the entire affair "a sorry spectacle."[14]

The Carter administration did not let the scathing editorial pass without delivering a response. The rebuttal came from Cleland in the familiar form of an op-ed. The tone of the missive was both defensive and bitter. "I do not know whether the author of The Post's editorial of March 21 on Agent Orange is a veteran of Vietnam. I am," Cleland angrily retorted. "I do not know whether the author of the editorial was exposed to Agent Orange. I was. And I can assure you that under my direction, the Veterans Administration has spared no effort, nor will we, in reaching a sound medical conclusion regarding the effect—or lack of effect—of exposure to this herbicide." Clearly, the administration was digging in its heels and had no intention of backing down from the position that Cleland outlined at the congressional hearing a month earlier. In fact, the op-ed included a bulleted summary of the administrator's major talking points from his previous testimony.[15]

A few weeks later, Colman McCarthy situated the Agent Orange ordeal "within the larger national tragedy of Vietnam." He called the morass of "lawsuits, memos and studies" a form of "judicial" warfare, "disturbingly similar to the jungle war our veterans were asked to fight." The solution, he suggested, was to examine the Agent Orange dilemma "more as a moral issue than a legal one" and issue a presumptive finding of causation.[16]

In late spring 1980, the National Academy of Sciences (NAS) released a report indicating that the Air Force's planned Agent Orange study was deeply flawed. Simply put, the Air Force was testing too few men and considering too many possible cancer-causing effects other than Agent Orange. As a result, the NAS determined that the study had a low probability of linking Agent Orange to cancer and birth defects.[17] Reacting to this latest news, the *Washington Post* editorialized that the "sorry spectacle" continued in the absence of "serious attention from the Pentagon and the Veterans Administration."[18] The newspaper endorsed the NAS's recommendation that the federal government fund independent and expedited studies. None of these revelations or renewed pressures moved the administration to adopt a new plan of action for dealing with the Agent Orange question. Instead, it chose to battle over this agenda item with Congress and the activist network. As the Agent Orange controversy intensified, another Vietnam veterans' issue came to the forefront—one that the White House eagerly embraced.

The Wall

In April 1979, Jan Scruggs and Robert Doubek incorporated the Vietnam Veterans Memorial Fund (VVMF). Their mission was to build a memorial in the nation's capital to honor all American service members who died during the Vietnam War. Both men were veterans of the conflict: Doubek had been an Air Force intelligence officer, and Scruggs was an Army noncommissioned combat officer. As the president of VVMF, Scruggs functioned as the organization's spokesman. Prior to founding VVMF, Scruggs completed a master's degree in counseling psychology and had published scholarly works examining the psychological effects of the war on Vietnam veterans.[19] He was open and candid about his own emotional connections to the war. He experienced "bitterness" over the memories of "carrying the lifeless bodies of close friends through the mire of Vietnam." He supposed those feelings would "never subside." Scruggs wondered if it was possible to derive "any purpose to all the suffering and death."[20] He wanted to erect a memorial displaying the names of the more than 57,000 Americans who died in Vietnam. In doing so, he hoped, "It would be a powerful reminder of that war and those who died, and that it would aid in reconciliation after that divisive period in our history."[21]

A project of this scale was no small endeavor. The VVMF decided from the start that private money, not tax dollars, would pay for the construction of the memorial. Thus, fundraising was a top priority and was a responsibility assumed by the organization. Securing a location for the memorial in the nation's capital, however, required congressional assistance. In August 1979 Scruggs met with Senator Charles McC. Mathias (R-MD) to discuss possibilities. Mathais, who had been an opponent of the war, was supportive of Scruggs's basic plan. They agreed that the best route forward was to pass congressional legislation authorizing federal jurisdiction of a memorial on public lands.²² Later that year, Mathias, with bipartisan cosponsors, introduced legislation to set aside a two-acre section of Constitutional Gardens on the Washington Mall for a Vietnam memorial. In proposing the legislation, Mathais explained that the memorial "will provide a long overdue acknowledgement by the American people of the sacrifice and service of Vietnam veterans. It will contribute greatly toward resolving the real and continuing divisions in our society as a result of the war."²³ Although some wanted to use the memorial deliberations as an opportunity to debate whether the United States had been right or wrong in waging war in Vietnam, these questions did not derail the process. In late June 1980 a joint resolution approving the placement of a Vietnam memorial on the Washington Mall passed by an overwhelming margin, unanimously in the Senate. The legislation preserved the original provision that the memorial construction be privately financed and upon completion be transferred to the Department of the Interior, which would then assume responsibility for the operation and maintenance of the memorial.²⁴

The president signed the legislation on July 1 during a Rose Garden ceremony at the White House. In his opening remarks, Carter congratulated Congress for the "broad and bipartisan support" that produced the legislation. Before he recognized any individuals who deserved special praise, he sought credit for himself by announcing that he and his wife Rosalynn were among the members of the National Sponsoring Committee, the fundraising arm of the VVMF. After acknowledging the important role played by Scruggs, Sen. Mathias, Rep. Bonior, and several others, Carter suggested that his administration had done much over the previous three-and-one-half years to encourage "an enormous change in the attitude of Americans toward those who served in Vietnam." He expressed satisfaction that the nation had reached a moment of "healing and reconciliation" after a difficult and "painful" period. "For too long," he explained, the country's desire to put the war "behind us" led to the disregard of those "who bravely answered" the call to service. By ignoring and in some cases shunning Vietnam veterans, the nation burdened them with additional "pain," the president contended. He encouraged Americans to overlook "whatever the rights and wrongs of the war" in order "to acknowledge more deeply and also more publicly the debt which we can never fully pay to those who served." In conferring his blessing on the creation of the memorial, the president denied that the nation was honoring war. The intent, as he defined it, was to "honor the peace they sought to preserve [and] the freedoms that they fought to preserve." Carter finished his remarks by paraphrasing the eulogy to Lt. Levy from Philip Caputo's *A Rumor of War*. Relying on his own words, Carter conveyed Caputo's lamentation that "no monuments, no statues, no plaques" had been erected to pay tribute "to the Walter Levys who died on the other side of the world, sacrificing themselves for others, sacrificing themselves for us and our children and our children's children." Now, Carter averred, we "will prove with this monument that we care, and that we will always remember." In doing so, the president wanted to emphasize the courage and sacrifice of the Vietnam veterans and offer them a measure of "overdue recognition."[25]

Journalist Bernard Weinraub, in his account of the signing ceremony, wrote, "Mr. Carter's remarks were greeted by some in the audience with coolness." Among the disaffected was Robert Muller. The executive director of the VVA said that the president's comments were "merely words" and that his Vietnam veterans' programs were just "a drop in the bucket."[26] Scruggs later complained that the signing ceremony gave the false impression that the White House, and not VVMF, VVC, and their allies, "had pushed" the authorization of the memorial through Congress. He was also angered by the administration's attempt to upstage the memorial ceremony.[27] Just hours before the Rose Garden event, the Veterans Administration released the results of a massive opinion survey entitled *Myths and Realities: A Study of Attitudes toward Vietnam Era Veterans*. Press coverage of the signing ceremony did in fact include details of the survey's findings, somewhat detracting from the significant achievement of the VVFW.[28] The administration's handling of the signing ceremony illustrated how important it was to showcase the president as a leader on Vietnam veterans' issues. In addition, the origins of the Vietnam Veterans Memorial was yet another example of how a host of individuals and groups had elevated the war's veterans in the national consciousness.

The VVMF still had many hurdles to climb and a long road to travel before reaching its ambitious goal. Fundraising was still a priority. In October 1980 the organization announced a national design competition for the memorial, which turned into a protracted and divisive process that prolonged the selection of the winning entry until May 1981. This contentious phase of the memorial's history transpired after the Carter presidency ended. Although the signing ceremony effectively completed the administration's role in this poignant undertaking, Vietnam veterans' issues continued to confront the president until his last days in office.

Another Vietnam Campaign

During the first half of 1980, the degree to which Agent Orange and the Vietnam Veterans Memorial dominated questions over the nation's obligation to the veterans of that conflict attested to how much both the answer and the parameters of the question had changed since Carter first ran for president four years earlier. In 1976 the Georgia governor made pardoning the Vietnam draft evaders part of his primary campaign. During the general election, the Democratic nominee berated the Ford administration for neglecting Vietnam veterans and offered himself as the candidate who would do the most as president to provide solutions to the readjustment struggles of those who had served in the unpopular war. In the intervening four years, Carter, as president, acted on a Vietnam veterans' agenda that funded job creation, expanded GI Bill benefits, and addressed psychological counseling. He conducted an executive-level readjustment study, and he had regularly employed the rhetoric of gratitude to honor the service of Vietnam veterans. These efforts exposed him to various degrees of political scrutiny. How Carter defended his record and how his Republican challenger assessed that record became part of the 1980 presidential campaign.

According to political scientist Andrew E. Busch, the 1980 election campaign revolved around "four interlocking national crises," which he identified as the troubled economy, the threats posed by the Soviet Union and Iran, "a crisis of public confidence," and a variety of social issues.[29] To win reelection, Carter had to navigate a maelstrom of attacks, coming mainly from Ronald Reagan. The former California governor denounced Carter's pursuit of détente and cuts to defense spending. He blamed the president for weakening the United States in the eyes of its enemies, which Reagan argued contributed to the Soviet invasion of Afghanistan and the hostage crisis in Iran. The Republican promised not only to restore American military might but to use that power to defend the nation's interest and to thwart Communist aggression. He pinned the calamities of rising inflation, high unemployment, fuel shortages, and declining family incomes on the president's failed economic programs. He railed against busing, welfare spending, and racial quotas, and he vowed to get burdensome liberal government off the backs of the American people. The Republican's prescriptions for recovery and prosperity were tax cuts, business and industry deregulation, and reductions in federal spending, except on matters of national defense.[30] Reagan rode this messaging to win twenty-nine of thirty-three primary contests.[31]

In mid-July Republicans convened in Detroit, Michigan, to nominate Reagan, draft a party platform, and await the selection of a vice president. The convention opened to "moments of passion and uncertainty" as delegates hammered out platform planks on abortion and the Equal Rights Amendment (ERA). Regarding the former, Republicans revised the "ambivalent" language from the previous platform and approved a plank that called for a constitutional amendment to protect the life of the unborn. Regarding the latter, delegates voted to oppose the ERA, ending what had been a forty-year endorsement. These decisions, as Busch notes, "demonstrated the degree to which the new Republican coalition revolved around the sudden power of the cultural Right." As significant as the plank positions were, "the greater drama" entailed the selection of a vice presidential candidate. For a while, Reagan considered picking Gerald Ford as his running mate, but the idea lost its appeal when the former chief executive began talking about a co-presidency. From a list of twenty-one possible candidates, the Republican nominee settled on George H. W. Bush, who added ideological and geographical balance to the ticket.[32]

To be expected, print journalists covering the convention focused on the controversial platform debates.[33] Peter Osnos, for example, who analyzed the Republican platform in four installments for the *Washington Post*, concentrated on economics, human rights, foreign policy, and the party's view of the proper role of the federal government. Despite his extensive coverage, he made no mention of the Republican plank on veterans, which had undergone a transformation since the previous election.[34] In 1976 the party platform on veterans coolly stated that Vietnam veterans "deserve[d] education, job, and housing benefits equivalent to those of World War II and the Korean conflict." It identified as a "top priority" the recovery of those "listed as Prisoners of War or Missing in Action in Vietnam." Otherwise, the plank reinforced the status quo.[35] The 1980 version of the Republican plank on veterans demonstrated a much different stance and strategy. Without providing specific policy prescriptions, the Detroit plank endorsed budgetary increases for health programs, rehabilitation care, and job training for all veterans as well as "continued and expanded health care for our Vietnam veterans."[36] These changes were significant, but the press overlooked or dismissed them because there was no controversy with their approval. Moreover, Reagan did not mention veterans at all in his nomination acceptance speech. Nevertheless, something was brewing with respect to how the Republican candidate intended to inject Vietnam veterans and the legacy of the war into the general election campaign. What exactly he intended to do became apparent in the immediate aftermath of the Democratic National Convention.

Notwithstanding the advantages of incumbency, Carter's path to his party's nomination had been "rockier" than that of his Republican challenger. On the first day of the Democratic National Convention, Senator Ted Kennedy, who had engaged in a contentious primary contest with the president, launched one last desperate attempt to replace Carter. When the Massachusettsan failed, he forced a scuffle over the party's platform. Kennedy wanted platform planks committing the party to comprehensive national health insurance, wage and price controls, Medicaid funding for abortions, and billions of dollars in additional spending for public works projects—all positions Carter did not favor, either ideologically or because they made him vulnerable to Reagan. In the end, the senator got most of what he wanted. Having been "upstaged" and overshadowed by Kennedy, Carter used his acceptance speech primarily as a way to reveal the guiding themes of the general election campaign.[37]

As was the case with the Republican convention, the press fixated on the Carter-Kennedy drama and the platform fights.[38] Writing in the *Washington Post*, Robert G. Kline examined the Democratic platform in a three-part series that focused on economics, human rights, and foreign policy.[39] His detailed assessment did not include a single reference to the veterans plank, a plank that had changed considerably from the previous four years and one that reflected how much Vietnam veterans had become part of the president's agenda. In 1976 Carter had not originally included a veterans plank in the proposed platform that he submitted to the Democratic National Convention. The plank eventually adopted by the party reflected the work of Senator Vance Hartke.[40] Although these positions originated with Hartke, Carter subsequently incorporated them into his campaign. Conversely, the 1980 veterans plank recounted the administration's achievements to date and highlighted areas of future commitment. The list of accomplishments included granting the Veterans Administration cabinet-level participation, expanding GI Bill education benefits, increasing VA compensation benefits, establishing drug and alcohol treatment programs, signing the Veterans and Survivors Pension Improvement Act, and initiating an upgrade process for Vietnam veterans with less than honorable discharges. Regarding ongoing priorities, there was a pledge to "complete promptly" Agent Orange studies and to "establish appropriate and sensitive VA health care programs" to those exposed to defoliants or nuclear radiation. The plank even mentioned the administration's commitment to the Vietnam Veterans Memorial. The message was plain and simple. As president, Carter had significantly strengthened the nation's commitment to all veterans and had honored his earlier promises to Vietnam veterans.[41]

Despite the meaningful changes that had taken place in the respective party planks on veterans over the past four years, large segments of the press completely ignored the differences. The conspicuous oversight by such newspapers as the *Washington Post* and the *New York Times* and such journalists as Bernard Weinraub and Philip Geyelin merits closer inspection. Having been such outspoken critics of Carter's stances on employment programs, bad discharge upgrades, the Veterans and Survivors Pension Improvement Act, the psychological and substance abuse counseling programs, and his handling of Agent Orange, their silence cannot be disregarded. Weinraub penned four articles on the Democratic National Convention for the *New York Times*, but he made no mention of Vietnam veterans in any of the pieces. Similarly, Geyelin, the editor of the *Washington Post* and advisor to Vietnam Veterans of America, twice offered commentary on platform-related matters, but in neither instance did he bring up Vietnam veterans' issues, although he offered a lengthy philosophical take on party platforms. "They are in a sense, the archaeological digs of American politics," he opined. "When you read them sequentially in the context of past pronouncements, they tell you quite a lot about how the thinking of the party's best (available) ideologues has been formed."[42] Why did Weinraub and Geyelin dismiss the major revisions to the party platforms? Why did they deny the articulation of a Vietnam veterans' agenda by the two parties? Regardless of the answers to these questions, their silence reveals a failure to foresee how veteran discontent was becoming part of the general election campaign. Similarly, they failed to anticipate Reagan's appeal to this unique constituency or his intention to cast Carter as the anti-veteran president.

A Noble Cause

With the party conventions over, the candidates moved on to the general election campaign. By mid- to late August, Carter had narrowed the gap substantially from a month earlier, when he trailed his Republican challenger by thirty points.[43] Most of the swing in public sentiment occurred because of Reagan's missteps.[44] With the race tightening, each candidate made noteworthy appearances before influential veterans organizations. On August 18, Reagan struck first with an address on national security delivered to the Veterans of Foreign Wars convention in Chicago, Illinois. The wide-ranging speech discussed the proper US response to the Soviet Union and Communist aggression around the world. Using Vietnam as a historical example of the "threatening pattern" of Communist intentions, Reagan declared that "it is time we recognized" that American involvement in Vietnam "was, in truth, a noble cause." Reagan insisted that the lesson of Vietnam was that the United States must always have "the means and the determination to prevail" or risk forfeiting the security of peace. "And while we are at it," the Republican proclaimed, "let use tell those who fought in that war we will never again ask young men to fight and possibly die in a war our government is afraid to let them win." Scholars have fixated on these comments, seeing them as a transformational moment in the contested memory of the Vietnam War. In doing so, they have neglected other parts of the speech, most importantly, where Reagan attacked Carter as the anti-veteran candidate.

Early in his speech, before he reached the US response to Communist aggression or the issue of Vietnam, Reagan examined the recent inability of the VFW to move forward its legislative agenda in Congress. He told the convention attendees that the reason for the organization's lack of success was simple; it's "solely because this present anti-veteran administration has stacked the deck against you." Reagan enumerated five areas where the administration failed to honor its obligation to veterans. Among the accusations, the Republican charged the White House with underfunding and undermining the mission of the Veterans Administration, of not defending veterans hiring preferences in the public sector, and of limiting veterans' access to national cemeteries. As for Vietnam veterans, Reagan remarked that they had been treated shabbily despite fighting "as well and as bravely as any Americans have ever fought in any war." They deserve "our gratitude, our respect, and our continuing concern," he stated. "To me it is the height of hypocrisy for the administration in high sounding words to repeatedly tell us how much we owe our Vietnam veterans" and then in an election year only make recommendations for "a stingy" increase in their educational benefits.[45] It was a damning and grossly misleading indictment of Carter's treatment of veterans and indicative of how Reagan intended to politicize veterans' issues during the campaign.

Just three days after Reagan spoke to the VFW, Carter appeared before the American Legion convention in Boston, Massachusetts. Four years earlier, as the Democratic challenger, he used the venue to present his national security vision for America and to affirm his decision to pardon the Vietnam draft evaders. Now, as the incumbent and in his first campaign appearance since his party's convention, the president needed to defend his record. He began with a rebuttal to Reagan's charges that he had failed the country's veterans. He was proud of his efforts and those of VA director Cleland for having raised pension benefits and disability compensation during his first term. Carter took credit for initiating the psychological counseling program for Vietnam veterans. The president also touted the success of the VA and Department of Labor in expanding employment opportunities for disabled veterans. The hurried rebuttal, however, sidestepped pressing matters for Vietnam veterans such as the epidemiological studies on Agent Orange exposure and VA protocols for treating those with suspected exposure to defoliants.[46] Carter's American Legion address failed to generate much interest among convention attendees or the press. "The president's speech was received politely but he aroused no fervor among the legionnaires," reported Lee Lescaze of the *Washington Post*. "He rarely strained for applause, and complete silence greeted his statements that an active diplomacy must accompany arms in winning a true peace." Moreover, the president received no plaudits for his past efforts on behalf of veterans.[47]

During the final month of the campaign, Carter strategists faced an array of political headwinds. The third-party candidacy of John Anderson complicated matters, as did Carter's refusal to participate in a three-person presidential debate.[48] These preoccupations left Carter exposed to the simmering discontent within the veteran community and Reagan's plan to exploit this discontent to his political advantage.

The Revolt of the Veterans

Immediately after the Republican National Convention, the Veterans of Foreign Wars formally endorsed Reagan for president.[49] Laws prohibiting tax-exempt organizations from making political endorsements discouraged veterans' groups from taking such actions in the past. But the VFW in 1979 established a political action committee, which afforded the group a legal means to endorse candidates and make campaign contributions. In addition to backing Reagan and making a $5,000 contribution to his campaign, the VFW endorsed approximately two hundred congressional candidates and contributed $200,000 to upcoming election bids. Cooper Holt, executive director of the VFW, explained his organization's decision to break the long-standing precedent and join the political fray: "Jimmy Carter has done more to destroy the veterans program than any President that ever sat in the White House."[50] The unprecedented move by the nation's oldest veterans' organization was the first salvo in an election-year veterans revolt.

On October 15 the immediate past commanders of the VFW, the American Legion, and American Veterans of World War II, Korea and Vietnam (AMVETS) appeared at the National Press Club and added their endorsement to the Reagan-Bush ticket. The three men spoke as individuals. Neither the American Legion nor AMVETS had political action committees. Still, they expressed their belief that many of their fellow members would join them in voting for the Republican challenger. Their purpose was to paint Carter as the anti-veteran candidate, and their opening statements were bitter and sometimes insular and unfair. Frank I. Hamilton of the American Legion remarked that he believed only a Republican White House could "reverse the outrageous and dehumanizing treatment" of veterans that had occurred under the Carter presidency.[51] Howard Vander Clute of the VFW slammed the administration for its "inability or unwillingness to address the legitimate needs of those who have served their country, especially the disabled and Vietnam-era veterans."[52]

Although the major veterans' organizations had long been identified as the guardians of older generations of veterans, they had in recent years made inroads into recruiting Vietnam veterans. The American Legion, which boasted the largest membership of any veterans' organization, counted 750,000 Vietnam veterans among its 2.7 million members. The VFW claimed 500,000 Vietnam veterans as part of its 1.8 million total membership. By comparison, Muller's Vietnam Veterans of American had fewer than 1,500 members. The multigenerational organizations packed a considerable political punch. Indeed, veterans, as part of the voting citizenry, represented 22 percent of the electorate. With less than a month before the election, polls showed 48 percent of veterans supported Reagan while only 28 percent favored Carter. Any concerted effort to organize veteran support for Reagan presented serious political ramifications to Carter's reelection bid.[53]

In addition to their remarks at the National Press Club, each of the former commanders issued carefully prepared press releases with a detailed list of grievances against the Carter administration. For instance, Joseph R. Koralewski of AMVETS maintained that the president's spending proposals for various types of veterans' benefits did not keep up with the rate of inflation. He panned a Carter-supported 10 percent increase in GI Bill education benefits pending before Congress, arguing that the cost of living "had risen more than 33 percent" in the previous three years, which was the last time the education benefits had been increased. Reagan, in his "noble cause" speech, had termed this legislation a "stingy increase." Offering another example, Koralewski conceded that VA disability benefits increased during Carter's first term in office but observed that "the value of these benefits has steadily decreased" because of rising inflation.[54] Similarly, Hamilton pointed out that inflation negated any funding increases to veterans' programs and further argued that the total allocation to the Veterans Administration as a percentage of the federal budget had fallen 50 percent in the four years under Carter, despite one-half million veterans being added to the VA system.[55]

They maintained that the president favored smaller increases to veterans' programs than those recommended by their organizations or advocated by Congress. They cited Carter's recent veto of the Veterans' Administration Health Care Amendments of 1980 as an example. The legislation increased salaries and incentive bonuses for VA doctors and dentists and created a scholarship program that offered financial assistance to medical students in return for their service in VA hospitals. Furthermore, it authorized the establishment of up to fifteen geriatric health centers. Proponents of the bill argued the measures were necessary to secure and retain exceptional medical personnel for the VA health-care system. Carter vetoed the legislation, saying it was not "essential" because VA physicians were already well compensated and the legislation as written did not further the administration's "goal of directly helping sick and disabled veterans."[56] Congress disagreed and overrode the veto, with only five members supporting the president. Koralewski used the case to argue that "President Carter's policies of fiscal restraint" constituted a "thoughtless and uncaring approach to veterans needs."[57] Hamilton considered the pay increases essential to halting "the outflow of trained VA doctors, dentists and technicians" from the VA system.[58]

The three former commanders also took umbrage with any attempt by the president to defend his record and denied him any policy successes. For example, Hamilton called Carter's claim that the Veterans and Survivors Pension Improvement Act of 1978 was an administration accomplishment a blatant misrepresentation of the truth. Hamilton pointed out that the White House lobbied successfully to reduce the benefit levels,[59] which led to one million fewer veterans receiving pensions. Koralewski derided the president for taking credit for the psychological counseling programs. He argued that the White House pushed for considerably less funding than requested by the legislation's sponsors and labeled the final bill a "bandaid on a sucking chest wound."[60] Some of these criticisms against Carter had been leveled before, but not by the multigenerational veterans' organizations. Interestingly, during Sen. Cranston's years-long attempt to pass drug and counseling programs, the VFW and American Legion had not been enthusiastic supporters, illustrating just how politicized veterans' issues had become in the presidential election year.

Somewhat surprisingly, Vander Clute tackled HIRE, the centerpiece of the administration's effort to reduce Vietnam veterans' unemployment. Relying on the erroneous claims previously posited by Carter's critics, he alleged that the reimbursable component of HIRE produced a miniscule number of jobs due to mismanagement and the fact that veteran unemployment was "a low priority" for the president. Although it was true that the reimbursable component of HIRE had not met the original targets set by Carter, the president had launched the veterans' program as part of his first national economic recovery program, and the number of jobs created by the reimbursable component was far greater than the critics avowed. Still, Carter certainly failed to ensure the proper execution of his own program, particularly the public-sector component that operated through CETA, and Vander Clute correctly pointed out that unspent HIRE funds continued to be returned to the US Treasury.[61] However, the president had helped Vietnam veterans tremendously in terms of improving their economic standing, probably more so than for the average American. In some respects, the criticisms of HIRE served as a guise for assailing the president's views on veterans' preference in federal job hiring.

Earlier in his presidency, Carter announced a plan for an overhaul of the civil service system. He proposed sweeping changes to encourage "the hiring of qualified women, minorities, and the handicapped." To accomplish this objective, Carter wanted "to reduce the preferential advantage given to non-disabled veterans . . . and to end this preference altogether for senior military officers who retired with pension benefits after a full military career."[62] In addition, veterans of World War II and the Korean Wars would no longer be able to use their preference status when applying for new federal jobs under the president's federal civil service reform plan, and the clock was ticking on how much longer Vietnam veterans had to utilize their advantage. As a result, the major veterans organizations vehemently opposed any attempt to end their lifetime employment advantages.[63] Hamilton assailed Carter for abandoning veterans, ignoring "the special nature" of their "sacrifices and hardships," and denying "their justly earned rights and benefits."[64] Vander Clute denounced Carter for betraying a campaign promise to defend the long-standing benefit, and further chastised him for seeking to award a new federal hiring preference to those "who had served in the Peace Corps."[65] In the end, Congress excluded the president's modifications on the veterans preference from the final version of the civil service reform bill, but in the eyes of many, the damage was irreparable.[66]

The outraged veterans added undermining the independence of the Veterans Administration to their list of grievances against Carter. Koralewski identified three instances where initiatives of the president posed a threat to the autonomy of the VA. The first was part of a "welfare reform" plan that proposed placing certain VA disability compensation and pension programs under the control of the Department of Health, Education and Welfare. A second transpired when the president considered transferring all VA educational programs to his newly created Department of Education. The final instance, introduced during the election year, involved the president's national health plan and the possibility of placing the VA hospital system into the general pool of health-care providers. Carter's obsession with restructuring and reorganizing government did him no favors when it came to veterans' policies. Vander Clute, Hamilton, and Koralewski believed their constituency deserved a "special distinction," and as Koralewski carped, "clearly, when one reflects on the Carter administration's attempt to dismantle the

VA's power to administer veterans benefits, it becomes evident just how little priority America's veterans have had under President Carter's leadership."[67]

By appearing before the National Press Club just a few weeks before the presidential election, the three immediate past commanders of the VFW, American Legion, and AMVETS were clearly attempting to sway voters. The White House could not afford to let their accusations go unchallenged; it seized an opportunity on October 17 when Carter signed the Veterans Rehabilitation and Education Amendments of 1980. As he opened his remarks, he defended his record on veterans' policy and expressed pride in signing into law "another of a series of legislative acts" benefiting the nation's veterans. The Veterans Rehabilitation and Education Amendments provided for a 10 percent cost-of-living increase for GI Bill education benefits, restructured VA vocational rehabilitation programs, and increased the living allowance for disabled veterans by 17 percent. He celebrated the changes to the vocational rehabilitation programs as "the first major reform of the program since it first began in 1943." Tellingly, Carter linked all aspects of the Veterans Rehabilitation and Education Amendments to recommendations contained in his Presidential Review Memorandum. In addition, he asserted that veterans' benefits and services "remain unsurpassed," and vowed that he "continued to support an independent VA hospital system." Carter also trumpeted the counseling and jobs programs for Vietnam veterans and took credit for signing the proclamation establishing Vietnam Veterans Week.[68]

In responding to Vander Clute, Hamilton, and Koralewski, not only did Carter touch on and attempt to rebut each of their charges, but both the speech and the signing ceremony were clear indications of a reaction to the National Press Club event. Exactly ten days earlier, the president chose not to give a speech or host a signing ceremony for the Veterans Disability Compensation and Housing Benefits Amendments of 1980. And the statement he released on signing the legislation failed to mention anything about his four-year record on veterans' policies.[69] However, Vander Clute, Hamilton, and Koralewski's endorsement of Reagan had changed the political calculus. A sense of urgency filtered through the domestic policy staff. Aides rushed to assemble a Veterans for Carter Committee as a form of damage control. The president introduced the group at the October 17 signing ceremony at the White House. The goal was to use past leaders of veterans' organizations to validate Carter's "deep commitment to meeting the needs of America's veterans, an independent high quality VA health care system, and recognition and support for Vietnam veterans."[70] The brief photo opportunity, however, lacked the drama of the National Press Club event.

During the final week of the campaign, the race was too close to call. On election day, which coincided with the one-year anniversary of the Iranian hostage crisis, voters turned sharply against Carter. Reagan received 51 percent to Carter's 41 percent of the popular vote; Anderson picked up nearly 7 percent. The electoral margin, 489 to 49, was a landslide for Reagan, the results at the time comparable only to Franklin Roosevelt's win in 1936 and Richard Nixon's in 1972. Reagan's victory was due in large measure to his ability to capture blue-collar, ethnic, Catholic, and evangelical voters. The two most important issues in the election were the economy and foreign policy. Reagan scored best on "strengthening national defense, reducing inflation, improving the economy, spending tax money wisely, increasing respect for the United States overseas, and reducing unemployment." Carter fared better on "improving things for minorities, keeping the United States out of war, helping the poor, fostering women's rights, dealing with racial problems, and advancing peace in the Middle East."[71]

Just two days after the election, Wanda Henderson, secretary of the American Legion Auxiliary of Louisiana, wrote to the president to convey her sadness that Carter had lost his reelection bid. "The people of our country did not vote against you as a person, but the state of affairs which you had no control over," she consoled. "You will always be remembered as a great human being . . . and we know what you have tried to do for our veterans."[72] There were similar letters from other veterans who had supported the president.[73] These expressions of consolation may have been heartfelt, and the explanation that fate had dealt Carter an unfair political hand surely resonated within the White House, but such sentiments did little to soothe the defeated president. How much the veterans' vote influenced the election cannot be determined by the available polling data. What needs to be emphasized as part of this 1980 election analysis is the complete reversal that occurred from the previous presidential campaign. In 1976 Carter declared himself the friend of the Vietnam veteran and raised expectations that he planned to deliver a comprehensive veterans' agenda, all while attacking President Ford as the anti-veteran candidate. In 1980 Reagan turned the tables. He—with the help of the VFW, and former leaders of American Legion, and AMVETS—branded Carter as the anti-veteran president. Although that charge was simply not true, the 1980 election did confirm that Vietnam veterans' issues had become a national agenda item. Indeed, two presidential candidates, armed with two political party platforms, sought the mantle of guardian and defender of Vietnam veterans. Jimmy Carter's role in this historic development cannot be denied.

Conclusion

Once considered in the same category as Herbert Hoover, Calvin Coolidge, and Chester Arthur,[1] Jimmy Carter's presidential reputation has been rehabilitated in recent years. A spate of authors have portrayed the Georgian as underrated, misunderstood, or underappreciated.[2] For example, political journalist Jonathan Alter writes that the thirty-ninth president deserves more praise "considering what came before (Vietnam and Watergate) and after (the Iran-Contra scandal, endless wars in Iraq and Afghanistan, [and] two impeachments)." With those bookends, Vice President Mondale's toast that the administration "told the truth . . . obeyed the law [and] kept the peace" constitutes meaningful successes.[3] Not everyone, however, has been as complimentary. While recognizing Carter's accomplishments, there has been no shortage of writers pointing out the Georgian's "consequential" failures.[4] Both Carter's personal and political character have complicated the assessments of his presidency. As Alter suggests, "Carter was often respected without being liked; afterward, he was admired without being loved."[5] In the spirit of reevaluation, *A Debt of Gratitude* explored Carter's role in making Vietnam veterans' issues a national agenda item, and how his actions and especially his rhetoric of gratitude presented the veterans of that controversial war in a new light.

Beginning with his days as governor, Carter appropriated himself as an advocate for Vietnam veterans. His appointment of the Georgia Advisory Committee on Vietnam Veterans signaled that he was prepared to take action. The free college tuition debate revealed his preference to have surrogates work out the policy details and proved that he was willing to accept compromise measures and avoid costly new programs. Without question, Carter set budgetary limits and sometimes accommodated elected legislatures with respect to his Vietnam veterans' agenda. Yet, he set no such limits nor acquiesced to concessions when it came to his public recognition of the war's veterans. He illuminated Vietnam veterans and their readjustment transition through highly symbolic commemorative events such as the Jobs for Veterans Year and the Salute to Vietnam Veterans Week. Most importantly, in all of these endeavors Carter employed a rhetoric of gratitude, which defined the Vietnam veteran as heroic and selfless. In formulating a Vietnam veterans' agenda, he conveyed appreciation and respect to those who served. He remained committed to this Georgia formula once he became president.

In 1976 Carter embarked on a run for the White House. The media fixated on his pledge to pardon Vietnam draft evaders and his newly adopted criticism of the war. However, as the general election unfolded, Carter made a concerted effort to paint Gerald Ford as an anti-veteran president. His campaign organized the National Committee of Veterans for Carter-Mondale, and the candidate promised to prioritize a Vietnam veterans' agenda. These decisions demonstrated that Carter intentionally politicized Vietnam veterans' issues. In raising expectations, he became accountable to Vietnam veteran activists and their allies in the media.

To fulfill his many campaign promises, Carter commenced his presidency by pardoning the draft evaders, which proved to be something of an anticlimactic event, although it stirred up old animosities. Conversely, his plan to address Vietnam veteran unemployment generated broad-based support. The general concept of HIRE, a private-public approach to job creation, was solid. However, slow implementation by the administration prompted criticism. The inability to engage Congress on amending CETA guidelines to set aside more public-sector jobs for Vietnam veterans prevented Carter from obtaining maximum results. Nevertheless, HIRE proved to be one of the president's most successful programs for Vietnam veterans, thanks in part to the efforts of the National Alliance of Businessmen. Unfortunately for him, Carter never received his due credit for this important initiative. When he failed to provide aggressive leadership in the face of congressional opposition to his bad-discharge upgrade proposal, his credibility took a hit. Rather than risk an embarrassing political defeat by having his first presidential veto overridden by Congress, Carter effectively abandoned the idea in order to maintain support for important domestic and foreign policy priorities. During his first year in office, a vociferous assortment of critics accused Carter of failing to deliver on his promises to Vietnam veterans. The intensity of the public relations battle confirmed the ascendency of Vietnam veterans' issues as a national agenda item.

In his 1978 State of the Union address, he lowered expectations for his second year in office. This basic tempering of expectations also applied to his Vietnam veterans' policies. As year two progressed, members of the administration changed their messaging, asserting that the vast majority of Vietnam veterans had readjusted successfully, with a much smaller percentage still struggling to transition into civilian life. The findings from the Presidential Review Memorandum validated this new strategy by confirming that Vietnam veterans had received more assistance than previous generations of veterans and that most former service members were better off than their nonveteran counterparts. Moreover, the administration used the findings to buttress the claim that the president's policies had contributed significantly to the successful readjustment of Vietnam veterans and that he had fulfilled his earlier campaign promises to Vietnam veterans. The PRM marked a watershed moment, but not only for the administration.

The Vietnam veterans' activist network rejected Carter's new narrative. In their eyes, he had not lived up to their expectations. The break between the White House and the Vietnam Veterans in Congress caucus may have been the most dramatic and telling example. Believing that the war's veterans had a low priority with Carter and that the PRM offered only administrative reform, the caucus members felt they had no alternative but to push forward with their own legislative agenda. From this point on in the Carter presidency, there were competing Vietnam veterans' agendas, and the White House increasingly saw the public relations battle over the Georgian's record on these issues as unwinnable. The final nail in the public relations coffin for the White House came with the Agent Orange controversy. The administration's opposition to a presumptive finding to allow for immediate VA benefits for those suffering or gravely ill from perceived exposure to Agent Orange expanded the network of Carter's critics. As a result, the president sustained damaging attacks to his credibility on and commitment to Vietnam veterans' issues.

Without question, the troubled American economy, the aggressiveness and threatening actions of the Soviet Union and Iran, and such social issues as abortion and the Equal Rights Amendment animated the presidential election of 1980. Still, Republican challenger Ronald Reagan chose to insert Vietnam and the treatment of the war's veterans into the election. As a testament to the pressure generated by the national debate over the Vietnam veterans' agenda, both candidates, both parties, and both platforms sought to establish electoral legitimacy with the war's veterans. What also seems obvious from this election and Carter's entire presidency is that the administration never seemed capable of managing the politics of victimhood. Ultimately, with respect to Vietnam veterans' policies, the goal posts kept moving—and the administration never overcame the perception manufactured by Carter's critics that he promised too much, delivered too little, and relied too heavily on symbolism.

Despite introducing or sponsoring more legislation, conducting more executive-level studies, and facilitating or endorsing more public ceremonies for Vietnam veterans than any prior president, scholars have ignored the range and scope of Carter's actions and words. Indeed, Carter afforded Vietnam veterans a higher place on the national agenda than at any other point during the decade of the 1970s. His efforts have been a conspicuous omission from the recorded history on Vietnam veterans. Carter clearly contributed to the transfiguration of the Vietnam veteran.[6] He reimagined the Vietnam veteran by practicing a "conventional ethics" of remembering the war. This type of memory, Pulitzer-prize author Viet Nguyen writes, constitutes a remembrance of "one's own" and a thinking "of war solely as combat and its main protagonist as the soldier."[7] Carter's ethics of remembering sought to redeem the American soldier, to erase the divisiveness of the past, and to "delegitimize and marginalize anti-war opinions."[8] He traced much of the pain, suffering, and bitterness that burdened Vietnam veterans to "the attitude of those who stayed behind" and opposed the war.[9] He encouraged Americans not to confuse "the war with the warrior"[10] and he instructed them to overlook "the rights or wrongs of the war."[11] Whether speaking on ceremonial occasions such as Veterans Day or at patriotic landscapes such as Arlington National Cemetery, he elevated the Americans who fought in Vietnam above the enemies in order to "to revitalize an American image which had been tarnished by the Vietnam experience."[12] His rhetoric of gratitude was an attempt to restore a "nationalist spirit" and reinforce a "shared identity."[13]

As part of the revitalization or restoration process, Carter contributed to a revisionist history of the American experience in Vietnam.[14] His rhetoric of gratitude sounded similar to the myth that the "real enemy" during the Vietnam War was a domestic foe,[15] but Carter did not peddle a version of the stab-in-the-back legend to explain America's defeat in Vietnam. He avoided Reagan's claims that an American victory could have been achieved if politicians had better managed the war or if generals had been allowed to fight more aggressively on the field of battle. These revisionist tropes, as chronicled by such scholars as Kathleen Belew, fueled the rise of white power movements and paramilitary groups in post-Vietnam America.[16] However, by focusing on the valor and selflessness of the Vietnam veteran, Carter built a hawkish defense of the war that ignored "the political complexities of U.S. intervention." He overturned orthodox understandings of the war when he equated the combat service of Vietnam veterans with that of the honored veterans of America's martial past. Thus, Carter's placement of Vietnam veterans on the national agenda foreshadowed many of Reagan's pronouncements. In the end, Reagan's "noble cause" speech seems less an inflection point on the evolution of the collective memory of Vietnam and the war's veterans than scholars have argued previously. In this regard, Carter's decade of policy antecedents and his rhetoric of gratitude are too important to ignore.

NOTES

INTRODUCTION

1. "Executive Order" [no date], RG 1-7-105, Box 9, GA.
2. "News Release," January 29, 1973, Box 54, MCP, JCL.
3. Jimmy Carter to Max Cleland, February 11, 1971, Box 55, MCP, JCL.
4. Proclamation, "Salute to Veterans Week," September 7, 1973, Box 49, MCP, JCL.
5. The theoretical foundation for my argument comes from Mary E. Stuckey, *Jimmy Carter, Human Rights, and the National Agenda* (College Station: Texas A&M University Press, 2009); George C. Edwards III, *On Deaf Ears: The Limits of the Bully Pulpit* (New Haven, CT: Yale University Press, 2003).
6. Meredith H. Lair, *Armed with Abundance: Consumerism and Soldiering in the Vietnam War* (Chapel Hill: University of North Carolina Press, 2011), 14, 13.
7. Lisa S. Villadsen and Jason A. Edwards, "Introduction," in Lisa S. Villadsen and Jason A. Edwards, eds., *The Rhetoric of Official Apology* (Lanham, MD: Lexington Books, 2020), 1–12.
8. A. Cheree Carlson and John E. Hocking, "Strategies of Redemption at the Vietnam Veterans' Memorial," *Western Journal of Speech Communication* 52 (Summer 1988): 208.
9. For background on the narrative of victimhood, see, Eric T. Dean Jr., "The Myth of the Troubled and Scorned Vietnam Veteran," *Journal of American Studies* 26 (April 1992): 59–74; Andrew J. Huebner, *The Warrior Image: Soldiers in American Culture from the Second World War to the Vietnam Era* (Chapel Hill: University of North Carolina Press, 2008), 194, 210, 232, 238, 256; Susan Jeffords, *The Remasculinization of America: Gender and the Vietnam War* (Bloomington: Indiana University Press, 1989), 116–120.
10. Robert J. McMahon, "Rationalizing Defeat: The Vietnam War in American Presidential Discourse, 1975–1995," *Rhetoric and Public Affairs* 2 (Winter 1999): 529–549; Robert J. McMahon, "Contested Memory: The Vietnam War and American Society, 1975–2001," *Diplomatic History* 26 (Spring 2002): 159–184.
11. Dan F. Hahn, "The Rhetoric of Jimmy Carter, 1976–1980," *Presidential Studies Quarterly* 14 (Spring 1984): 265–288; Kai Bird, *The Outlier: The Unfinished Presidency of Jimmy Carter* (New York: Crown Publishing, 2021), 314–315.
12. Stuckey, *Jimmy Carter, Human Rights, and the National Agenda*, xv–xxvii.
13. Gerald Nicosia, *Home to War: A History of the Vietnam Veterans*

Movement (New York: Crown Publishing, 2001); Myra MacPherson, *Long Time Passing: Vietnam and the Haunted Generation* (Garden City, NY: Doubleday, 1984), 4; Wilbur J. Scott, *Vietnam Veterans since the War: The Politics of PTSD, Agent Orange, and the National Memorial* (Norman: University of Oklahoma Press, 2003), xvi.

14. Ronald Reagan, "Peace: Restoring the Margin of Safety," August 18, 1980, https://www.reaganlibrary.gov/archives/speech/peace-restoring-margin-safety.

15. Sandra Scanlon, *The Prowar Movement: Domestic Support for the Vietnam War and the Making of Modern American Conservatism* (Amherst: University of Massachusetts Press, 2013), 4; Patrick Hagopian, *The Vietnam War in American Memory: Veterans, Memorials, and the Politics of Healing* (Amherst: University of Massachusetts Press, 2009), 12; Joseph Darda, *How White Men Won the Culture Wars: A History of Veteran America* (Oakland: University of California Press, 2021), 154; Lair, *Armed with Abundance*, 142. Gregory A. Daddis, *Pulp Vietnam: War and Gender in Cold War Men's Adventure Magazines* (Cambridge, UK: Cambridge University Press, 2020), 172–173, 225.

16. Darda, *How White Men Won the Culture Wars*, 3–4, 51.

17. Jerry Lembcke, *The Spitting Image: Myth, Memory, and the Legacy of Vietnam* (New York: New York University Press, 1998), 173–174.

18. The quote is from Christian G. Appy, *Working-Class War: American Combat Soldiers and Vietnam* (Chapel Hill: University of North Carolina Press, 1993), 320. Appy is not the only one to claim the 1970s were a decade of silence. Penny Lewis described America's cultural response to Vietnam as one of "repressed silence and anxiety" until 1978. Her claims are based in large measure on an inventory of articles on the Vietnam War published in the American Sociological Review; see Penny Lewis, *Hardhats, Hippies, and Hawks: The Vietnam Antiwar Movement as Myth and Memory* (Ithaca, NY: Cornell University Press, 2013), 11, 29, 198n13. See also John Robert Greene, *The Presidency of Gerald Ford* (Lawrence: University Press of Kansas, 1994), 37, to mention just a few examples.

CHAPTER 1. ILLUMINATING VIETNAM VETERANS

1. For more on the return of the American prisoners and the media response, see Glenn Robins, *The Longest Rescue: The Life and Legacy of Vietnam POW William A. Robinson* (Lexington: University Press of Kentucky, 2013), 127–159; Craig Howes, *Voices of the Vietnam POWs: Witnesses to Their Flight* (New York: Oxford University Press, 1993), 159.

2. "Nixon Throws a Party," *Time*, June 4, 1973, 32.

3. Tom Wicker, "Red Carpets and Other Hypocrisies," *New York Times*, February 15, 1973, 43.

4. "The Vets: Heroes as Orphans," *Newsweek*, March 5, 1973, 22, 24; "Veterans: Forgotten Warriors?," *Time*, March 12, 1973, 17–18; Garry Settle, "Postwar U.S.: The Scapegoat," *Time*, February 5, 1973, 21.

5. "For Veterans Seeking Work, the Picture Is Brighter," *U.S. News & World Report*, June 4, 1973, 76–78; "How Aid to Veterans Is Rising," *U.S. News & World Report*, July 9, 1973, 57.

6. "Home From Vietnam," *U.S. News & World Report*, February 12, 1973, 21–23.

7. Leonard C. Lewin, "The Heroes of Our Time," *Nation*, April 2, 1973, 421; Wicker, "Red Carpets and Other Hypocrisies," "The Vets: Heroes as Orphans," *Newsweek*, March 5, 1973, 22, 24; "Veterans: Forgotten Warriors?," *Time*, March 12, 1973, 17–18; "For Veterans Seeking Work, the Picture Is Brighter"; "How Aid to Veterans Is Rising."

8. "Executive Order" [no date], RG 1-7-105, Box 9, GA.

9. Press Release, "U.S. Census Shows 562,358 Veterans Living in Georgia," June 17, 1972, RG 036-03-006, Box 1, GA.

10. Memorandum, "Purpose of Georgia Advisory Committee on Vietnam Veterans," [no date], RG 036-03-006, Box 1, GA.

11. For background on Jimmy Carter's early life, see E. Stanly Godbold Jr., *Jimmy and Rosalynn Carter: The Georgia Years, 1924–1974* (New York: Oxford University Press, 2010).

12. Eric T. Dean Jr., "The Myth of the Troubled and Scorned Vietnam Veteran," *Journal of American Studies* 26 (April 1992): 62.

13. Cleland Testimony, August 7, 1973, Box 55, MCP, JCL.

14. Comparative Data on State Benefits for Veterans [no date], Box 49, MCP, JCL; "Welcome Home," *State Government News*, January 1974, newspaper clipping, Box 55, MCP, JCL.

15. Conference Program, "Problems of the Returning Veteran," March 13–14, 1972, RG 1-7-105, Box 9, GA.

16. Max Cleland, *Strong at the Broken Places* (Lincoln, VA: Chosen Books, 1980). For specifics on Cleland's Senate run, see Pat Potter, "Max Cleland Will Be Youngest Senator when Legislature Opens in January," *DeKalb New Era*, December 10, 1970, 1, 9.

17. "Vietnam Veterans Turned Off by Red Tape," *Lithonia Observer*, December 28, 1972, 7.

18. "Subcommittee Report on Drug Abuse," March 2, 1973; "Problems of the Mental and Physical Handicapped"; "Report of the Employment Sub-Committee"; all in RG 1-7-105, Box 9, GA.

19. "News Release," January 29, 1973, Box 54, MCP, JCL.

20. Mark Boulton, *Failing Our Veterans: The G.I. Bill and the Vietnam Generation* (New York: New York University Press, 2014), 97–99, 117.

21. "Vietnam Veterans Turned Off by Red Tape," 7.

22. Max Cleland to James H. Floyd, January 26, 1973, Box 54, MCP, JCL.

23. Legislative Fact Sheet, "Veterans' Educational Benefits" [no date], RG 036-03-006, Box 1, GA.

24. Legislative Fact Sheet, "Veterans' Educational Benefits" [no date], RG 036-03-006, Box 1, GA.

25. Bart Snead to Max Cleland, January 5, 1973, Box 55, MCP, JCL.

26. Margaret Shannon, "After the War, What?," *Atlanta Journal and Constitution Magazine*, February 11, 1973, 8, 9, 37, 39.

27. Max Cleland to James H. Floyd, January 26, 1973, Box 54, MCP, JCL.
28. "Vet Scholarship Bill Is Sent Back," *Columbus Enquirer*, February 17, 1973, newspaper clipping, Box 53, MCP, JCL.
29. "Press Release," March 6, 1973, Box 54, MCP, JCL.
30. Dallas Lee, "Senator Attacks Tuition Bill Stall," *Macon Telegraph*, March 14, 1973, 3.
31. Max Cleland, "The Senate," March 5, 1973, Box 54, MCP, JCL.
32. "Vet Scholarship Bill Is Sent Back."
33. Legislative Fact Sheet, "Veterans' Educational Benefits" [no date], RG 036-03-006, Box 1, GA.
34. Paul Raymon, "A Realistic Way to Help Vietnam Veterans," March 7, 1973, Box 54, MCP, JCL; Elmo Ellis, "Georgia Veterans Educational Assistance Bill" [no date], Box 53, MCP, JCL; "Let's Help Vets," *Dekalb New Era*, February 22, 1973, newspaper clipping, Box 53, MCP, JCL; Ken Walton, "Cleland Explains Problems of Vets Home from 'Nam," *Clarkston Neighbor*, March 8, 1973, newspaper clipping, Box 53, MCP, JCL.
35. Sharon J. Sayler, "Tuition Bill for Vets Trapped in Committee," *Alpharetta Neighbor*, newspaper clipping, Box 55, MCP, JCL.
36. "Georgia Vets Seek Free Tuition," *Bell Ringer*, January 12, 1973, newspaper clipping, Box 53, MCP, JCL; "State Senator Max Cleland Speaks in Savannah," *Sou'wester*, October 23, 1973, 3; "Free Tuition," *Red and Black*, February 1, 1973, 4; "Veterans Need Stipend Increase," *Signal*, newspaper clipping, Box 53, MCP, JCL.
37. Max Cleland to James R. Lanzer, June 25, 1973, Box 57, MCP, JCL.
38. "The Big Issues, *Atlanta Journal*, February 26, 1974, 16.
39. Max Cleland to James R. Lanzer, June 25, 1973, Box 57, MCP, JCL.
40. Press Release, "School Aid to Veterans Approved," February 21, 1974, Box 54, MCP, JCL.
41. Bert Westbrook to Max Cleland, January 15, 1973, Box 55, MCP, JCL.
42. "Report of the Employment Sub-Committee," RG 1-7-105, Box 9, GA.
43. "Ford, Owens-Illinois among Georgia Companies Hiring Vet, *The JFV Report*, May 1972, 6; "Patriotism, Expanding Economy, Helps Job-Hunting Ex-GIs in Georgia," *The JFV Report*, May 1972, 7,15, both in Box 53, MCP, JCL.
44. "President Extends Vets Program for One Year," *The JFV Report*, May 1972, 1, Box 53, MCP, JCL.
45. "Salute to Veterans Week Proclamation," September 7, 1973, Box 49, MCP, JCL.
46. W. G. Ashmore and Max Cleland to Gentlemen, September 4, 1973, Box 49, MCP, JCL.
47. "Radio/TV Spots," Box 49, MCP, JCL.
48. Jimmy Carter to Max Cleland, February 11, 1971, Box 55, MCP, JCL.
49. David E. Rosenbaum, "Carter's Position on Issues Designed for Wide Appeal," *New York Times*, June 11, 1976, 1, 16.

50. Kevin M. Kruse and Julian E. Zelizer, *Fault Lines: A History of the United States since 1974* (New York: W. W. Norton, 2019), 37, 35.

51. Caddell quoted in Kandy Stroud, *How Jimmy Won: The Victory Campaign from Plains to the White House* (New York: William Morrow, 1977), 191.

52. Laura Kalman, *Right Star Rising: A New Politics, 1974–1980* (New York: W. W. Norton, 2010), 111–113.

53. Kenneth E. Morris, *Jimmy Carter: American Moralist* (Athens: University of Georgia Press, 1996), 215–220.

54. Godbold, *Jimmy and Rosalynn Carter*, 228.

CHAPTER 2. THE VIETNAM CAMPAIGN

1. "Formal Announcement," December 12, 1974, *The Presidential Campaign 1976* (Washington, DC: Government Printing Office, 1977), vol. 1, pt. 1, 3–11.

2. Charles C. Jones, *The Trusteeship Presidency: Jimmy Carter and the United States Congress* (Baton Rouge: Louisiana State University Press, 1988), 18.

3. Kevin M. Kruze and Julian E. Zelizer, *Fault Lines: A History of the United States since 1974* (New York: W. W. Norton, 2019), 35.

4. Burton I. Kaufman and Scott Kaufman, *The Presidency of James Earl Carter, Jr.* (Lawrence: University Press of Kansas, 2006), 16.

5. David E. Rosenbaum, "Carter's Position on Issues Designed for Wide Appeal," *New York Times*, June 11, 1976, 16.

6. Elizabeth Drew, *American Journal: The Events of 1976* (New York: Vantage Books, 1976), 41, 63, 106.

7. Quotes from Rosenbaum, "Carter's Position on Issues Designed for Wide Appeal"; see also Helen Dewar, "Jimmy Carter's Broad Rhetoric," *Washington Post*, June 4, 1976, 4. The charges of fuzziness on the issues followed Carter after the primary contest into the general election; see Stanley Cloud, "Jimmy's Mixed Signals," *Time*, October 4, 1976, 28; Mark J. Rozell, *The Press and the Carter Presidency* (Boulder, CO: Westview Press, 1989), 12–15.

8. Drew, *American Journal*, 43.

9. "Jimmy Carter: The Candidate on the Issues: An Interview," *Washington Post*, March 21, 1976, B1, B5.

10. Barry Werth, *31 Days: Gerald Ford, the Nixon Pardon, and a Government in Crisis* (New York: Anchor Books, 2006), 195.

11. Sandra Scanlon, *The Prowar Movement Domestic Support for the Vietnam War and the Making of Modern American Conservatism* (Amherst: University of Massachusetts Press, 2013), 305, 324.

12. Gordon L. Weil, *The Long Shot: George McGovern Runs for President* (New York: W. W. Norton, 1973), 97–99, 132, 227.

13. "How Radical Is McGovern?," *Newsweek*, June 19, 1972, 24–25.

14. Rick Perlstein, *Nixonland: The Rise of a President and the Fracturing of America* (New York: Scribner, 2008), 652

15. *The Gallup Poll: Public Opinion 1972–1977*, 2 vols. (Wilmington, DE: Scholarly Resources, 1978), 1:48–48, 51–52.

16. Robert Mason, *Richard Nixon and the Quest for a New Majority* (Chapel Hill: University of North Carolina Press, 2004), 183, 189, 184; Edward D. Berkowitz, *Something Happened: A Political and Cultural Overview of the Seventies* (New York: Columbia University Press, 2006), 19.

17. *The Gallup Poll: Public Opinion*, 1:99–100.

18. "Amnesty—Latest in a Hot Debate," *U.S. News & World Report*, March 12, 1973, 34–35.

19. *The Gallup Poll: Public Opinion*, 1:252–253.

20. Carter quoted in "Candidates Tell Views on Deserters' Fate," *Army Times*, March 22, 1976, newspaper clipping, Records of the 1976 Campaign Committee to Elect Jimmy Carter, Noel Sterrett's Domestic Clippings Files, Box 127, JCL.

21. Carter quotes in L. Amber Roessner and Lindsey M. Bier, "Pardon Me, Mr. Carter: Amnesty and Unfinished Business of Vietnam in Jimmy Carter's 1976," Campaign," *Journalism History* 43 (Summer 2017): 90.

22. For background on the legal and criminological aspects of Carter's pardon policy, see David Shichor and Donald R. Ranish, "President Carter's Vietnam Amnesty: An Analysis of a Public Policy Decision," *Presidential Studies Quarterly* 10 (Summer 1980): 443–450.

23. Memorandum, Bill Strauss to Peter Bourne, "Our Discussion about What a Good Position on Amnesty Might Be," February 17, 1976, Records of the 1976 Campaign Committee to Elect Jimmy Carter, Noel Sterrett's Domestic Clippings Files, Box 127, JCL. For background on the Vietnam Offender Study, see Lawrence M. Baskir and William A. Strauss, *Reconciliation after Vietnam: A Program of Relief for Vietnam Era Draft and Military Offenders* (Notre Dame, IN: University of Notre Dame Press, 1977).

24. Rosenbaum, "Carter's Position on Issues Designed for Wide Appeal."

25. Martin Schram, *Running for President 1976: The Carter Campaign* (New York: Stein & Day, 1977), 82.

26. Rowland Evans and Robert Novak, "Carter's Campaign: The McGovern Factor," *Washington Post*, March 16, 1976, 19; Dewar, "Jimmy Carter's Broad Rhetoric."

27. E. Stanly Godbold Jr., *Jimmy and Rosalynn Carter: The Georgia Years, 1924–1974* (New York: Oxford University Press, 2010), 232.

28. Statement, Governor Jimmy Carter [to] Democratic Platform Committee, June 9, 1972, RG 0001-01-045, Box 13, GA. For the text of the plank, see 1972 Democratic Party Platform, https://www.presidency.ucsb.edu/documents/1972-democratic-party-platform.

29. Candidate quotes are from "Candidates Tell Views on Deserters' Fate," *Army Times*, March 22, 1976, newspaper clipping, Records of the 1976 Campaign Committee to Elect Jimmy Carter, Noel Sterrett's Domestic Clippings Files, Box 127, JCL. For the core of the party's liberal agenda, see Daniel K. Williams, *The Election of the*

Evangelical: Jimmy Carter, Gerald Ford and the Presidential Contest of 1976 (Lawrence: University Press of Kansas, 2020), 6–8, 14, 199–207.

30. "Jimmy Carter: The Candidate on the Issues: An Interview."

31. Steven Brill, "Jimmy Carter's Pathetic Lies: The Heroic Image Is Made of Brass," *Harper's*, March 1976, 77.

32. The Nevada events are covered in Charles Mohr, "Calley and Vietnam War," *New York Times*, May 21, 1, 16. For a summary of the April 2, 1971, events in Columbus, Georgia, see "2,500 Hear Wallace at Calley Rally," *Atlanta Constitution*, April 3, 1971, 1, 11. For his Carter quotations Mohr relied on Duane Riner, "Carter Decrees Day of Tribute," *Atlanta Constitution*, April 2, 1971, 1, 24.

33. Mohr, "Calley and Vietnam War." For his Carter quotations Mohr relied on Duane Riner, "Carter Decrees Day of Tribute," *Atlanta Constitution*, April 2, 1971, 1, 24.

34. Mohr, "Calley and Vietnam War."

35. James Reston, "On Carter's Amnesty and Pardon Views," *New York Times*, October 2, 1976, 25.

36. Mohr, "Calley and Vietnam War."

37. Memorandum, "Vietnam Veterans Need Campaign Attention" [n.d.], Box 71, MCP, JCL.

38. Williams, *The Election of the Evangelical*, 222–228.

39. "The Democratic Platform," *Washington Post*, June 20, 1976, 38. See also David E. Rosenbaum, "Democrats Adopt a Platform Aimed at Unity Farty," *New York Times*, June 16, 1976, 1, 19.

40. Rosenbaum, "Democrats Adopt a Platform Aimed at Unity Farty."

41. John Robert Greene, *The Presidency of Gerald Ford* (Lawrence: University Press of Kansas, 1994), 37–39.

42. "Proclamation 4313, Announcing a Program for the Return of Vietnam Era Draft Evaders and Military Deserters," September 16, 1974, *PPPUS, Gerald Ford, 1974*, 138–140.

43. Kalman, *Right Star Rising*, 18; George C. Wilson, "Minority Hits Clemency Panel Actions," *Washington Post*, September 19, 1975, 1, 9; Greene, *The Presidency of Gerald Ford*, 42.

44. "Candidates View Veterans' Issues," *American Legion Magazine*, October 1976, 8.

45. Rosenbaum, "Democrats Adopt a Platform Aimed at Unity Party." For Carter's proposed platform, see "A New Beginning: Presentation by Jimmy Carter to the Platform Committee of the Democratic Party," June 16, 1976, Records of the 1976 Campaign Committee to Elect Jimmy Carter, Noel Sterrett Subject File, Box 70, JCL.

46. "1976 Democratic Party Platform," https://www.presidency.ucsb.edu/documents/1976-democratic-party-platform.

47. Richard Reeves, *Convention* (New York: Harcourt Brace Jovanovich, 1977), 147, 156.

48. Stan Hinden, "New Sight at Democratic Convention: Delegates from Americans Abroad," *Washington Post*, July 15, 1976, 22.

49. Reeves, *Convention*, 82–83, 119–120, 146–147, 162.

50. "Nominating Speech for Fritz Efaw by Louise Ransom," in Dorothy Vredenburgh Bush, *The Official Proceedings of the Democratic National Convention, New York City, July 1976* (Washington, DC: Democratic National Convention, 1976), 378–379.

51. "Nominating Speech for Fritz Efaw in Support of His Own Nomination," Bush, *The Official Proceedings of the Democratic National Convention*, 380–381.

52. Reeves, *Convention*, 120, 201–202.

53. Austin Scott and Peter Milius, "Carter's Forces Move to Smooth Convention Path," *Washington Post*, July 14, 1976, 1.

54. "Address of Jimmy Carter, in Acceptance of the Presidential Nomination of the Democratic Party," Bush, *The Official Proceedings of the Democratic National Convention*, 401–406.

55. Jimmy Carter, "Patriotism and National Security," *The Presidential Campaign 1976* (Washington, DC: Government Printing Office, 1977), vol. 1, pt. 1, 510–516.

56. Carter, "Patriotism and National Security," 517.

57. James T. Wooten, "Legionnaires Boo Carter and Pardon for Draft Defiers," *Washington Post*, August 25, 1976, 1, 18.

58. Dole quoted in Douglas E. Kneeland, "Dole Attacks Carter on Pardon for Draft Evaders," *New York Times*, August 26, 1976, 22.

59. Williams, *The Election of the Evangelical*, 301.

60. Presidential Campaign Debate, September 23, 1976, https://www.presidency.ucsb.edu/documents/presidential-campaign-debate-1.

61. Presidential Campaign Debate, September 23, 1976, https://www.presidency.ucsb.edu/documents/presidential-campaign-debate-1.

62. "1976 Democratic Party Platform," https://www.presidency.ucsb.edu/documents/1976-democratic-party-platform.

63. "Statement of Senator Vance Hartke, Chairman, Senate Committee on Veteran's Affairs Before the Committee on Resolutions and Platform, Democratic National Convention," May 20, 1976, Box 71, MCP, JCL. "A New Beginning: Presentation by Jimmy Carter to the Platform Committee of the Democratic Party," June 16, 1976, Box 70, Records of the 1976 Campaign Committee to Elect Jimmy Carter, Noel Sterrett Subject File, JCL.

64. Memorandum, "Vietnam Veterans Need Campaign Attention" [n.d.], Box 71, MCP, JCL.

65. James H. Webb, "The Invisible Vietnam Veteran," *Washington Post*, August 4, 1976, 11.

66. Memorandum, "Vietnam Veterans Need Campaign Attention."

67. Memorandum, "Vietnam Veterans Need Campaign Attention." For background on the Ford veto see Mark Boulton, *Failing Our Veterans: The G.I. Bill and the Vietnam Generation*. New York: New York University Press, 2014, 180–198.

68. Quotes from "For Ronald W. Drach, National Director of Employment Disabled American Veterans," October 15, 1976. See also Press Release, "Jimmy Carter's Statement on Veterans Employment, October 14, 1976, both in Box 71, MCP, JCL. For polling data, see "President Gains in the Polls," October 19, 1976, newsletter, Box F13, President Ford Committee Records, GFL.

69. "Carter Would Put Viet Vets in Key VA Posts," *Waco Tribune-Herald*, October 25, 1976, newspaper clipping, Box 71, MCP, JCL.

70. "Candidates View Veterans' Issues," *American Legion Magazine*, October 1976, 8–9. For Ford's perspective on the GI Bill, see Boulton, *Failing Our Veterans*, 198.

71. For background and context on the Playboy interview, see Williams, *The Election of the Evangelical*, 291–299.

72. "Playboy Interview," *The Presidential Campaign 1976*, vol. 1, pt. 2, 939–964.

73. "Playboy Interview," *The Presidential Campaign 1976*, vol. 1, pt. 2, 948–952.

74. Playboy Interview," *The Presidential Campaign 1976*, vol. 1, pt. 2, 949.

75. Jack Carter Oral History Interview, June 25, 2003, pp. 10–11, Carter Library Oral History Project, JCL.

76. Williams, *The Election of the Evangelical*, 333–346.

77. *The Gallup Poll, Public Opinion 1972–1977*, 2: 911.

CHAPTER 3. THE VIETNAM AGENDA

1. Robert Shogan, *Promises to Keep: Carter's First 100 Days* (Springfield, OH: Crowell, 1977), 117–119.

2. Mercer Cross, "Carter Aide Lists Domestic Priorities," *Congressional Quarterly Weekly Report*, January 15, 1977, 85–86.

3. Burton I. Kaufman and Scott Kaufman, *The Presidency of James Earl Carter, Jr.* (Lawrence: University Press of Kansas, 2006), 33.

4. Lee Lescaze, "President Pardons Viet Draft Evaders: Total Unknown; Plan Excludes All Deserters," *Washington Post*, January 22, 1977, 1, 4.

5. "Presidential Proclamation of Pardon," January 21, 1977, *PPPUS, Jimmy Carter, 1977*, pt. 1, 5; "Executive Order Relating to Proclamation of Pardon," January 21, 1977, *PPPUS, Jimmy Carter, 1977*, pt. 1, 6.

6. "Jimmy Carter: The Candidate on the Issues: An Interview," *Washington Post*, March 21, 1976, B5.

7. Press Release, "Presidential Pardon," February [sic?] 20, 1977, Box 1, White House Press Office—Media Liaison Office, Background Report Mass Mailings File, JCL.

8. "The Vietnam Pardon," *Washington Post*, January 24, 1977, 22.

9. Quoted in Peter G. Bourne, *Jimmy Carter: A Comprehensive Biography from Plains to the Post-Presidency* (New York: Scribner, 1997), 366.

10. Shogun, *Promises to Keep*, 120.

11. Austin Scott, "Reaction to the Pardon Runs Gamut from Joy to Outrage," *Washington Post*, January 22, 1977, 5.

12. Lee Lescaze, "Draft Pardon Foes Fail to Obtain Senate Vote," *Washington*

Post, January 25, 1977, 4; "House Bars Use of New Appropriation in Carter's Vietnam Pardon Program," *Washington Post*, March 17, 1977, 7; *Congress and the Nation: 1977–1980* (Washington, DC Government Printing Office, 1980), 181.

13. Jeff Sallot, "Deserters Call Carter Plan Too Little, Too Late, and a Sham," *Washington Post*, February 1, 1977, 18.

14. Quote from Sallot, "Deserters Call Carter Plan Too Little, Too Late, and a Sham." Exile numbers from Charles Mohr, "Mr. Carter Spoke Softly, Effectively on Discharges," *New York Times*, April 3, 1977, E4.

15. Susan Fraker, Jon Lowell, Eleanor Clift, and Mary Lord, "After the Pardon," *Newsweek*, January 31, 1977, 28–29; Martin Schram, "Pardon Granted, Promise Kept," *Newsday*, news Paralyzed Veterans of American (PVA) clipping, Box 39, Records of the White House Office of Counsel to the President, Robert J. Lipshutz's Files, JCL.

16. "The Vietnam Pardon," *Washington Post*, January 24, 1977, 22.

17. "Ask President Carter," March 5, 1977, *PPPUS, Jimmy Carter, 1977*, pt. 1, 299–300.

18. W. Carl Bevin, *Jimmy Carter's Economy: Policy in an Age of Limits* (Chapel Hill: University of North Carolina Press, 2014), 69, 83–85.

19. "Economic Recovery Program: Message to Congress," January 31, 1977, *PPPUS, Jimmy Carter, 1977*, pt. 1, 47–55.

20. Department of Labor, "Jobs for Vietnam Vets," January 28, 1977, press release, Box 29, White House Press Office—Media Liaison Office, Eleanor Weaver Subject Files, JCL; Memorandum, Media Liaison Office to Editors, News Directors, "Employment for Vietnam-Era Veterans," February 22, 1977, Box 29, White House Press Office, Media Liaison Office, Eleanor Weaver Subject Files, JCL. For background on CETA, see Donald C. Baumer and Carl E. Van Horn, *The Politics of Unemployment* (Washington, DC: Congressional Quarterly, 1985), 59–72.

21. Department of Labor, "Jobs for Vietnam Vets," January 28, 1977, press release, Box 29, White House Press Office—Media Liaison Office, Eleanor Weaver Subject Files, JCL.

22. Memorandum, Stuart Eizenstat to Jimmy Carter through Rick Hutcheson and Jody Powell, "Vietnam Veterans Jobs Program," January 21, 1977, Box 39, Records of Robert Lipshutz, JCL.

23. Mary Rose Oakar to the President, January 21, 1977, Box VA-1, White House Central Files—Veteran Affairs, JCL.

24. Sam Nunn and Henry M. Jackson to the President, January 21, 1977, Box VA-1, White House Central Files—Veteran Affairs, JCL.

25. For a non-pardon-related discussion of the Vietnam veteran jobs program during the presidential transitional phase, see Memorandum, "A Suggested Carter Administration Agenda," [n.d.], Box 55, Records of Ellen Goldstein, JCL.

26. "Economic Recovery Program: Message to Congress," January 31, 1977, *PPPUS, Jimmy Carter 1977*, pt. 1, 52–53.

27. See, for examples, "The Restraints of Carter's Economic Policy," *Business*

Week, January 24, 1977, 62–66; Allan J. Mayer and Richard Thomas, "A Boast, but a Moderate One," *Newsweek*, January 17, 1977, 59–60.

28. James R. Dickenson, "Carter Seeks 200,000 Jobs for Veterans," *Washington Star*, January 27, 1977, 1.

29. Mary McGrory, "A Glimmer of Light for Vietnam Vets," *Washington Star*, January 31, 1977, newspaper clipping, Box 29, White House Press Office—Media Liaison Office, Eleanor Weaver Subject Files, JCL.

30. Quote from "Ask President Carter," March 5, 1977, *PPPUS, Jimmy Carter 1977*, pt. 1, 300. See also "Administrator of Veterans Affairs: Nomination of Max Cleland," February 18, 1977, *PPPUS, Jimmy Carter 1977*, pt. 1, 192–193.

31. Max Cleland, *Heart of a Patriot: How I Found the Courage to Survive Vietnam, Walter Reed, and Karl Rove* (New York: Simon & Schuster, 2009), 128; Bourne, *Jimmy Carter*, 341.

32. Quotes from "For Ronald W. Drach, National Director of Employment Disabled American Veterans," October 15, 1976, Box 71, MCP, JCL. See also "Candidates View Veterans' Issues," *American Legion Magazine*, October 1976, 8–9.

33. *Hearing Before the Committee on Veterans' Affairs: The Nomination of Joseph Maxwell Cleland to be Administrator of Veterans' Affairs*, Ninety-Fifth Congress, First Session (Washington, DC: Government Printing Office, 1977), 1–27.

34. Garry Clifford, "Near Death on a Vietnam Battlefield, Max Cleland Comes Back to Take Over the V.A.," *People*, March 28, 1977, 26–28.

35. *Arkansas Gazette*, April 23, 1977, newspaper summary; *Miami News*, April 4, 1977, newspaper summary; *Tampa Tribune-Times*, February 20, 1977, newspaper summary; *Johnson City Press-Chronicle*, March 19, 1977, newspaper summary; all in Box 27, MCP, JCL.

36. "Exclusive Interview with New V.A. Head," *Reveille*, March-April 1977, 6–7, 28–29.

37. "Cleland First at VA," *American Legion Magazine*, April 1977, 39.

38. Memorandum, Jon Steinberg, Michael Burns, Mack Fleming, Guy McMichael to Al Stern, "Issues Requiring Decision in the VA in the First Six Months," December 15, 1976, Box 71, MCP, JCL

39. "Candidates View Veterans' Issues, *American Legion Magazine*, October 1976, 8.

40. Lawrence M. Baskir and William A. Strauss, *Reconciliation after Vietnam: A Program of Relief for Vietnam Era Draft and Military Offenders* (Notre Dame, IN: University of Notre Dame Press, 1977), 229–230.

41. Quotes from June A. Willenz, "A New Deal for Vietnam Veterans," February 27, 1977, *Washington Post*, 40. See also Peter Slavin, "The Stigmas of Discharge," April 18, 1976, *Washington Post*, 25; Mary McGrory, "A Glimmer of Light for Vietnam Veterans," newspaper clipping, Box 29, White House Press Office—Media Liaison Office, Eleanor Weaver Subject Files, JCL; John Robert Greene, *The Presidency of Gerald Ford* (Lawrence: University Press of Kansas, 1994), 37–39.

42. Memorandum, Charles Kirbo to Governor Carter, "Discharges" [no date], Box 230, Staff Offices—Presidential Transition Files, JCL.

43. Memorandum, Stu Eizenstat and Frank Raines to Robert Lipshutz, "Proposal to Review Administrative Discharges during the Vietnam Era," March 16, 1977, Box 39, Records of the White House Office of Counsel to the President, Robert J. Lipshutz Files, JCL.

44. Memorandum, Stu Eizenstat and Frank Raines to Robert Lipshutz, "Proposal to Review Administrative Discharges during the Vietnam Era," March 16, 1977, Box 39, Records of the White House Office of Counsel to the President, Robert J. Lipshutz Files, JCL. For examples of the studies, see Lawrence M. Baskir and William A. Strauss, "Vietnam: A Legacy of 'Bad Discharges,'" *Washington Post*, April 11, 1977, 21; Baskir and Strauss, *Reconciliation after Vietnam*.

45. Memorandum, Griffin B. Bell to Mr. Lipshutz, "Discharge Review Program," March 25, 1977, Box 39, Records of the White House Office of Counsel to the President, Robert J. Lipshutz Files, JCL.

46. George C. Wilson, "Carter Authorizes Upgrading Many Viet Discharges," *Washington Post*, March 29, 1977, 1; Charles Mohr, "Most Deserters of Vietnam Years Eligible for Improved Discharges," *New York Times*, April 2, 1977, 1, 12.

47. Quote from Wilson, "Carter Authorizes Upgrading Many Viet Discharges." See also Charles Mohr, "Mr. Carter Spoke Softly, Effectively on Discharges," *New York Times*, April 3, 1977, E4.

48. Lynn quoted in Wilson, "Carter Authorizes Upgrading Many Viet Discharges."

49. "Those Who Served (Cont.)," *Washington Post*, April 11, 1977, 20.

50. "On Discharging a Vietnam Duty," *New York Times*, April 5, 1977, 32.

51. Mohr, "Most Deserters of Vietnam Years Eligible for Improved Discharges"; Mohr, "Mr. Carter Spoke Softly, Effectively on Discharges."

52. Jack Anderson, "The Other Military Offenders: Will Carter Extend the Pardon," *Washington Post*, February 13, 1977, 35.

53. Jack Carter Oral History Interview, June 25, 2003, p. 15, Carter Library Oral History Project, JCL, https://www.jimmycarterlibrary.gov/assets/documents/oral_histories/project/jackcarter.pdf.

54. "Jack Carter Declines Offer," *Washington Post*, April 7, 1977, 12.

55. Alan Cranston to Jimmy Carter, March 2, 1977, Records of the Domestic Policy Staff, Ellen Goldstein Subject Files, Box 45, JCL.

56. Lee Lescaze, "Skirmish on Veterans' Benefits to Begin," *Washington Post*, June 12, 1977, 6.

57. William Greider, "Promises of Jobs Go Unfilled, Veterans Assert," *Washington Post*, April 28, 1977, 1.

58. Greider, "Promises of Jobs Go Unfilled, Veterans Assert."

59. Memorandum, Stu Eizenstat and Bob Ginsburg to the President, "Secretary Marshall's Recommendation to Launch the HIRE PROGRAM with a White House Conference," February 8, 1977, Box VA-1, White House Central Files—Veterans Affairs, JCL.

60. Memorandum, Stuart Eizenstat to the President, "First 100 Days," April 26, 1977, Box 17, White House Press Office—Media Liaison Office, Eleanor Weaver Subject Files, JCL.

61. "Conference on HIRE," June 14, 1977, *PPPUS, Jimmy Carter 1977*, pt. 1, 1115–1117.

62. Second Annual Report, National Alliance of Businessmen, 2, Box 069, Lugar Collection, Institute for Civic Leadership and Digital Mayoral Archives, University of Indianapolis, https://uindy.historyit.com/item.php?id=353505.

63. G. William Miller to President Carter, January 16, 1978, Box VA-3, White House Central Files—Veterans Affairs, JCL.

64. Memorandum, Larry Bailey to Bob Linder, "Incoming Mail for the President's Committee on HIRE, July 6, 1977; "HIRE Monthly Report," July 15, 1977; "HIRE Monthly Report," August 15, 1977; all in Box VA-1, White House Central Files—Veterans Affairs, JCL.

65. Wayne King, "Jobs Plan for Vietnam Veterans Gets a Slow Start," *New York Times*, August 11, 1977, B6.

66. "Those Who Served (Cont.)," *Washington Post*, May 30, 1977, 12.

67. Memorandum, Max Cleland to Jimmy Carter, May 31, 1977, Box 31, MCP, JCL.

68. Memorandum, Rick Hutcheson to Max Cleland, June 4, 1977, Box 44, Records of the Domestic Policy Staff, Ellen Goldstein Subject Files, JCL.

69. *Congressional Record—House*, June 15, 1977, 19077–19080.

70. *Congressional Record—House*, June 15, 1977, 19079–19080.

71. Mary Russell, "Taking 'Joy Rides' on the Floor," *Washington Post*, June 16, 1977, 1.

72. "Bad Paper Discharges (Con't)," *Washington Post*, June 14, 1977, 18.

73. Lee Lescaze, "Upgrading Vietnam Discharges Chills '40s Vets in House," *Washington Post*, June 21, 1977, 6.

74. Quotes from Alan Cranston to Clifford Alexander, June 14, 1977, Box 45, Records of the Domestic Policy Staff, Ellen Goldstein Subject Files, JCL. See also *Congressional Quarterly Almanac*, 1977, 384–386.

75. *Congressional Quarterly Almanac*, 1977, 386–387.

76. Memorandum, Margaret McKenna to Bob Lipshutz, "Cranston-Thurmond Legislation," [n.d], Box 39, Records of the White House Office of Counsel to the President, Robert Lipshutz Subject Files, JCL.

77. Memorandum, Stu Eizenstat to the President, October 6, 1977, "Enrolled Bill S. 1307 Veterans Discharge Amendments," Box 45, Records of the Domestic Policy Staff, Ellen Goldstein Subject Files, JCL.

78. Memorandum, Stu Eizenstat to the President, October 6, 1977, "Enrolled Bill S. 1307 Veterans Discharge Amendments," Box 45, Records of the Domestic Policy Staff, Ellen Goldstein Subject Files, JCL.

79. Memorandum, Stu Eizenstat to the President, October 6, 1977, "Enrolled Bill S. 1307 Veterans Discharge Amendments," Box 45, Records of the Domestic Policy Staff, Ellen Goldstein Subject Files, JCL.

80. "Veterans Benefits," October 8, 1977, *PPPUS, Jimmy Carter*, pt. 1, 1757–1758.

81. "A Setback for Ex-Servicemen," *Washington Post*, October 11, 1977, 18.

82. Mary McGrory, "Hawks Cut the Heart out of 'Compassion,'" *Washington Star*, October 17, 1977, newspaper clipping, Box 71, White House Press Office—News Summary Office, Janet McMahon's Newspaper Columnists Files, JCL.

83. Mary McGrory, "Congress Ambushes Discharge Review," *Baltimore Sun*, October 1, 1977, newspaper clipping, Box 71, White House Press Office—News Summary Office, Janet McMahon's Newspaper Columnists Files, JCL.

84. "Veterans Day," October 24, 1977, *PPPUS, Jimmy Carter*, pt. 1, 1900–1902.

85. "'A Special Debt,'" *Washington Post*, October 30, 1977, 82.

86. *Congress and the Nation, 1977–1980* (Washington, DC: Congressional Quarterly Press, 1981), 179.

87. *Congress and the Nation, 1977–1980*, 179–180.

88. Memorandum, Stu Eizenstat and Frank Raines to the President, November 22, 1977, "Enrolled Bill H.R. 8701 G.I. Bill Improvement Act," Box 45, Records of the Domestic Policy Staff, Ellen Goldstein Subject Files, JCL.

89. "GI Bill Improvement Act of 1977," November, 23 1977, *PPPUS, Jimmy Carter*, pt. 1, 2048–2049.

90. "Vietnam Veterans and the GI Bill, *Washington Post*, July 19, 1977, 16; Colman McCarthy, "Vietnam Veterans: Who Listens to Them in Washington?" *Washington Post*, September 27, 1977, 19.

91. Colman McCarthy, "The Continuing Neglect of Our Newest Veterans," *Washington Post*, October 24, 1977, 19.

92. McCarthy, "The Continuing Neglect of Our Newest Veterans."

93. Kaufman and Kaufman, *The Presidency of James Earl Carter, Jr.*, 63, 83.

94. David S. Broder, "'Serious Concerns' about the Carter Presidency," *Washington Post*, October 23, 1977, C7.

95. Frank Greve, "A Legacy of 'Lost' Veterans," *Washington Post*, November 18, 1977, 19.

96. "The Class That Went to War," *Washington Post*, December 2, 1977, 16.

97. Margaret Shannon, "Max Cleland: New Image at the VA," *Atlanta Journal and Constitution Magazine*, April 30, 1978, 14.

CHAPTER 4. BATTLING EXPECTATIONS

1. Kenneth Crawford, "Can Carter's Presidency Be Redeemed?," *Washington Post*, May 16, 1978, 13.

2. "The Year's First Lessons," *Washington Post*, January 13, 1978, 12.

3. "The State of Mr. Carter's Country," *New York Times*, January 22, 1978, E18.

4. "The State of the Union," January 19, 1978, *PPPUS, Jimmy Carter, 1978*, pt. 1, 90–98.

5. "A Theory of Limited Government," *Washington Post*, January 21, 1978, 16.

6. Barry M. Hager, "Carter's State of the Union Stresses Government Limits, Need to Act on Problems," *Congressional Quarterly Weekly Review*, January 21, 1978, 99–100, 141.

7. "Congress Returns to Face Energy, Canal, Korea, Other Tough Election-Year Issues," *Congressional Quarterly Weekly Review*, January 14, 1978, 43–52.

8. "HIRE Report," January 16, 1978, Box VA-3, White House Central Files—Veterans Affairs, JCL.

9. G. William Miller to President Carter, February 15, 1978, Box VA-3, White House Central Files—Veterans Affairs, JCL.

10. Jack H. Watson, Jr. to G. William Miller, January 31, 1978, Box VA-3, White House Central Files—Veterans Affairs, JCL.

11. Memorandum, Jack H. Watson to Tim Kraft and Fran Voorde, "Request for Meeting with the President by Bill Miller and Ruben Mettler," March 10, 1978, Box VA-3, White House Central Files—Veterans Affairs, JCL.

12. "Veterans' Unemployment," *Washington Post*, March 6, 1978, 18.

13. Ray Marshall to the President, March 8, 1978, Box VA-3, White House Central Files—Veterans Affairs, JCL.

14. Ray Marshall to Philip L. Geyelin, March 9, 1978, Box VA-3, White House Central Files—Veterans Affairs, JCL.

15. Ray Marshall, "HIRE *Is* Helping the Jobless Vietnam Vet, *Washington Post*, March 25, 1978, 11.

16. "HIRE, Promises and Jobs," *Washington Post*, March 25, 1978, 10.

17. Donia Mills, "Vietnam Vets: Is Help Coming 10 Years Too Late?," *Washington Star*, March 26, 1978, 1, 3. For information on the presidential transition lobbying contact, see Stuart F. Feldman to Gail Harrison, December 16, 1976, Box 75, MCP, JCL.

18. Warren Brown, "Range of Intangibles Said Hurting Viet Vets the Most," *Washington Post*, May 29, 1978, 9; "First Year a Busy One for VA Chief," *Clearwater Sun*, April 6, 1978, and Jerry T. Baulch, "VA Focuses on Task of Aiding 'Hard-Core' Vets," *Tampa Times* [n.d.], both newspaper clippings in Box 31, MCP, JCL.

19. "Are Vietnam Veterans Getting a Raw Deal?," *U.S. News & World Report*, May 29, 1978, 39–40.

20. "Are Vietnam Veterans Getting a Raw Deal?," *U.S. News & World Report*. The term "hard core" was used commonly; see "V.A. Target: Vietnam 'Hard-Core' Who Can't Readjust," *New York Times*, March 30, 1978, 13.

21. Robert H. Charles to President Carter, March 15, 1978; "HIRE Progress Summary," March 28, 1978, both in Box VA-3, White House Central Files—Veterans Affairs, JCL.

22. "HIRE Report," May 1, 1978, Box VA-3, White House Central Files—Veterans Affairs, JCL.

23. Olin Teague to President Jimmy Carter, February 24, 1978; Olin Teague to President Jimmy Carter April 24, 1978; Gregory J. Ahart to John Conyers, March 9, 1978; all in Box VA-3, White House Central Files—Veterans Affairs, JCL.

24. "109 Polled Congressmen Upbraid U.S. on Veterans," *New York Times*, May 29, 1978, 9.

25. Colman McCarthy, "Vietnam Vets: Does Congress Finally Understand?," *Washington Post*, May 29, 1978, 21.

26. Statement of Charles P. Collins III Before the Subcommittee on Employment and Training of the Committee on Veteran Affairs, US House of Representatives, May 3, 1978, Box VA-3, White House Central Files—Veterans Affairs, JCL.

27. Statement of Charles P. Collins III Before the Subcommittee on Employment and Training of the Committee on Veteran Affairs, US House of Representatives, May 3, 1978, Box VA-3, White House Central Files—Veterans Affairs, JCL.

28. Memorandum, Ray Marshall to the President, "May 29 Jack Anderson Column on Administration's Veterans' Programs, June 6, 1978, Box VA-3, White House Central Files—Veterans Affairs, JCL.

29. Jack Anderson, "Carter, and U.S., Forget Vietnam Vets," *Washington Post*, May 29, 1978, D12.

30. Memorandum, Ray Marshall to the President, "May 29 Jack Anderson Column on Administration's Veterans' Programs, June 6, 1978, Box VA-3, White House Central Files—Veterans Affairs, JCL.

31. Anderson, "Carter, and U.S., Forget Vietnam Vets"; Jack Anderson, "Veterans Job Statistics Disputed," *Washington Post*, July 3, 1978, D10.

32. Anderson, "Veterans Job Statistics Disputed."

33. Memorandum, Ray Marshall to the President, "May 29 Jack Anderson Column on Administration's Veterans' Programs, June 6, 1978, Box VA-3, White House Central Files—Veterans Affairs, JCL.

34. Anderson, "Veterans Job Statistics Disputed."

35. Rueben F. Mettler to the President, November 10, 1978; Memorandum, Ray Marshall to the President, "May 29 Jack Anderson Column on Administration's Veterans' Programs, June 6, 1978, both in Box VA-3, White House Central Files—Veterans Affairs, JCL. See also Edward D. Berkowitz, *Something Happened: A Political and Cultural Overview of the Seventies* (New York: Columbia University Press, 2006), 124–125.

36. "The State of the Union: Annual Message to the Congress," January 19, 1978, *PPPUS, Jimmy Carter, 1978*, pt. 1, 107.

37. Memorandum, Frank Raines to Stu Eizenstat, "PRM Study on the Status of Vietnam Veterans," January 20, 1978, Box VA-2, White House Central Files—Veterans Affairs, JCL.

38. David S. Broder, "New Process for Domestic Issues," *Washington Post*, February 12, 1978, 14.

39. Memorandum, Stu Eizenstat to the Secretary of Defense, the Attorney General, the Secretary of Labor, the Secretary of Health, Education, and Welfare, the Director of OMB, the Administrator of the VA, the Administrator of the Community Services Administration, the Assistant to the President for Public Liaison, "Draft Issue Definition-Memorandum on the Status of Vietnam-era Veterans," January 20, 1978, Box VA-2, White House Central Files—Veterans Affairs, JCL.

40. Memorandum, Stu Eizenstat to the President, "Vietnam Veteran PRM Study," March 17, 1978, Box 142, Records of the White House Office of Counsel to the President, Margaret McKenna Files, JCL.

41. Memorandum, Bill Spring to Bert Carp, "VEV PRM," June 30, 1978, Box 45, Kitty Higgins and William Spring Subject Files, Records of the Domestic Policy Staff, JCL.

42. Memorandum, Stu Eizenstat to the President, "Vietnam-Era Veterans PRM," July 31, 1978, Box VA-3, White House Central Files-Veterans Affairs, JCL.

43. Bernard Weinraub, "Congressman Hopes to Get a Break for Vietnam Veterans," *Washington Star*, August 8, 1978, newspaper clipping, Box 55, Ellen Goldstein Subject Files, Records of the Domestic Policy Staff, JCL.

44. "Vietnam Veterans in Congress," *Washington Post*, May 8, 1978, 22.

45. Memorandum, Bill Spring, Ellen Goldstein, Kitty Higgins to Jerry Rafshoon and Greg Schneiders, "Public Presentation of Vietnam Veteran PRM," August 8, 1978, Box VA-3, White House Central Files—Veterans Affairs, JCL.

46. Fred Barbash, "Vietnam Veterans a Neglected Cause, Carter Told," *Washington Post*, August 2, 1978, 3.

47. Memorandum, Bill Spring, Ellen Goldstein, Kitty Higgins to Jerry Rafshoon and Greg Schneiders, "Public Presentation of Vietnam Veteran PRM," August 8, 1978, Box VA-3, White House Central Files—Veterans Affairs, JCL.

48. Burton I. Kaufman and Scott Kaufman, *The Presidency of James Earl Carter, Jr.* (Lawrence: University Press of Kansas, 2006), 128, 101, 126.

49. Memorandum, Jerry Rafshoon to the President, "Vietnam Era Veterans PRM Announcement," September 1, 1978, Box 7, Records of the Office of the Assistant to the President for Communication, Gerald Rafshoon Subject Files, JCL.

50. Mills, "Vietnam Vets: Is Help Coming 10 Years Too Late?"

51. Robert Muller, "Letters to the Editor," *Washington Post*, August 20, 1978, C6; "Giving Vietnam Veterans a Break," *Washington Post*, August 11, 1978, 14.

52. Stuart F. Feldman, "Our Failure to Discuss Vietnam," *Washington Post*, July 27, 1978, 27.

53. "The Unbearable Colman McCarthy," *Washingtonian*, November 1977, 70; McCarthy, "An Advocate for Vietnam Veterans," 15.

54. Memorandum, Jerry Rafshoon to the President, "Vietnam Era Veterans PRM Announcement," September 1, 1978, Box 7, Records of the Office of the Assistant to the President for Communication, Gerald Rafshoon Subject Files, JCL.

55. See handwritten note on Memorandum, Stu Eizenstat to the President, "Vietnam Veterans PRM," September 1, 1978; Box 7, Records of the Office of the Assistant to the President for Communication, Gerald Rafshoon Subject Files, JCL.

56. Stu Eizenstat to Mr. President, September 12, 1978, Box 7, Records of the Office of the Assistant to the President for Communication, Gerald Rafshoon Subject Files, JCL.

57. See handwritten note on Memorandum, Stu Eizenstat to the President, "Vietnam Veterans PRM," September 1, 1978, Box 7, Records of the Office of the Assistant to the President for Communication, Gerald Rafshoon Subject Files, JCL.

58. Spencer Rich, "Carter Urges $250 Million Veterans Aid," *Washington Post*, October 11, 1978, 2.

59. "Vietnam Era Veterans: Message to the Congress," October 10, 1978, *PPPUS, Jimmy Carter, 1978*, pt. 2, 1737–1742.

60. Muller quoted in Rich, "Carter Urges $250 Million Veterans Aid."

61. Muller quoted in "President Outlines Proposals for Helping Vietnam Veterans, *Atlanta Journal*, October 11, 1978, 6.

62. Muller quoted in Mary McGrory, "Carter's Dealings with Vietnam Veterans Still at Arm's Length," *Washington Star*, October 13, 1978, 4.

63. Colman McCarthy, "Carter's 'Concern' for Vietnam Veterans," *Washington Post*, October 19, 1978, 19.

64. McGrory, "Carter's Dealings with Vietnam Veterans Still at Arm's Length."

65. Rich, "Carter Urges $250 Million Veterans Aid."

66. McCarthy, "Carter's 'Concern' for Vietnam Veterans," 19.

67. McGrory, "Carter's Dealings with Vietnam Veterans Still at Arm's Length."

68. "Veterans Day," November 11, 1978, *PPPUS, Jimmy Carter, 1978*, pt. 2, 2012–2014.

69. On the Carter-Cleland encounter, see Stephanie Mansfield, "Veterans Day: 'Ignored' Men of Vietnam Owed a Debt, Carter Says," *Washington Post*, November 12, 1978, C1, C4.

70. Roger Stahl, "Why We 'Support the Troops': Rhetorical Evolutions," *Rhetoric and Public Affairs* 12 (Winter 2009): 535, 548, 551.

71. Memorandum, Stu Eizenstat to the President, July 31, 1978, Box VA-3, White House Central Files—Veterans Affairs, JCL.

72. Edward Walsh and Susanna McBee, "Increase in Veterans Pensions, Called Inflationary, Signed," *Washington Post*, November 7, 1978, 7.

73. George F. Will, "Those Austerity Rumors," *Washington Post*, November 9, 1978, 19.

74. "A Veto for Veterans' Pensions," *Washington Post*, November 3, 1978, 22.

75. "PVA Calls for Veto of Pension Bill," *Stars and Stripes*, October 12, 1978.

76. Bernard Weinraub, "Vietnam G.I.: From Idealism to Bitterness," *New York Times*, November 15, 1978, 18.

77. Memorandum, Bert Carp and Ellen Goldstein to Pat Bario and Mike Chanin, "Media Distortions on Veterans Pension Legislation," November 14, 1978, Box VA-4, White House Central Files—Veterans Affairs, JCL. See also Background Report, Office of Media Liaison, "Veterans Pension Reform," December 27, 1978, Box VA-4, White House Central Files—Veterans Affairs, JCL.

78. Terrence Smith, "Rafshoon Resists the Label of Image Maker," *New York Times*, November 27, 1978, A1, B16.

79. Martin Schram, "Rafshoon Country: Where Policy Meets Image," *Washington Post*, November 26, 1978, C7.

80. Weinraub, "Vietnam G.I.: From Idealism to Bitterness."

81. Bernard Weinraub, "Angry Vietnam Veterans Charging Federal Policies Ignore Their Needs," *New York Times*, February 5, 1979, 15.

CHAPTER 5. LOSING CONTROL OF THE AGENDA

1. George Gallup, "Carter Rated Better Than Ford, Nixon, LBJ," *Washington Post*, January 18, 1979, 2.
2. Joseph Kraft, "'79: The Year of 'What Next?,'" *Washington Post*, January 2, 1979, 19.
3. "The State of the Union," January 23, 1979, *PPPUS, Jimmy Carter, 1979*, pt. 1, 103–109. For background on the adoption of the New Foundation theme, see Jonathan Alter, *His Very Best: Jimmy Carter, a Life* (New York: Simon & Schuster, 2020), 458–459.
4. Charles O. Jones, *The Trusteeship Presidency: Jimmy Carter and the United States Congress* (Baton Rouge: Louisiana State University Press, 1988), 173.
5. "The President's News Conference," January 26, 1979, *PPPUS, Jimmy Carter, 1979*, pt. 1, 172.
6. "Budget Message," January 22, 1979, *PPPUS, Jimmy Carter, 1979*, pt. 1, 96–101.
7. "The President's News Conference," January 17, 1979, *PPPUS, Jimmy Carter, 1979*, pt. 1, 50–58.
8. "Vietnam Veterans—Peace at Last?," *U.S. News & World Report*, January 29, 1979, 36–37.
9. Stuart F. Feldman to Gail Harrison c/o Senator Mondale, December 16, 1976, Box 75, MCP, JCL.
10. Memorandum, Stu Eizenstat to the President, July 31, 1978, Box VA-3, White House Central Files—Veterans Affairs, JCL.
11. Public Law 95–513.
12. Quotes from "Operational Plans: Vietnam Veterans Week," March 5, 1979, Records of the Domestic Policy Staff, Ellen Goldstein Subject Files, Box 58, JCL. See also Working Paper, "Veterans Service Organizations Meeting on Vietnam Veterans Week," February 20, 1979, Records of the Domestic Policy Staff, Ellen Goldstein Subject Files, Box 58, JCL.
13. William E. Lawson to Bill Spring, February 2, 1979, Box 45, Records of the Domestic Policy Staff, Ellen Goldstein Subject Files, JCL.
14. John M. Carey to James Earl Carter, January 30, 1979, Box 58, Records of the Domestic Policy Staff, Ellen Goldstein Subject Files, JCL.
15. Memorandum with handwritten comments, Ellen [Goldstein] to Rick [ ], [n.d.], Box 58, Records of the Domestic Policy Staff, Ellen Goldstein Subject Files, JCL.
16. Quotes from Bernard Weinraub, "Highly Decorated Veteran Ousted; U.S. Denies His Charge of a Purge," *New York Times*, January 25, 1979, 1, 16. See also Emily Yoffe, "Vietnam Veteran Disputed on Dismissal Charges," *Washington Post*, February 2, 1979, 3.
17. Memorandum, Bill Spring, Ellen Goldstein, Gene Eidenbrg to Stu Eizenstat, Jack Watson, Tim Kraft, March 14, 1979, Box 58, Records of the Domestic Policy Staff, Ellen Goldstein Subject Files, JCL.
18. Memorandum, Max Cleland to the President, "Participation in Vietnam

Veterans Week," March 15, 1979, Box 58, Records of the Domestic Policy Staff, Ellen Goldstein Subject Files, JCL.

19. Memorandum, Stu Eizenstat, Anne Wexler, Jack Watson, Tim Kraft to the President, "Vietnam Veterans Week" [n.d.], Box 58, Records of the Domestic Policy Staff, Ellen Goldstein Subject Files, JCL.

20. Wilbur J. Scott, *Vietnam Veterans since the War: The Politics of PTSD, Agent Orange, and the National Memorial* (Norman: University of Oklahoma Press, 2003), 86–87.

21. "Angry Vietnam Veterans form Group to Spur Jobs," *New York Times*, May 2, 1979, 25.

22. Ward Sinclair, "Vietnam Veterans Still Feel Chill from the White House," *Washington Post*, April 28, 1979, 2.

23. Sinclair, "Vietnam Veterans Still Feel Chill from the White House." For the quote on the PRM, see "Vietnam Veterans Week Resolution Passes House and Senate: Bonior," *Stars and Stripes*, October 19, 1978.

24. Memorandum, Bill Spring and Ellen Goldstein to Jody Powell, "Ward Sinclair Article on Vietnam Veterans," May 3, 1979, Box 55, Records of the Domestic Policy Staff, Ellen Goldstein Subject Files, JCL.

25. Memorandum, Bill Spring and Ellen Goldstein to Jody Powell, "Ward Sinclair Article on Vietnam Veterans," May 3, 1979, Box 55, Records of the Domestic Policy Staff, Ellen Goldstein Subject Files, JCL.

26. Bernard Weinraub, "Now, Vietnam Vets Demand Their Rights," *New York Times Magazine*, May 27, 1979, 31–33, 66, 68.

27. Memorandum, Bill Spring and Ellen Goldstein to Jody Powell, "Ward Sinclair Article on Vietnam Veterans," May 3, 1979, Box 55, Records of the Domestic Policy Staff, Ellen Goldstein Subject Files, JCL; see also "Vietnam Veterans Week, 1979, Proclamation 4647," March 20, 1979, *PPPUS, Jimmy Carter, 1979*, pt. 1, 445–446; "Statistical Data on Vietnam Era Veterans, March 1979, Box 38, White House Press Office, Media Liaison Office, Jim Parks Subject Files, JCL; "Fact Sheet Vietnam Era Veterans," May 30, 1979, Box 17, White House Press Office—Lower Press Office, Kate King's Office Files, JCL.

28. "Vietnam Veterans Week, 1979, Remarks at a White House Reception," May 30, 1979, *PPPUS, Jimmy Carter, 1979*, pt. 1, 972–973.

29. "Vietnam Veterans Week, 1979, Remarks at a White House Reception," May 30, 1979, *PPPUS, Jimmy Carter, 1979*, pt. 1, 974–975.

30. Myra MacPherson, "Honoring that 'Extra Measure of Sacrifice,'" *Washington Post*, May 31, 1979, D1, D10.

31. "Welcoming the Viet Vets Home at Last," *New York Times*, May 30, 1979, 23.

32. "We Love You: New View of the Viet Nam Vet," *Time*, June 11, 1979, 21.

33. MacPherson, "Honoring that 'Extra Measure of Sacrifice.'"

34. "NACV Questions Carter's Intent," *Stars and Stripes*, June 14, 1979, 8.

35. Larry Pressler to Jimmy Carter, May 30, 1979, Box VA-4, White House Central Files—Veterans Affairs, JCL.

36. Colman McCarthy, "Vietnam Veterans: A Change in Morale," *Washington Post*, May 30, 1979, 19.

37. "Vietnam Veterans Week, 1979, Remarks at a White House Reception," May 30, 1979, *PPPUS, Jimmy Carter, 1979*, pt. 1, 975.

38. For background on the Cranston bill, see Scott, *Vietnam Veterans since the War*, 38–39, 52–55.

39. Elizabeth Wehr, "'Pork Barrel' Provision Sparks Fight: Psychological Aid for Vietnam Vets Approved," *Congressional Quarterly Weekly Review*, May 26, 1979, 1015–1017.

40. David S. Broder, "The Pork-Barrel Price for Helping the Vets," *Washington Post*, June 3, 1979, D7.

41. McCarthy, "Vietnam Veterans: A Change in Morale."

42. Alter, *His Very Best*, 456–487.

43. Bernard Weinraub, "Vietnam Veterans Found to Have Major Problems," *New York Times*, September 26, 1979, 16.

44. Ward Sinclair, "Study Says Vietnam Vets Face Difficulty," *Washington Post*, September 26, 1979, 7.

45. Max Cleland to Alan Cranston, September 17, 1979, Box 55, Records of the Domestic Policy Staff, Ellen Goldstein Subject Files, JCL.

46. *Congressional Record—Senate*, September 28, 1979, 26767–26768.

47. Colman McCarthy, "Casualties Still," *Washington Post*, October 30, 1979, 15.

48. Muller quoted in Weinraub, "Vietnam Veterans Found to Have Major Problems."

49. Sinclair, "Study Says Vietnam Vets Face Difficulty."

50. Bernard Weinraub, "New Bill Would Aid Vietnam Veterans," *New York Times*, October 11, 1979, 9.

51. "Forgotten Veterans Remembered," *New York Times*, October 13, 1979, 18. For the handwritten comments on a photocopy of the editorial, see Box 55, Records of the Domestic Policy Staff, Ellen Goldstein Subject Files, JCL.

52. Memorandum, Bill Spring and Ellen Goldstein to Jody Powell, "Ward Sinclair Article on Vietnam Veterans," May 3, 1979, Box 55, Records of the Domestic Policy Staff, Ellen Goldstein Subject Files, JCL.

53. Ronald B. Frankum Jr., *Like Rolling Thunder: The Air War in Vietnam, 1964–1975* (Lanham, MD: Rowman & Littlefield Publishers, 2005), 68, 88–92; Peter H. Schuck, *Agent Orange on Trial: Mass Toxic Disasters in the Courts* (Cambridge, MA: Belknap Press, 1986), 16–18; Fred A. Wilcox, *Waiting for an Army to Die: The Tragedy of Agent Orange* (1983; repr., New York: Seven Stories Press, 2011), 148; Edwin A. Martini, *Agent Orange: History, Science, and the Politics of Uncertainty* (Amherst: University of Massachusetts Press, 2012), 97–101.

54. Martini, *Agent Orange*, 152–159.

55. "500 Vets Claim Herbicide Effects," *Washington Post*, October 12, 1978, 9.

56. A copy of the memorandum Cleland circulated throughout the VA can be found in Wilcox, *Waiting for an Army to Die*, 191–194.

57. Schuck, *Agent Orange on Trial*, 37–34; Scott, *Vietnam Veterans since the War*, 89–92.

58. The author of the series was Richard Severo; see "Two Crippled Lives Mirror Disputes on Herbicides," "U.S., Despite Claims of Veterans Says None Are Herbicide Victims," "Herbicides Pose a Bitter Mystery in U.S. Decades after Discovery," *New York Times*, May 27, 1979, 1, 42; May 28, 1979, 1, D8; May 29, 1979, 1, 18.

59. "Welcoming the Viet Vets Home at Last," *New York Times*, May 30, 1979, 22.

60. "Vietnam Veterans Week, 1979, Remarks at a White House Reception," May 30, 1979, *PPPUS, Jimmy Carter, 1979*, pt. 1, 974.

61. Martin Tolchin, "Carter Vows to Focus on Vietnam Veterans Rights," *New York Times*, May 31, 1979, 16.

62. Margot Hornblower, "A Sinister Drama of Agent Orange Opens in Congress," *Washington Post*, June 27, 1979, 3.

63. "On the Agent Orange Trail," *New York Times*, July 5, 1979, 16.

64. "Agent Orange and the Vets," *Washington Post*, July 21, 1979, 14.

65. Richard Severo, "H.E.W. Is Urged to Study Problem over a Herbicide Used in Vietnam," *New York Times*, June 27, 1979, 14.

66. "Agent Orange and the Vets," *Washington Post*, July 21, 1979, 14.

67. Severo, "H.E.W. Is Urged to Study Problem over a Herbicide Used in Vietnam."

68. "Coalition to Study Effect of Agent Orange on G.I.'s," *New York Times*, July 17, 1979, 10.

69. "Vietnam Veterans Sue for Disability Claims Involving Agent Orange," *Washington Post*, June 1, 1979, 6.

70. Bernard Weinraub, "Pentagon Is Disputed on Exposure of Troops to Herbicide in Vietnam," *New York Times*, November 25, 1979, 1.

71. Joanne Omang, "Thousands of U.S. Vietnam Troops May Have Been Exposed to Herbicide," *Washington Post*, November 25, 1979, 24.

72. Memorandum, Stu Eizenstat to the President, "Agent Orange/FYI," December 26, 1979, Box VA-4, White House Central Files—Veteran Affairs, JCL.

CHAPTER 6. THE REVOLT OF THE VETERANS

1. Carter quoted in Hamilton Jordan, *Crisis: The Last Year of the Carter Presidency* (New York: G. P. Putnam's Sons, 1982), 1.

2. Charles O. Jones, *The Trustee Presidency: Jimmy Carter and the United States Congress* (Baton Rouge: Louisiana State University Press, 1988), 192.

3. "The State of the Union," January 23, 1980, *PPPUS, Jimmy Carter, 1980–81*, pt. 1, 194–200.

4. Kenneth A. Weiss, "Carter's Domestic Agenda Contains Few New Proposals," *Congressional Quarterly Weekly Review*, January 26, 1980, 177–179.

5. "Budget Message," January 28, 1980, *PPPUS, Jimmy Carter, 1980–81*, pt. 1, 227–232.

6. Irwin B. Arieff, "Uncertain Agenda Faces Hill as Foreign Issues Presses In," *Congressional Quarterly Weekly Review*, January 19, 1980, 115–116.

7. "Carter Legislative Message to Congress," *Congressional Quarterly Weekly Review*, January 26, 1980, 203–229.

8. Elizabeth Wehr, "Victims of Radiation, Other Environment-Related Illness Seeking Help from Congress," *Congressional Quarterly Weekly Review*, February 23, 1980, 549–556.

9. Colman McCarthy, "A Debt Owed Vietnam Veterans," *Washington Post*, April 10, 1980.

10. *Oversight Hearing to Receive Testimony on Agent Orange*, Hearing Before the House Subcommittee on Medical Facilities and Benefits of the Committee on Veterans Affairs, Ninety-Sixth Congress, Second Session, February 25, 1980 (Washington, DC: Government Printing Office, 1980), 1–3.

11. *Oversight Hearing to Receive Testimony on Agent Orange*, 41–46.

12. *Oversight Hearing to Receive Testimony on Agent Orange*, 98–104.

13. *Oversight Hearing to Receive Testimony on Agent Orange*, 3–4.

14. "More on Agent Orange," *Washington Post*, March 21, 1980, 18.

15. "Max Cleland on Agent Orange," *Washington Post*, March 30, 1980, C6.

16. McCarthy, "A Debt Owed Vietnam Veterans."

17. "Air Force Faulted on Agent Orange Study Proposal," *Washington Post*, May 8, 1980, 40.

18. "The Saga of Agent Orange," *Washington Post*, May 13, 1980, 16.

19. Patrick Hagopian, *The Vietnam War in American Memory: Veterans, Memorials, and the Politics of Healing* (Amherst: University of Massachusetts Press, 2009), 79–84.

20. Jan C. Scruggs, "'We Were Young. We Have Died. Remember Us,'" *Washington Post*, December 11, 1979, B4.

21. Jan C. Scruggs, "A Vietnam Memorial," *Washington Post*, March 22, 1980, 13.

22. Jan C. Scruggs and Joel L. Swerdlow, *To Heal a Nation: The Vietnam Veterans Memorial* (New York: Harper & Row, 1985), 8–14.

23. Donald P. Baker, "Vietnam War Memorial: Senate Bill Proposes Site on Mall," *Washington Post*, November 9, 1979, C1.

24. Hagopian, *The Vietnam War in American Memory*, 79–84.

25. "Vietnam Veterans Memorial Bill: Remarks on Signing," July 1, 1980 *PPPUS, Jimmy Carter, 1980–81*, pt. 2, 1268–1271.

26. Bernard Weinraub, "Carter Hails Veterans of Vietnam in Signing Bill for a War Memorial," *New York Times*, July 2, 1980, 14.

27. Scruggs and Swerdlow, *To Heal a Nation*, 42–43.

28. For examples. see "Carter Clears Vietnam Memorial," *Washington Post*, July 2, 1980, 21; Weinraub, "Carter Hails Veterans of Vietnam in Signing Bill for a War Memorial."

29. Andrew E. Busch, *Reagan's Victory: The Presidential Election of 1980 and the Rise of the Right* (Lawrence: University Press of Kansas, 2005), 1.

30. Kevin M. Kruse and Julian E. Zelizer, *Fault Lines: A History of the United States since 1974* (New York: W. W. Norton, 2019), 98–104.

31. Busch, *Reagan's Victory*, 73.
32. Busch, *Reagan's Victory*, 80–85.
33. See, for example, "Platform-Making in Detroit," July 10, 1980, 16, "The GOP's Man Who," July 20, 1980, E6, both in the *Washington Post*; Adam Clymer, "Emotional Issue for G.O.P.," July 10, 1980, A1, B18; "The Conservatives' Message," July 16, 1980, 1, 17, both in the *New York Times*.
34. The four-part series appeared in the *Washington Post* as follows: Peter Osnos, "The Republican Platform: Economic Solution Lies in Incentives to Business," July 14, 1980, 14; "GOP Platform: Commitment to Racial Equality," July 15, 1980, 11; "GOP's Platform Urges Arms Lead over Soviets," July 16, 1980, 17; "Free Enterprise Is Platform's Energy Source, July 17, 1980, 12.
35. "Republican Party Platform of 1976," https://www.presidency.ucsb.edu/documents/republican-party-platform-1976.
36. "Republican Party Platform of 1980," https://www.presidency.ucsb.edu/documents/republican-party-platform-1980.
37. Busch, *Reagan's Victory*, 86–92.
38. See, for example, "And Now the Democrats," August 10, 1980, C6, "Jobs, Dollars and Platforms," August 14, 1980, both in the *Washington Post*; "Democratic Gestures," *New York Times*, August 17, 1980, E20.
39. Robert G. Kline, "Platform Promises: Hold down Spending and Attack Inflation," *Washington Post*, August 12, 1980, A11. Robert G. Kline, "The Platform Liberal Views, Fiscal Curbs," *Washington Post*, August 12, 1980, A14. "Democrats' Defense Stance: Military Parity, Not Superiority," *Washington Post*, August 14, 1980, A16.
40. "1976 Democratic Party Platform," https://www.presidency.ucsb.edu/documents/1976-democratic-party-platform.
41. "1980 Democratic Party Platform," https://www.presidency.ucsb.edu/documents/1980-democratic-party-platform.
42. Quote from Philip Geyelin, "Digging into the Platform," *Washington Post*, August 13, 1980, 21. See also his "'Trigger-Unhappy Cowboy,'" *Washington Post*, July 17, 1980, 17.
43. Barry Sussman, "New Polls Show Closer '80 Race," *Washington Post*, August 10, 1980, 1, 3.
44. Howell Raines, "Reagan Campaign Problems," *New York Times*, August 27, 1980, 17; Lou Cannon, "Reagan Working Hard at Underdog Role," *Washington Post*, August 31, 1980, 1, 4.
45. Ronald Reagan, "Peace: Restoring the Margin of Safety," August 18, 1980, https://www.reaganlibrary.gov/archives/speech/peace-restoring-margin-safety.
46. "Remarks at the Annual Convention of the American Legion," August 21, 1980 *PPPUS, Jimmy Carter, 1980–81*, pt. 2, 1550–1556.
47. Lee Lescaze, "Carter, on Stump, Vows to Enlarge Defense Outlays," *Washington Post*, August 22, 1980, 1–2.
48. Busch, *Reagan's Victory*, 74–75, 102–103, 111–116.
49. "Veterans' Group Endorses Reagan," *Washington Post*, July 17, 1980, 11.

50. Marjorie Hunter, "Veterans Lobby Dug in, Battle Ready," *New York Times*, July 27, 1980, E2.

51. Press Release, "Statement of Frank I. Hamilton Immediate Past Commander-in-Chief of the American Legion," Box 49, Records of the Domestic Policy Staff, Ellen Goldstein Subject Files, JCL.

52. Press Release, "Statement of Howard Vander Clute Immediate Past Commander-in-Chief of the Veterans of Foreign Wars," Box 49, Records of the Domestic Policy Staff, Ellen Goldstein Subject Files, JCL.

53. Marjorie Hunter, "Reagan Endorsed by Ex-Leaders of Three Major Veterans' Groups," *New York Times*, October 16, 1980, B8; Bill Keller, "Chinks in the 'Iron Triangle'?," *Congressional Quarterly Weekly Review*, June 14, 1980, 1627–1634.

54. Press Release, "Statement of Joseph R. Koralewski, Immediate Past National Commander of the American Veterans," Box 49, Records of the Domestic Policy Staff, Ellen Goldstein Subject Files, JCL.

55. Press Release, "Statement of Frank I. Hamilton Immediate Past Commander-in-Chief of the American Legion," Box 49, Records of the Domestic Policy Staff, Ellen Goldstein Subject Files, JCL.

56. "Veterans Administration Health Care Legislation," August 22, 1980, *PPPUS, Jimmy Carter, 1980–81*, pt. 2, 1563.

57. Press Release, "Statement of Joseph R. Koralewski, Immediate Past National Commander of the American Veterans," Box 49, Records of the Domestic Policy Staff, Ellen Goldstein Subject Files, JCL.

58. Press Release, "Statement of Frank I. Hamilton Immediate Past Commander-in-Chief of the American Legion," Box 49, Records of the Domestic Policy Staff, Ellen Goldstein Subject Files, JCL.

59. Press Release, "Statement of Frank I. Hamilton Immediate Past Commander-in-Chief of the American Legion," Box 49, Records of the Domestic Policy Staff, Ellen Goldstein Subject Files, JCL. See also Edward Walsh and Susanna McBee, "Increase in Veterans Pensions. Called Inflationary, Signed," *Washington Post*, November 7, 1978, 7; Memorandum for the President, "Enrolled Bill H.R. 10173—Veterans' and Survivors' Pension Improvement Act of 1978," Box VA-4, White House Central Files—Veterans Affairs, JCL.

60. Press Release, "Statement of Joseph R. Koralewski, Immediate Past National Commander of the American Veterans," Box 49, Records of the Domestic Policy Staff, Ellen Goldstein Subject Files, JCL.

61. Press Release, "Statement of Howard Vander Clute Immediate Past Commander-in-Chief of the Veterans of Foreign Wars," Box 49, Records of the Domestic Policy Staff, Ellen Goldstein Subject Files, JCL.

62. "Federal Civil Service Reform," March 2, 1978, *PPPUS, Jimmy Carter, 1978*, pt. 2, 435–438.

63. Stephen J. Lynton, "Proposal Angers Veterans, Splits Federal Unions," *Washington Post*, March 3, 1978, 1, 18.

64. Press Release, "Statement of Frank I. Hamilton Immediate Past Com-

mander-in-Chief of the American Legion," Box 49, Records of the Domestic Policy Staff, Ellen Goldstein Subject Files, JCL.

65. Press Release, "Statement of Howard Vander Clute Immediate Past Commander-in-Chief of the Veterans of Foreign Wars," Box 49, Records of the Domestic Policy Staff, Ellen Goldstein Subject Files, JCL.

66. Kathy Sawyer, "House Sustains Vet Preference in Civil Service," *Washington Post*, September 12, 1978, 1, 7. *Congress and the Nation, 1977–1980*, 831–837, 852–853.

67. Press Release, "Statement of Joseph R. Koralewski, Immediate Past National Commander of the American Veterans," Box 49, Records of the Domestic Policy Staff, Ellen Goldstein Subject Files, JCL.

68. "Veterans Rehabilitation and Education Amendments of 1980," October 17, 1980, *PPPUS, Jimmy Carter, 1980*, pt. 3, 2315–2318.

69. "Veterans' Disability Compensation and Housing Benefits Amendments of 1980," October 7, 1980, "*PPPUS, Jimmy Carter, 1980*, pt. 3, 2097–2098.

70. Memorandum, "Meeting with Veteran Supporters," Anne Wexler and Stuart Eizenstat to the White House," October 17, 1980, Box 49, Records of Domestic Policy Staff, Ellen Goldstein Subject Files, JCL.

71. Busch, *Reagan's Victory*, 116–130.

72. Wanda Henderson to Hon. Jimmy Carter, November 6, 1980, Box 49, Records of the Domestic Policy Staff, Ellen Goldstein Subject Files, JCL.

73. Walter W. Stachacz to the President, November 6, 1980; Claude L. Callegary to President James E. Carter, November 25, 1980, both in Box 49, Records of the Domestic Policy Staff, Ellen Goldstein Subject Files, JCL.

CHAPTER 7. CONCLUSION

1. Robert W. Merry, *Where They Stand: The American Presidents in the Eyes of Voters and Historians* (New York: Simon & Schuster, 2012), 244–245.

2. For an introduction to the Carter revisionism, see Peter Baker, "Was Jimmy Carter the Most Underrated President in History?," *New York Times*, June 10, 2021, BR 16.

3. Jonathan Alter, *His Very Best: Jimmy Carter, a Life* (New York: Simon & Schuster, 2020); ix, 602.

4. Kai Bird, *The Outlier: The Unfinished Presidency of Jimmy Carter* (New York: Crown Publishing, 2021), 622–624.

5. Alter, *His Very Best*, 662.

6. Joseph Darda, *How White Men Won the Culture Wars: A History of Veteran America* (Oakland: University of California Press, 2021), 3–4, 35.

7. Viet Thanh Nguyen, *Nothing Ever Dies: Vietnam and the Memory of War* (Cambridge, MA: Harvard University Press, 2016), 9.

8. Sandra Scanlon, *The Pro-War Movement: Domestic Support for the Vietnam War and the Making of Modern American Conservatism* (Amherst: University of Massachusetts Press, 2013), 340.

9. "Veterans Day," November 11, 1978, *PPPUS, Jimmy Carter, 1978*, pt. 2, 2014.

10. "Vietnam Era Veterans: Message to the Congress," October 10, 1978, *PPPUS, Jimmy Carter, 1978*, pt. 2, 1737.

11. Here Carter was quoting from Philip Caputo's *Rumor of War*; see "Vietnam Veterans Memorial Bill: Remarks on Signing," July 1, 1980, *PPPUS, Jimmy Carter, 1980–81*, pt. 2, 1269.

12. Mary E. Stuckey, *Jimmy Carter, Human Rights, and the National Agenda* (College Station: Texas A&M University Press, 2009), xx–xxv.

13. Nguyen, *Nothing Ever Dies*, 16, 11, 32.

14. George N. Dionisopoulos and Steven R. Goldzwig, ""The Meaning of Vietnam": Political Rhetoric as Revisionist Cultural History," *Quarterly Journal of Speech* 78 (February 1992): 61–79.

15. Jerry Lembcke, *The Spitting Image: Myth, Memory, and the Legacy of Vietnam* (New York: New York University Press, 1998), 91–93.

16. Kathleen Belew, *Bring the War Home: The White Power Movement and Paramilitary America* (Cambridge: Harvard University Press, 2018).

BIBLIOGRAPHY

Georgia Archives, Morrow, Georgia
    Record Groups (RGs):
        RG 1-7-105 (Legal Division–Executive Minutes)
        RG 036-03-006 (Veterans' Services-Public Information Section-News Releases)
Gerald Ford Presidential Library, Ann Arbor, Michigan
    President Ford Committee Records
Jimmy Carter Presidential Library, Atlanta, Georgia
    Carter Library Oral History Project
    Jack Carter Oral History Interview, June 25, 2003
    Max Cleland Papers
    Records of Ellen Goldstein
    Records of Robert Lipshutz
    Records of the 1976 Campaign Committee to Elect Jimmy Carter
        Noel Sterrett's Domestic Clippings Files
        Noel Sterrett Subject File
    Records of the Domestic Policy Staff
        Ellen Goldstein Subject Files
        Kitty Higgins and William Spring Subject Files
    Records of the Office of the Assistant to the President for Communication
        Gerald Rafshoon Subject Files
    Records of the White House Office of Counsel to the President
        Robert J. Lipshutz Files
        Margaret McKenna Files
    Staff Offices—Presidential Transition Files
    White House Central Files—Veterans Affairs
    White House Press Office—Lower Press Office
        Kate King's Office Files
    White House Press Office—Media Liaison Office
        Jim Parks Subject Files
        Eleanor Weaver Subject Files
    White House Press Office—News Summary Office
        Janet McMahon's Newspaper Columnists Files
Ronald Reagan Presidential Library, Simi Valley, California
    Digitized Textual Material
        Major Pre-Presidential Speeches, 1964–1980

GOVERNMENT PUBLICATIONS
Congress and the Nation: 1977–1980
Congressional Quarterly Almanac
Congressional Quarterly Weekly Report
Congressional Record
Hearing Before the Committee on Veterans' Affairs: The Nomination of Joseph Maxwell Cleland to be Administrator of Veterans' Affairs, Ninety-Fifth Congress, First Session. Washington, DC: Government Printing Office, 1977.
Myths and Realities: A Study of Attitudes toward Vietnam Era Veterans. Washington, DC: Government Printing Office, 1980.
Oversight Hearing to Receive Testimony on Agent Orange. Hearing Before the House Subcommittee on Medical Facilities and Benefits of the Committee on Veterans Affairs, Ninety-Sixth Congress, Second Session, February 25, 1980. Washington, DC: Government Printing Office, 1980.
The Presidential Campaign 1976

DIGITAL
American Presidency Project (University of California, Santa Barbara)
Institute for Civic Leadership and Digital Mayoral Archives (University of Indianapolis)
Public Papers of the Presidents of the United States (University of Michigan Digital Library)

NEWSPAPERS
Alpharetta Neighbor (Georgia)
Arkansas Gazette
Atlanta Constitution
Atlanta Journal
Atlanta Journal and Constitution
Atlanta Journal and Constitution Magazine
Clarkston Neighbor (Georgia)
Clearwater Sun (Florida)
Columbus Enquirer (Georgia)
DeKalb New Era (Georgia)
Johnson City Press-Chronicle (Tennessee)
Lithonia Observer (Georgia)
Macon Telegraph
Miami News
New York Times
Newsday
Tampa Tribune-Times
Waco Tribune-Herald
Washington Post

Washington Star
The Washingtonian

COLLEGE NEWSPAPERS
Bell Ringer (Augusta State College)
Red and Black (University of Georgia)
Signal (Georgia State College)

MAGAZINES AND NEWSLETTERS
American Legion Magazine
Army Times
Business Week
Harper's
JFV Report
Nation
Newsweek
People
Reveille
Stars and Stripes
State Government News
Time
U.S. News & World Report

MEMOIRS AND PARTICIPANT ACCOUNTS
Bourne, Peter G. *Jimmy Carter: A Comprehensive Biography from Plains to the Post-Presidency*. New York: Scribner, 1997.
Bush, Dorothy Vredenburgh. *The Official Proceedings of the Democratic National Convention, New York City, July 1976*. Washington DC: Democratic National Convention, 1976.
Carter, Jimmy. *White House Diary*. New York: Farrar, Straus & Giroux, 2010.
Cleland, Max. *Heart of a Patriot: How I Found the Courage to Survive Vietnam, Walter Reed, and Karl Rove*. New York: Simon & Schuster, 2009.
———. *Strong at the Broken Places*. Lincoln, VA: Chosen Books, 1980.
Drew, Elizabeth. *American Journal: The Events of 1976*. New York: Vantage Books, 1976.
Eizenstat, Stuart E. *President Carter: The White House Years*. New York: Thomas Dunne Books, 2018.
Jordan, Hamilton. *Crisis: The Last Year of the Carter Presidency*. New York: G. P. Putnam's Sons, 1982.
Reeves, Richard. *Convention*. New York: Harcourt Brace Jovanovich, 1977.
Schram, Martin. *Running for President 1976: The Carter Campaign*. New York: Stein & Day, 1977.
Scruggs, Jan C. and Joel L. Swerdlow. *To Heal a Nation: The Vietnam Veterans Memorial*. New York: Harper & Row, 1985.

Shogan, Robert. *Promises to Keep: Carter's First 100 Days*. Springfield, OH: Crowell, 1977.
Stroud, Kandy. *How Jimmy Won: The Victory Campaign from Plains to the White House*. New York: William Morrow, 1977.

BOOKS

Alter, Jonathan. *His Very Best: Jimmy Carter, a Life*. New York: Simon & Schuster, 2020.
Appy, Christian G. *Working-Class War: American Combat Soldiers and Vietnam*. Chapel Hill: University of North Carolina Press, 1993.
Balmer, Randall. *Redeemer: The Life of Jimmy Carter*. New York: Basic Books, 2014.
Baskir, Lawrence M., and William A. Strauss. *Reconciliation after Vietnam: A Program of Relief for Vietnam Era Draft and Military Offenders*. Notre Dame, IN: University of Notre Dame Press, 1977.
Baumer, Donald C., and Carl E. Van Horn. *The Politics of Unemployment*. Washington, DC: Congressional Quarterly, 1985.
Belew, Kathleen. *Bring the War Home: The White Power Movement and Paramilitary America*. Cambridge, MA: Harvard University Press, 2018.
Berkowitz, Edward D. *Something Happened: A Political and Cultural Overview of the Seventies*. New York: Columbia University Press, 2006.
Bevin, W. Carl. *Jimmy Carter's Economy: Policy in an Age of Limits*. Chapel Hill: University of North Carolina Press, 2014.
Bird, Kai. *The Outlier: The Unfinished Presidency of Jimmy Carter*. New York: Crown Publishing, 2021.
Boulton, Mark. *Failing Our Veterans: The G.I. Bill and the Vietnam Generation*. New York: New York University Press, 2014.
Busch, Andrew E. *Reagan's Victory: The Presidential Election of 1980 and the Rise of the Right*. Lawrence: University Press of Kansas, 2005.
Daddis, Gregory A. *Pulp Vietnam: War and Gender in Cold War Men's Adventure Magazines*, Cambridge, UK: Cambridge University Press, 2020.
Darda, Joseph. *How White Men Won the Culture Wars: A History of Veteran America*. Oakland: University of California Press, 2021.
Edwards, George C., III. *On Deaf Ears: The Limits of the Bully Pulpit*. New Haven, CT: Yale University Press, 2003.
Flippen, J. Brooks. *Jimmy Carter, the Politics of Family, and the Rise of the Religious Right*. Athens: University of Georgia Press, 2011.
Frankum Jr., Ronald B. *Like Rolling Thunder: The Air War in Vietnam, 1964–1975*. Lanham, MD: Rowman & Littlefield Publishers, 2005.
The Gallup Poll: Public Opinion 1972–1977. 2 vols. Wilmington, DE: Scholarly Resources, 1978.
Godbold Jr., E. Stanly. *Jimmy and Rosalynn Carter: The Georgia Years, 1924–1974*. New York: Oxford University Press, 2010.
Greene, John Robert. *The Presidency of Gerald Ford*. Lawrence: University Press of Kansas, 1994.

Hagopian, Patrick. *The Vietnam War in American Memory: Veterans, Memorials, and the Politics of Healing*. Amherst: University of Massachusetts Press, 2009.
Hess, Stephen. *Washington Reporters*. Washington, DC: Brookings Institute Press, 1981.
Howes, Craig. *Voices of the Vietnam POWs: Witnesses to Their Flight*. New York: Oxford University Press, 1993.
Huebner, Andrew J. *The Warrior Image: Soldiers in American Culture from the Second World War to the Vietnam Era*. Chapel Hill: University of North Carolina Press, 2008.
Jeffords, Susan. *The Remasculinization of America: Gender and the Vietnam War*. Bloomington: Indiana University Press, 1989.
Jones, Charles O. *The Trusteeship Presidency: Jimmy Carter and the United States Congress*. Baton Rouge: Louisiana State University Press, 1988.
Kalman, Laura. *Right Star Rising: A New Politics, 1974–1980*. New York: W. W. Norton, 2010.
Kaufman, Burton I., and Scott Kaufman. *The Presidency of James Earl Carter, Jr.* Lawrence: University Press of Kansas, 2006.
Kinder, John M. *Paying with Their Bodies: American War and the Problem of the Disabled Veteran*. Chicago: University of Chicago Press, 2015.
Kruse, Kevin M., and Julian E. Zelizer. *Fault Lines: A History of the United States since 1974*. New York: W. W. Norton, 2019.
Lair, Meredith H. *Armed with Abundance: Consumerism and Soldiering in the Vietnam War*. Chapel Hill: University of North Carolina Press, 2011.
Lembcke, Jerry. *The Spitting Image: Myth, Memory, and the Legacy of Vietnam*. New York: New York University Press, 1998.
Lewis, Penny. *Hardhats, Hippies, and Hawks: The Vietnam Antiwar Movement as Myth and Memory*. Ithaca, NY: Cornell University Press, 2013.
MacPherson, Myra. *Long Time Passing: Vietnam and the Haunted Generation*. Garden City, NY: Doubleday, 1984.
Martini, Edwin A. *Agent Orange: History, Science, and the Politics of Uncertainty*. Amherst: University of Massachusetts Press, 2012.
Mason, Robert. *Richard Nixon and the Quest for a New Majority*. Chapel Hill: University of North Carolina Press, 2004.
Merry, Robert W. *Where They Stand: The American Presidents in the Eyes of Voters and Historians*. New York: Simon & Schuster, 2012.
Morris, Kenneth E. *Jimmy Carter: American Moralist*. Athens: University of Georgia Press, 1996.
Nguyen, Viet Thanh. *Nothing Ever Dies: Vietnam and the Memory of War*. Cambridge, MA: Harvard University Press, 2016.
Nicosia, Gerald. *Home to War: A History of the Vietnam Veterans Movement*. New York: Crown Publishing, 2001.
Perlstein, Rick. *Nixonland: The Rise of a President and the Fracturing of America*. New York: Scribner, 2009.

Pressman, Matthew. *On Press: The Liberal Values That Shaped the News.* Cambridge, MA: Harvard University Press, 2018.

Robins, Glenn. *The Longest Rescue: The Life and Legacy of Vietnam POW William A. Robinson.* Lexington: University Press of Kentucky, 2013.

Roessner, Amber. *Jimmy Carter and the Birth of the Marathon Media Campaign.* Baton Rouge: Louisiana State University Press, 2020.

Rozell, Mark J. *The Press and the Carter Presidency.* Boulder, CO: Westview Press, 1989.

Scanlon, Sandra. *The Prowar Movement: Domestic Support for the Vietnam War and the Making of Modern American Conservatism.* Amherst: University of Massachusetts Press, 2013.

Schuck, Peter H. *Agent Orange on Trial: Mass Toxic Disasters in the Courts.* Cambridge, MA: Belknap Press.

Scott, Wilbur J. *Vietnam Veterans since the War: The Politics of PTSD, Agent Orange, and the National Memorial.* Norman: University of Oklahoma Press, 2003.

Stuckey, Mary E. *Jimmy Carter, Human Rights, and the National Agenda.* College Station: Texas A&M University Press, 2009.

Weil, Gordon L. *The Long Shot: George McGovern Runs for President.* New York: W. W. Norton, 1973.

Werth, Barry. *31 Days: Gerald Ford, the Nixon Pardon, and a Government in Crisis.* New York: Anchor Books.

Wilcox, Fred A. *Waiting for an Army to Die: The Tragedy of Agent Orange.* 1983; repr. New York: Seven Stories Press, 2011.

Williams, Daniel K. *The Election of the Evangelical: Jimmy Carter, Gerald Ford and the Presidential Contest of 1976.* Lawrence: University Press of Kansas, 2020.

ARTICLES AND BOOK CHAPTERS

Bloodworth, Jeffery. "Jimmy Carter's 1976 Presidential Campaign: The Saint, the Sinner, and the Hopeless Dreamer." In Scott Kaufman, *A Companion to Gerald R. Ford and Jimmy Carter*, 229–250. Malden, MA: Wiley-Blackwell, 2015.

Carlson, A. Cheree, and John E. Hocking. "Strategies of Redemption at the Vietnam Veterans' Memorial." *Western Journal of Speech Communication* 52 (Summer 1988): 203–215.

Dean Jr., Eric T. "The Myth of the Troubled and Scorned Vietnam Veteran." *Journal of American Studies* 26 (April 1992): 59–74.

Dionisopoulos, George N., and Steven R. Goldzwig. "The Meaning of Vietnam: Political Rhetoric as Revisionist Cultural History," *Quarterly Journal of Speech* 78 (February 1992): 61–79.

Hahn, Dan F. "The Rhetoric of Jimmy Carter, 1976–1980." *Presidential Studies Quarterly* 14 (Spring 1984): 265–288.

McMahon, Robert J. "Contested Memory: The Vietnam War and American Society, 1975–2001," *Diplomatic History* 26 (Spring 2002): 159–184.

———. "Rationalizing Defeat: The Vietnam War in American Presidential Discourse, 1975–1995." *Rhetoric and Public Affairs* 2 (Winter 1999): 529–549.

Roessner, L. Amber, and Lindsey M. Bier. "Pardon Me, Mr. Carter: Amnesty and Unfinished Business of Vietnam in Jimmy Carter's 1976 Campaign." *Journalism History* 43 (Summer 2017): 86–96.

Shichor, David, and Donald R. Ranish. "President Carter's Vietnam Amnesty: An Analysis of a Public Policy Decision." *Presidential Studies Quarterly* 10 (Summer 1980): 443–450.

Stahl, Roger. "Why We 'Support the Troops': Rhetorical Evolutions." *Rhetoric and Public Affairs* 12 (Winter 2009): 535–551.

Villadsen, Lisa S., and Jason A. Edwards. "Introduction," in Lisa S. Villadsen and Jason A. Edwards, eds., *The Rhetoric of Official Apology*. Lanham, MD: Lexington Books, 2020. 1–19.

INDEX

Abzug, Bella, 32
Addleston, David F., 93
Afghanistan, Soviet invasion of, 120–122, 130, 143
Agent Orange, 3–4, 113–119, 122–127, 130, 133, 135, 145
Agent Orange Victims International (AOVI), 3, 116
Agent Orange: Vietnam's Deadly Fog, 115, 120
Alexander, Clifford, 67
Alter, Jonathan, 143
American Association of Minority Veterans Programs Administrators (AAMVPA), 100–101
American Civil Liberties Union, 93
American Legion, 34–35, 40, 42, 53, 55, 101, 107, 135–136, 138, 140–141
American Veterans of World War II, Korea and Vietnam (AMVETS), 136–137, 140–141
Anderson, Jack, 60, 83
Anderson, John, 135
Aspin, Les, 88

Bailey, Tyrone, 108
Beard, Robin, 66–69
Belew, Kathleen, 147
Bell, Griffin, 57
Benjamin, T. Garret, Rev., 28
Bleier, Rocky, 101
Bonior, David E., 88, 97, 100, 105, 109, 111–113, 128
Boulton, Mark, 13
Bourne, Peter, 10
Brill, Steven, 26
Broder, David, 74, 110
Brown, Sam, 30

Brzezinski, Zbigniew, 86
Bundy, McGeorge, 86
Bush, George H. W., 131, 136
Busch, Andrew E., 130–131
Byrd, Robert C., 25

Caddell, Pat, 18
Calley, William, xi, 27–28
Caputo, Philip, 108, 129
Carey, John M., 101
Carter, Jimmy
  Agent Orange, response to, 117, 119–120, 122–123, 125–127
  appearances at Arlington National Cemetery, 94, 102, 146
  attacked by Reagan, 8, 130
  campaign strategy, veterans, (1976), 38–40
  Congressional opposition to pardon policy, 46–47
  criticisms of Ford, 6, 35, 37, 39, 130, 141, 144
  decision to run for president, 18–19
  on draft evaders, 6, 42–43, 45–49, 51–52, 55–57, 59–60, 62, 65, 69–70, 100, 104, 130, 135, 144
  economic recovery plan, 49–50, 52, 54
  fiscal conservatism, 17, 76–77, 98, 138
  Georgia Advisory Committee on Vietnam Veterans (GACVV), 1, 6–7, 11–12, 16–18, 53, 143
  GI Bill Improvement Act (1977), 71–73
  as governor of Georgia, 1, 14–18
  Iran hostage crisis, 120, 130, 143, 145
  legislative priorities, 20, 44, 77, 98–99, 121
  on George McGovern, 24–26

[185]

Carter, Jimmy, *continued*
  media coverage of, 21, 24, 76
  military background, 11
  on My Lai Massacre, 6, 27–28, 41
  pardon of draft evaders, 23–27, 35, 43, 45–49
  Playboy interview, 40–42
  public view of pardon policy, 46
  presidential ranking, 143
  record on Vietnam veterans' policies, 3–8, 143–147
  relationship with Max Cleland, 53, 94
  relationship with Vietnam Veterans of America, 104–107
  rhetoric of gratitude, 2, 5, 8, 18, 52, 91–93, 95, 99, 108, 130, 143–144, 146–147
  Special Discharge Review Process, 55–61, 66–71
  State of the Union Addresses of, 74, 76, 86–87, 98–99, 121–122, 145
  on Veterans Administration, 64–65
  Veterans and Survivors Pension Improvement Act (1978), 95–96
  Veterans Day Addresses of, 40, 71, 91, 94, 102, 146
  Veterans Disability Compensation and Housing Benefits Amendments (1980), 140
  Veterans Health Care Amendments (1979), 109–111
  Veterans Rehabilitation and Education Amendments (1980), 140
  Vietnam Veterans Memorial, 127–130
  Vietnam Veterans Presidential Review Memorandum, 7, 86–94, 96, 99, 101–103, 105–106, 108, 113, 122, 140, 145
  Vietnam Veterans Week, 99–103, 107–109
  on Vietnam veteran unemployment, 49–52, 54, 61–64, 77–86
  on Vietnam War, 19–20, 28–29, 38, 41, 93
  See also media coverage of Vietnam veterans
Carter, John William (Jack), 11, 41–42, 60
Christian, David A., 102, 104, 106, 107
Clark, Ramsey, 32
Class that Went to War, The, 74–75
Cleland, Max
  Agent Orange, 112, 115, 117–118, 123–126
  as administrator of Veterans Administration, 57, 64–65, 69, 75, 80–81, 91–92, 94, 102, 107–109, 135
  military service, 12, 123
  nomination to Veterans Administration, 7, 44, 52–55
  relationship with Jimmy Carter, 53, 94
  veterans' activism of in Georgia, 12, 14–18, 71
  on Vietnam veterans' readjustment, 80–81
  See also Veterans Administration
Collins, Charles P., 82
Comprehensive Employment Training Act (CETA), 50, 54, 61, 63, 79, 83–85, 92, 138, 144
Council of Vietnam Veterans (CCV), 3, 90, 95–97, 99, 103
Cranston, Alan, 53, 61, 67–68, 75, 109–110, 112–113, 123
Crawford, Kenneth, 76

Darda, Joseph, 5
Daschle, Thomas A., 124–125
Dean, Eric T. Jr., 5
Democratic National Convention (1976)
  vice presidential nomination, 31–34, 118
Democratic party platform (1976), 29–31, 55

INDEX [187]

Democratic party platform (1980), 132–133
Democratic presidential primary (1972), 22–23, 24–25, 59
Democratic presidential primary (1976), 20–21, 25–29
Democratic presidential primary (1980), 121–122, 132
DeVictor, Maude, 115
Dewar, Helen, 52
Disabled American Veterans (DAV), 62
Dole, Robert, 35–36. 67
Doubek, Robert, 127
draft evaders
 amnesty for, 21–23
 public view of amnesty, 22–23
 response to Carter pardon policy, 47
Drach, Ronald W., 62
Drew, Elizabeth, 21

Eckhardt, Bob, 118
Efaw, Fritz, 31–34, 118
Eisenhower, Dwight D., 41
Eizenstat, Stuart, 51–52, 62, 68–69, 73, 86–88, 91, 96, 102–103, 106
election, presidential, 1976
 debates, 36–37
 reasons for Carter's victory, 42
 Vietnam veterans' issues, 36–43
election, presidential, 1980
 reasons for Carter's defeat, 141, 143, 145–147
 Vietnam veterans' issues, 130–142
Evans, Frank, 66
Evans, Rowland, 24

Feldman, Stuart, 90, 96–97, 99, 103
Ford, Gerald, 131
 1976 election defeat, 42
 1976 presidential debate, 36
 attacked by Carter, 6, 35–37, 39, 130, 141, 144

clemency program, 30, 36, 58
 comparison to Carter, 98
 veterans' policy, 40, 63, 73, 109
Fouse, Ronald, 49, 51

Georgia Advisory Committee on Vietnam Veterans (GACVV), 1, 6–7, 11–12, 16–18, 53, 143
Georgia college tuition debate, 14–16
Georgia Jobs for Veterans Year, 17
Georgia Salute to Vietnam Veterans Week, 17–18
Geyelin, Philip L., 3, 103, 133
GI Bill Improvement Act (1977), 71–73
Glenn, John, 31
Godbold, E. Stanly, 19
Goldstein, Ellen, 89
Goldwater, Barry, 46
Gore, Albert, Jr., 88
Greenspun, Hank, 27–28
Greider, William, 61

Hamilton, Frank I., 136–140
Hammerschmidt, John Paul, 125
Harkin, Thomas, 88
Hartke, Vance, 38, 132
Heckler, Margaret, 113
Heinz, John, 89, 109, 113
Help Through Industrial Retraining and Employment (HIRE), 49–50, 54, 61–63, 77–79, 81–83, 85, 87, 99, 138, 144
Henderson, Wanda, 141
Higgins, Kitty, 89
Holt, Cooper, 136
Hornblower, Margot, 117
Humphrey, Hubert, 25

Jackson, Henry "Scoop," 25, 51
Johnson, Charles, 101
Johnson, Lyndon, 13, 32
Jones, Charles O., 98
Jordan, Hamilton, 53

Jordan, Vernon E. Jr., 97
Kalman, Laura, 19
Kennedy, Ted, 111, 120–122, 132
Kirbo, Charles, 56
Kissinger, Henry, 41, 86
Kline, Robert G., 132
Koralewski, Joseph R., 137–140
Kovner, Sarah, 32, 34
Kraft, Joseph, 98
Kurtis, Bill, 115

Lawson, William E., 100–101, 105
Lembcke, Jerry, 5
Lescaze, Lee, 67, 135
Lester, James, 15
Lukert, Otto, 108
Lynn, Barry, Rev., 58

MacPherson, Myra, 4
Maddox, Greg, 101
Maddox, Lester, 15
Maguire, Andrew, 117
Marshall, Ray, 50–51, 62–63, 78–80, 84, 85
Martini, Edwin, 115
Mathias, Charles McC., 127–128
McCain, John, 38
McCarthy, Colman, 3, 73–74, 90, 108–111, 113, 126
McCarthy, Frank, 116–118
McCloskey, Jack, 109
McGovern, George, 22–26, 29
McGrory, Mary, 52, 70, 73, 93
media coverage of Vietnam veterans, 3, 4, 10, 21, 24–30, 38, 46, 48, 52, 59–61, 64–65, 67–68, 70–71, 73–81, 83–84, 89, 90, 93, 95–96, 102–103, 106, 108, 110–114, 116–119, 125–126, 131–133, 135
Mettler, Ruben, 77, 85
Miller, G. William, 63–64, 77
Mills, Donia, 80

Mohr, Charles, 4, 28–29, 59–60
Mondale, Walter, 31, 34, 39–40, 91–92, 99, 104, 144
Moore, Frank, 69
Mora, Roland, 104, 106
Moynihan, Daniel Patrick, 113
Muller, Robert, 7, 90, 92–93, 96–97, 99, 103–106, 112–113, 117, 129
Murtha, John, 66, 88–89
Myers, John T., 46

National Alliance of Businessmen (NAB), 63, 77, 79, 82–83, 85
New York Times, 4, 10, 21, 24, 28–29, 38, 59, 68, 76, 96, 102, 106, 108, 112, 114, 116, 118–119, 133
Nguyen, Viet, 146
Nicosia, Gerald, 4
Nixon, Richard, 9, 18, 22–23, 25–26, 35–37, 39, 41, 63, 73–74, 109
North, Oliver, 38
Novak, Robert, 24
Nunn, Sam, 51

Oakar, Mary Rose, 51
Osnos, Peter, 131

Panetta, Leon, 88
Paralyzed Veterans of America (PVA), 61–62, 95–96
Paris Peace Accords, 9–10, 13, 23, 41
Percy, Charles H., 119–120
Phillips, Paul D., 67
Powell, Jody, 24, 53, 106
Pressler, Larry, 108–109

Rafshoon, Gerald, 89–91, 96, 102
Raines, Frank, 80, 86–87
Ransom, Louise, 32–33, 118
Reagan, Ronald,
    1980 election, 121, 131–132, 137, 140–141

attacks Carter, 8, 130
supported by VFW, 136
Vietnam as a noble cause, 5, 134
on Vietnam veterans, 134–135, 146
Republican Party platform (1976), 131
Republican Party platform (1980), 131–132
Reston, James, 29
Reutershan, Paul, 116, 120
Reynolds, Frank, 36
Roffee, Larry, 95–96
Rosenbaum, David E., 24
Rostow, Walt, 85
Roufee, Lawrence W., Jr., 61
Russo, Martin A., 117
Ryan, Kerry, 117, 120
Ryan, Michael, 117

Satterfield, David E. III, 123, 125
Schram, Martin, 24, 96
Scott, Wilbur, 4
Scruggs, Jan, 127–129
Shriver, Sargent, 25
Sinclair, Ward, 3, 103–104, 106, 111–113
Spring, Bill, 88
Stahl, Roger, 94
Staubach, Roger, 101
Strauss, Robert, 33
Strauss, William A., 24
Stuckey, Mary, 2

Thompson, William, 93
Thurmond, Strom, 54–55, 57–68
Time, 108

Udall, Morris (Mo), 25, 34
U.S. News & World Report, 10, 80, 81, 89

Vander Clute, Howard, 136, 138–140
Veterans Administration, 7, 35, 40, 45, 52–57, 64–66, 68–69, 71–73, 75, 80–81, 87, 90–91, 93, 102, 108–112,

115–119, 121–126, 129, 132–135, 137–140, 145. *See also* Cleland, Max
Veterans Disability Compensation and Housing Benefits Amendments (1980), 140
Veterans Health Care Amendments (1979), 109–111
Veterans of Foreign Wars (VFW), 5, 22, 134–136, 138, 140–141
Veterans Rehabilitation and Education Amendments (1980), 140
Veterans Survivors Pension Improvement Act (1978), 95–96
Vietnam GI Bill, 13, 71–73
Vietnam Veterans Act, 7, 105, 113, 116, 123
Vietnam Veterans in Congress Caucus (VVC), 3, 7, 88–89, 97, 99, 105, 108–109, 111, 113, 123–124, 129, 145
Vietnam Veterans Memorial, 127–130
Vietnam Veterans Memorial Fund (VVMF), 127–129
Vietnam Veterans of America, (VVA) 3, 7, 103–105, 112, 117, 129, 133
Vrieze, Kevin, 47

Wallace, George, 27
Washington Post, 3, 4, 21, 24–26, 30, 38, 46, 48, 59, 61, 64–65, 67–68, 70–71, 73–80, 84, 89, 90, 95–96, 103, 106, 112, 118, 125–126, 131–133, 135
Webb, James, 38–39
Weinraub, Bernard, 3, 5, 106, 111–112, 119, 129, 133
Weiss, Kenneth A., 121
Werth, Barry, 22
Westbrook, Bert, 14, 16–17
Wicker, Tom, 9–10
Williams, Daniel K., 30

Willenz, June A., 56
Wincek, Thomas J., 62
Woods, John, 117
Wooten, James T., 35

Yannacone, Victor J., Jr., 116

Zengerle, Joseph C., 104, 106–107
Zumwalt, Elmo, 97